MICHAEL WAKELIN produces ~~~~~~~~
and is executive producer for the BBC's
Religious Broadcasting Department's output
on Radio 1 and Radio 2. He read Theology
at Birmingham University and served for
two years as a missionary in South Korea
before joining the BBC as a researcher in
1986. Involved with various parts of the
Methodist Church, he has had a long-term
interest in Methodism's most famous son—
J. Arthur Rank. Michael lives, with his wife
Jacqui, in Cheshire.

In memory of my father
Dr Paul Oasland Wakelin

J. ARTHUR RANK

The Man Behind the Gong

Michael Wakelin

A LION BOOK

Copyright © 1996 Michael Wakelin

The author asserts the moral right
to be identified as the author of this work

Published by
Lion Publishing plc
Sandy Lane West, Oxford, England
ISBN 0 7459 3134 0 (hardback)
ISBN 0 7459 3135 9 (paperback)

First hardback edition 1996
First paperback edition 1997
10 9 8 7 6 5 4 3 2 1 0

Acknowledgments
Text from *J. Arthur Rank and the British Film Industry* by Geoffrey McNab
used by permission of Routledge
Text from *Mr Rank—A Study of J. Arthur Rank and British Films* by Alan Wood
copyright © The Estate of the late Alan Wood

A catalogue record for this book is available
from the British Library

Printed and bound in Great Britain by Caledonian

Acknowledgments

I would like to thank Maurice Lyon and Felicity Henderson at Lion Publishing for asking me to write this book and for working so hard on it; Rosemary Foxcroft for all her tremendous research; Bernard Jackson for making the original radio documentary with me and for giving me his tapes; Robin and Shelagh Cowen for their patient assistance and for allowing me access to the family; Patrick O'B. Baker for the historic interview with Walter Knights; Andrew Youdell at the British Film Institute for his expertise; Richard Lawry and the Rev. Howard Booth for reading the early drafts; and Jacqui Jouannet for being a light at the end of the tunnel.

In the course of my research for this book I spoke to many people who gave me their time and much helpful information. I would like to acknowledge the following sources: the Rev. Barry Allcott, CTVC; Patrick O'B. Baker, Rank enthusiast; Joyce Bank of the Wesley Historical Society; Paul Bartlett Lang, the Secretary of the Joseph Rank Benevolent Trust and former Vice-President of the Methodist Conference; Canon Peter Buckler of the Royal Agricultural Society of England; the Business Archives Council; the Right Rev. the Lord Donald Coggan; Major Robin Cowen, Rank's son-in-law; the Hon. Mrs Shelagh Cowen, Rank's daughter; Ted Critchley, Rank's farm manager; the Rev. David Cruise of the West London Mission, formerly a Sunday school pupil under Rank; Sir John Davis, former Chairman of the Rank Organisation; the Rev. Dr Donald English, formerly of Methodist Home Mission and President of the Methodist Conference; John Farrell of the Wesley College Archive; Kathy Fowler of the Church of England Records Centre; Joy Fox of the Methodist Church Overseas Division; the Rev. Dr Kenneth Greet, former President of the Methodist Conference; Michael Harnett, Rank's butler; Sir Anthony Havelock-Allan, film director; Geoff Houghton, The Leys School Archivist; Hull City Library; Colonel Douglas Hutchinson, CBE, MC, TD, Rank's nephew and Chairman of the Joseph Rank Benevolent Trust; Wilson Impey, miller; Ann Jeater; Sid Kenrick, former Ranks Hovis McDougall employee; The Leys School; the Rev. Dr Kingsley Lloyd, former President of the Methodist Conference; Martin Ludlow, of Methodist Home Mission; Sir John Mills, actor; the Rev. Dr Colin Morris, former President of the Methodist Conference; the National Register of Archives; Brian Owers, former Company Secretary of the Rank Organisation; Fred Packard, Rank's grandson; Sir Francis Pemberton, a family friend; Eric Pigott, formerly of the *Methodist Recorder*; Joan Powell, a family friend; Valentine Powell, a family friend; Colin Rank, Rank's great-nephew; Tony Reddall, Treasurer at Westminster Central Hall; the Rev. Edward Rogers of Methodist Home Mission; Dinah Sheridan, actress and former wife of Sir John Davis; the Rev. Dr Donald, the Lord Soper; M.J.M. Thompson, consultant land surveyor; May Thornton Smith, former Sunday school teacher under Rank; Humphrey Trembath, trustee of the Joseph Rank Benevolent Trust and former Sunday school teacher under Rank; the Rev. Dr John Tudor of Westminster Central Hall; Alan Watt of Wesley's Chapel; John Wheeler of the Rank Foundation; Andrew Youdell of the British Film Institute; Edgar Youdell, former researcher for Rank.

CONTENTS

INTRODUCTION

Constructing the life of J. Arthur Rank has not been an easy task. His family have kept his memory a closely guarded secret since his death in 1972. One of the first things his daughter Shelagh did when her father had passed away was to burn all his papers. Other writers' attempts to put his life in words have been met with a cold shoulder and a strong feeling from those closest to him that no one could ever do him justice.

I confess to a long-time fascination with 'the man behind the gong' who had heralded several exciting childhood adventures in the cinema. I remember once, when the famous bombadier struck the improbably large instrument behind the title 'J. Arthur Rank Presents', my mother whispering to me, 'He's a Methodist.' The village chapel we attended as a family only had twelve members and my early experiences of Methodism were of this and other similarly gloomy but loving places subsiding slowly into forgotten fields with congregations that only changed in number when somebody died. It struck me as extraordinary that someone so rich and glamorous could have emerged from a Christian tradition so poor and dwindling. Who was this man?

As I grew older and saw a wider vision of the Methodist Church it became clear to me that there probably wouldn't have been much of a Methodist Church without the Rank connection. Everywhere you go there is a Rank room and people who will tell you that Rank money paid for this extension and that new building; the great Central Halls were the work of Rank's father, Joseph, and the old projector in the store cupboard had been provided by J. Arthur. When I realized that the bread we ate, the bingo halls we were not allowed in and the photocopier in the study were all connected with the same family, I was intrigued.

In 1989, as a new producer in the BBC's Religious Broadcasting Department, I was suddenly aware of the possibilities of my position and decided to exercise my curiosity. Having never sold a programme idea to anyone before, I was delighted when the Controller of Radio 4 bought my documentary 'J. Arthur Rank Presents', and I set about with a reporter, Bernard Jackson, to try and find out what sort of man J. Arthur Rank was. At first we were struck by the mysterious silence that surrounded him. What was the family trying to hide? I must admit it was Bernard's badgering, not mine, that finally convinced the family that our intentions were honourable and at last some of the Rank story could be told. Listening to the programme now I realize how inadequate it was and what a great opportunity this has been to go much deeper into the subject.

Apart from the family's initial reticence, we discovered then that there is precious little written or recorded information of any kind on J. Arthur Rank. There is coverage of his involvement with films in various books on the British movie industry but in fact this is not much to do with the man himself. He didn't know anything about films and very little of his heart was in the actual process of movie production. So this book in no way intends to be a comprehensive study of Rank's dealings with films. The coverage of the 'golden age' of British cinema is used as a component in building up a much wider picture of the man. A picture that must include the image of his impressive if awkward figure almost singlehandedly taking on the American movie industry as no-one has ever done since, but must leave the detail to others.

Rank was certainly a powerful businessman, but at heart he was a simple miller, and a fish out of water in the glitzy world of show business. Great insight into his character can be obtained in studying the life of his father, Joseph, and in drawing back the curtains on his rich, loving and loyal family life which, along with his deep Christian faith, was the bedrock on which he built his extraordinary career.

Joseph's career was circumstantially very different to that of his younger son. Joseph's parents couldn't have cared less about him and provided him with virtually no heritage, but he still made his way from having almost nothing to becoming a very wealthy man. Arthur, however, began his career with money and parents who expected a great deal from him—but the reason for his fame came as quite a shock to them.

Arthur could have remained an ordinary, though very rich, businessman for the whole of his life. As a young man in his father's firm, he was already an important figure in the City and involved in various big church concerns. He could easily have tucked himself away in his Surrey home and indulged in his many hobbies and interests. The fact that he became involved in such a public business and turned into an international figure was, as will become clear, rather an accident.

It is said by some that this strange twist of fate provided the British film industry with its golden years. It is hard to name a film from the forties and fifties which was not funded in some way by Rank. *Great Expectations, The Red Shoes, Brief Encounter, Hamlet, Oliver Twist* and hundreds of other films bore his name.

Some were awful. Too many of them were produced at once, just to keep filling Rank's screens round the country. Overnight best boys became directors and extras became stars. Mistakes were made and, as a result, some say that Rank was just about the worst thing that could have happened to British movies. But, whatever else, he was truly a major figure in the film world for twenty years and his money was responsible for giving freedom to many of the great names in British film acting.

It is impossible to say what would have happened if he hadn't got involved. Maybe there would have been far fewer but far better quality pictures made. Even with his massive financial input and his attempts at silver-screen diplomacy, the Americans still dominated the market and never gave his films the respect they deserved.

What is remarkable is the fact that such an important and well-known name in the twentieth century has remained such a mystery. This biography should help to put some character behind the well-known name and find out what made up the man. There is, of course, a view that the kind of wealth he had could not have come without exploitation of some kind and therefore his theology and even his Christianity are in question. Such opinions are also represented here.

In the absence of written source material I have travelled many hundreds of miles to interview some fifty or so people who knew J. Arthur Rank. Some were old and some have died since I began the process. Dates of events have been forgotten and exact accuracy could not always be expected. Some anecdotes have clearly taken on a life of their own and may not be word-perfect on the utterances of the man, but here you have, in the main, an oral tradition about someone who made an enormous impression on those who knew him best.

Michael Wakelin
Kerridge, June 1996

1 THE SON OF HIS FATHER

A servant with this clause
Makes drudgery divine;
Who sweeps a room, as for thy laws,
Makes that and the action fine.
GEORGE HERBERT

At the memorial service held in honour of J. Arthur Rank, the Rev. Dr Maurice Barnett opened his address by saying:

> I have no difficulty in paying this tribute. Sometimes
> one has to scrape the barrel to find the left-over relics
> of goodness and usefulness. This is one of those happy
> occasions when the barrel is full, pressed down, and
> running over with unsolicited attributes of goodness.
> The question is what to leave out.

This has been my problem in writing this biography. He was, as has been said to me many times, an extraordinary man; he was not without his failings and weaknesses nor without enemies, but by and large it is hard to be anything other than impressed by his character and faith and by what he achieved.

There is only one other biography of J. Arthur Rank, written by Alan Wood in 1952. In it he writes: 'The essential facts are that he embarked on a film career from the start as a miller, a millionaire, a Methodist and a Yorkshireman.'[1] This is all true, but inadequate. There are other important characteristics one needs to know about J. Arthur Rank at the start of

13

this record of his life. He was not only a miller: he was an excellent miller who in the end loved flour more than anything else in his business world. He was not only a millionaire: he was an incredibly generous one, with a penchant for taking risks and with a nose for making money. He was not only a Methodist: he was a strong evangelical Christian with, in his opinion, a direct line to the Almighty and with a desire to convert the nation, if not the world, to his understanding of the Christian faith. He was not only a Yorkshireman: he was also a profound patriot who believed that Britain was the best country in the world with potentially the greatest workforce, the highest moral standards and the noblest life-style. All these attributes provided J. Arthur Rank with a confidence and security that guided him throughout his life and made him an extraordinary man to know and a quite remarkable figure in the twentieth century.

There is one more essential fact: J. Arthur Rank was very much his father's son. It is his father, Joseph Rank, who is the subject of this first chapter. We need to put Rank in context to have any understanding of what lay behind his desires and drove him on to his achievements. His family history and his father's life in particular are important keys to understanding Rank's personality. He shared a number of character traits with his father including a narrow evangelical faith and a deep-rooted integrity. The differences, too, are illuminating, and stem largely from the contentments and frustrations of their respective childhoods.

Joseph Rank was not quite the happy man his son turned out to be. He was dour, stern and more than a little awesome. From virtual penury, public ridicule and an apparently hopeless one-man business, he became one of the most successful businessmen this century, known for being an extraordinarily generous benefactor and one of Hull's most famous and respected citizens. He was a driven man, spurred on by childhood tragedy and family in-fighting which left him with a burning desire to succeed.

But Joseph was not the first Rank to put the family name on a bag of flour. The history of the Rank family is steeped in farming and milling. In Kingston-upon-Hull, in the early nineteenth century, the mayor and aldermen received a petition which read:

> We the poor inhabitants of the said town have lately experienced much sorrow in ourselves and families on the occasion of the exorbitant price of flour. We judge it needful to take every precaution to preserve ourselves from the invasions of covetous and merciless men. In consequence thereof, we have entered into a subscription for the purpose of building a mill.[2]

In order to buy flour at a cheaper rate than in the market the Anti-Mill Society was formed. This was not entirely satisfactory, because the poor people could not afford the subscription and, in the year of 1800, an additional society came together in order to build a 'Subscription Mill'. A card, printed in 1801 to celebrate the opening of this Subscription Mill, was carefully preserved by Joseph Rank, and it is thought that his grandfather, John Rank, may well have been foreman of the 'Hull Subscription Mill'. So John Rank (Arthur's great-grandfather) became the first Rank miller in 1825 when, at the age of twenty-four, he rented a windmill at Sproatly, a hamlet seven miles north-east of Hull. Up until that time, going back to the sixteenth century, the Rank family had been farmers.[3] John married Margaret Wreghit of Partington who produced their eldest son James (J. Arthur's grandfather) in 1829.

The introduction of steam power increased trade through the port of Hull, and John Rank purchased his first mill in town in 1841 on Holderness Road. He added a second on Southcoates Lane five years later.[4] John's son, James Rank, began assisting his father in the mill and was to continue in the family business, becoming a very successful flour miller. In 1851, James married Mary Ann Parrott, the daughter of Joseph Parrott, a local ship owner and master of one of the first schooners to put to sea with paddle-wheel engines. He has been described as 'a man of the sea, there was salt of adventure in his blood and some of his courage and independence was to descend through his daughter to his grandson.'[5]

James and Mary Ann's first son died at the age of four months and the sorrow that resulted from this tragedy caused Mary Ann to show an enormous indulgence to their next child, Joseph (J. Arthur Rank's father), who was born on 28 March 1854. The relationship between Joseph and his mother was intense and had a lasting effect, although tragically she died when Joseph was only four years old. Apparently he often spoke about her and it is said that her influence was with him throughout his life. James Rank married again, but Joseph pined for his real mother, and his childhood cannot be described as happy. According to the story, he developed trouble with his feet. This was said to be a direct consequence of having to squeeze into boots which were always far too small for him, because his stepmother would not buy new ones. It seems that his aching feet were just the outward manifestation of his crippled spirit. This general unhappiness affected his entire development. He walked with a limp; and he had a burning desire to prove his worth. His father, however, did not feel able to encourage him and spoke of him as being 'good for nowt!' He told colleagues that 'he'll never be much use in the world'. His stepmother went on to bear nine more children.

Joseph's unfortunate childhood was to get worse with a bizarre turn of events. As a young lad he was put to work in the mill and given the most menial tasks.

> I started with mending bags and sweeping floors and went on to grinding, packing and the dressing of old millstones... In those days we had no overtime in milling, and we had to work as long as the wind blew. No Saturday afternoons off, but if there was no wind we were allowed to leave at six o'clock.[6]

Despite this gruelling work there was no excuse for being tired. Once he was found fast asleep on a sack of flour when he should have been working. This angered his father, James. Around that time James met a miller from Aberdeen. They were comparing notes about how their sons were getting on, and the miller from Scotland declared that his son was no better than Joseph sounded. Extraordinarily, the two millers decided to swap sons. This was actually quite a good move for Joseph. He worked hard in the new environment and became fascinated by the Scottish milling techniques. As he became more interested, so his adopted Scottish father took him more seriously and Joseph was able to exchange notes with him on what he had learned, and they considered becoming partners. The Aberdonian wrote to James Rank saying that he had got the better of the bargain. In 1874 James died and left his property in the hands of Joseph's two uncles who had married his father's sisters. In this heartless move by his father, Joseph, aged twenty, was excluded from any future ownership of the mills. But he ran the mills on behalf of his uncles until he was twenty-one, when they gave him £500 and kicked him out of the firm. In addition, they placed an advertisement in the paper to say that Joseph was no longer with them.

His natural resentment led Joseph to break all links with the family. In 1875 he bought a windmill, but things did not go well for him and four years later he had lost £200 of his investment and, uncharacteristically, he decided to give up on it. Meanwhile he asked an elderly miller by the name of West if he could borrow his mill for three days a week when West retired. The old man agreed and even allowed Joseph to choose which three days he wanted. Joseph decided to do his milling in the early part of the week and used the other days for sales. He began working this mill entirely alone: he ground the wheat, collected the flour in sacks, canvassed for orders and delivered them himself. In the space of thirty years, from having the smallest milling business in the country he acquired the biggest personal investment in flour milling of any individual in the world.

In 1880, Joseph married Emily Voase, the daughter of a farmer at Ouborough, whom he met whilst buying grain for his mill. There is only praise for Emily: she was said to be patient, loving and resourceful; a devoted and loving wife and mother, who remained completely unaffected by the wealth that eventually came to surround her. Without the quiet, gentle, self-sacrificing partnership of his wife, Burnett (his biographer) believed Joseph might not have achieved success. They were to have three sons (James, Joseph Arthur and Rowland) and four daughters.

Joseph Rank had been brought up in the Wesleyan Methodist tradition but regular church attendance had become a duty without much meaning. Things were different after his marriage to Emily. They both became increasingly interested in the Christian religion, reading together passages from the Bible and having family prayers. They began married life attending the local parish church until the vicar preached a sermon emphasizing pre-destination. 'I've done with that church... I can't believe that stuff,' Joseph told his wife. They then began attending Kingston Chapel, at least a mile away. This religious reawakening coincided with Joseph's business expanding and becoming more successful. The two things grew together, his faith and his business. There was no question that Joseph considered these two events to be linked.

Joseph Rank's actual conversion took place at Waltham Street Methodist Chapel in 1883, when he was present at an evening service taken by the minister, Simpson Johnson. It was during the singing of one of Ira Sankey's hymns:

> 'Tis the promise of God full salvation to give
> Unto him who on Jesus His Son will believe

with the chorus:

> Hallelujah, 'tis done
> I believe on the Son
> I'm saved by the blood of the Crucified One...

It was then and there that Joseph made his decision to serve God always, and this stayed with him for the rest of his life. He had a clear vision of the Christian message, expressed in Charles Wesley's lines, 'For all my Lord was crucified, for all, for all my Saviour died'. His religion became a consuming passion that infiltrated every part of his life at home and at work. It coloured everything he thought and did. Joseph was later to say that he found it difficult to obey, but he never gave up trusting in God. 'If I take anything to prayer,' he was to say, 'I always succeed.'

His commitment to both his business and his God had a cost, as he admitted to *Milling* magazine:

> I have not much time to spare as most of my time is filled with business and church work... I am afraid, to a certain extent, the social side of my life has been neglected.[7]

At this time Hungary was at the forefront of European milling, producing excellent white flour of the highest quality. This was because they had started to use the 'new technology' of the day: rollers instead of grindstones. During Joseph's father's and grandfather's days, milling had been carried out by the old medieval method of millstones being moved by wind- or water-power. The first roller mill was built in Hull in 1884. This damaged Joseph's trade but in 1885 he retaliated by employing Simon Engineering from Manchester to build a six-sack roller mill which made proper patent, high-grade, white flour.

The new mill was named the Alexandra Mill and it was to be the start of Rank's phenomenal success. Joseph introduced this modern method to his milling business only after an enormous study of the details and the processes involved. But while many millers shunned the new ways of working, Joseph went forward full of confidence in himself and in the business, for he realized that it was necessary for British millers to adapt to the new machinery in their industry. If they didn't, the superior flour that these machines were able to produce would come in from abroad—the United States or Hungary—instead of the British mills. However, local opinion of Rank was still very low and his new mill was nicknamed 'Rank's folly'. How sweet it must have felt when his business grew so big he had to plan new mills to cope with demand. The Clarence Mills were put into operation in 1891 and were recognized at the time as the finest in the country. By now his income had begun to grow and poverty had been replaced with a much more comfortable lifestyle.

Joseph Rank was not, it is said, an easy man to live with. His job was stressful; he would bring his worries and problems home with him and he was not good at keeping them to himself. Nor did he suffer fools gladly. He would, according to R.G. Burnett, 'lash with an unmerciful tongue, not only his closest associates, but even his sons'.[8] There is no doubt that Joseph's wife, Emily, was the stabilizing force who dominated and protected her children's lives. She was the mediator and confidante dealing with all their difficulties and troubles. It was she who would write to the boys away at boarding school, providing them with news of day-to-day life at home.

Joseph's and Emily's children were not allowed to go to the theatre or public dances, but the circus was allowed and once a year Joseph took them all to the circus in Hull. Watching cricket was encouraged and dances were acceptable so long as they were in the home. Joseph encouraged the children in sporting activities, but punished anyone who was suspected of cheating. He himself played tennis, croquet, billiards, golf and cricket.

Joseph Rank's material success was largely to do with his energy and hard work, but it was also partly due to an uncanny knack of knowing exactly when to make certain decisions. There is a story of a board meeting when Joseph sat with his two sons, James and Arthur, and told them that a man was coming over from Belfast to buy a mill in Liverpool. 'Don't you think we should get it and buy it before him?' he asked his offspring. They both thought it was a bad idea, so the board decided not to buy. Later the brothers realized they had made an error of judgement and came to their father to arrange for the purchase he had suggested. They then discovered that he had in fact gone ahead anyway and had made a tidy profit.

The great secret of Joseph's success was to get the right wheat and then damp it and keep it until it was in perfect condition. It had to be just right and Rank had cracked the technique. His prowess on the wheat markets was legendary, and his ability to gauge risk-taking was due to a combination of genius, hard background study and common sense—and some have added that it was also an inclination to gamble. For instance, he would suddenly, seemingly at whim, buy in grain, just hours before the price was due to rise. This 'sixth sense' was something he used when interviewing would-be employees. He had the ability of always picking the right sort of person for the job in hand; his employees were important and vital for the business, and he spent much time choosing and deciding on the right person. J. Arthur was to inherit the penchant for gambling but only some of his father's sixth sense.

Joseph's knowledge of the trade, and his influence, spread far beyond his native Hull. He knew that the Americans had not only already adapted to the new reform of the industry, but they had also the advantage of fine quality wheat grown in their own country. In an interesting parallel with a trip his son Arthur was later to make, Joseph visited the States in 1902, making it clear that to see US flour on sale in Britain would be very unpopular. The repeal of the Corn Laws in 1845 had made Britain a free-trade nation, so cheap imports of wheat could be used legally. This had ruined some British farmers and Joseph is known to have supported protection for home agriculture, insisting that all the wheat we needed could be grown in Britain and the Empire. His son was to have similar views about British films.

In 1905 Joseph Rank moved to London with the headquarters of his company, leaving the Hull end of the business in the hands of J.S. Kemp. The first decade of the century was a time of great growth for Joseph Rank Ltd and in June 1908 the capital was increased from £900,000 to £1,100,000. In 1912 a fourth mill was built at Birkenhead in order to serve Ireland and the north-west of England. By 1914 Joseph had four or five mills in Hull. His six-sack mill, Alexandra Mill, had become a fifty-sack mill, and he had new mills in London and Cardiff.

Throughout all this business success Joseph Rank's faith and practice of religion was never neglected. The Sabbath was very important to him. He and Emily would do the accounts every Saturday evening, but they never worked after midnight. His mills would be closed on Sunday, but they started again at

1 a.m. on Monday mornings, closing at 9 p.m. on Saturday nights. Joseph's faith provided him with a security and a discipline in the volatile world of business, and it allowed him to see farther ahead than most of his competitors, giving him the courage of his perceptions. His money and his faith were bound together. He saw God as helping him to make the money—in order for him to give it away in God's service. Joseph had an Old Testament view of wealth; it came with the territory of a committed faith and dedicated service to God. *The Methodist Recorder* reflected on this theme of the marriage of money and faith in their obituary of Joseph Rank:

> Together with his friend T.R. Ferens he gave a conspicuous example of the 'exceeding broad' injunction concerning Christian fellowship, (of which John Wesley was an outstanding illustration in precept and practice), which teaches that the good things a Christian should be ready to communicate include not only spiritual knowledge but also material wealth. As riches increased his heart was not set on them but on the good he could do by their means.

As religion was being instilled into his children's consciousness so was good business practice and sometimes it must have been hard to distinguish between them. When the First World War broke out in 1914, Joseph was in Austria having treatment for his rheumatism. He did not at the time believe that the political situation was very serious, and he found himself interned. But his main concern was neither his own safety or worry about returning to Britain, but whether his sons would obey his parting instructions not to buy any more wheat until he returned, or overrule his commands and take advantage of buying immediately before the prices began to rise. It was a great relief and a cause of thankful praise to God for Joseph to hear that those in charge had bought while the going was good.

After he returned to Britain and war was under way Joseph was asked to join the Wheat Board. He told the government, 'You want to [should] stuff wheat into every building that you can find.' This would then form a second line of supply in the food blockade. But Lloyd George's government thought he was being silly, since they believed it would all be over by Christmas. Joseph Rank then said: 'Well, if the government will not buy it, I shall!'[9] So Joseph began storing wheat and eventually sold it to the government when they needed it.

Joseph Rank did all he could to preserve the production of flour during the war years. His influence as a major, worldwide customer for wheat played a vital role in obtaining wheat during those dark days. Due to his precise knowledge of all the neutral markets Rank was continually able to outwit the enemy. It transpired that during the war, Joseph Rank had made £2 million profit. (His son Jimmy was to have similar foresight at the time of the Second World War.).

Joseph Rank now employed 2,800 people. He lost his beloved Emily in July 1916 when she died suddenly from a stroke. In 1918 he married her sister Annie and was now rich enough to be able to say to his new wife, 'We've got enough money to live on for the rest of our lives.' He used his wealth to start one of his biggest philanthropic ventures, the Joseph Rank Trust.

His granddaughter Shelagh Cowen thought he was a wonderful man, though rather stern and imposing. She remembers being absolutely terrified of him, with his forbidding, leonine features.

He would say 'Come here, little girl, and what have you been doing?' and then he'd give me £1 to go back to school with.

He was once described as a 'bewhiskered tyrant who carried his lunch in a paper bag and refused to install elevators in his office buildings lest his workers become lazy.' Former president of the Methodist Conference, the Rev. Dr Kingsley Lloyd, formed his own impression of this hard businessman:

Joseph Rank was rather a narrow evangelical, a real Victorian and not a very good employer. He was all for grinding the faces of the poor and making money.

He was ruthless and, while there were other big milling businesses his grew while they failed. He was to pass his business ethics onto his sons as well as his fierce and somewhat ugly patriotism. Joseph told *Milling* magazine:

We must remember that we cannot get away from the law of the survival of the fittest, whether we like it or not. It is a natural law, and human nature without competition would soon become effete. 'Ca' canny' may last for a time, but if it is carried on for two or three generations, Englishmen, who are perhaps the quickest and the most adaptable workers in the world, will lose their capacity for work, and other nationalities will rise to the top.[10]

Not all his workers could cope with this, and some found little mercy in this Christian capitalist. There is a story of one of his long-term employees in Cardiff who developed a lung condition due to inhaling too much flour dust. When he complained he was dismissed without any compensation. Nevertheless, there were very few strikes in the firm he created and there were good relations with the unions. Joseph Rank Ltd was the first industry to introduce a pension scheme. The company was also very keen on welfare and recreation, holding frequent sporting events and days out for the workers and their families. And, because the company was so spread out around the country, an internal magazine was issued, named after a popular brand of flour, *As You Like It*. This was designed to keep all staff aware of the size of the operation and to feel part of the Rank 'family'.

Joseph was sometimes a hard taskmaster with his staff and he could be equally tough with his bankers. Robin Cowen, Rank's son-in-law, remembers hearing one story about Joseph Rank which was again to have an interesting parallel in Arthur's life.

One mill he built he managed to put in the wrong place without a deep-water berth, and he needed money for another. So he barged into one of the banks during a board meeting and said, 'I want to borrow some money. I make £10,000 a year, I live on £2,500, I have a thriving business—what else do you need to know?' He got the money forthwith!

But Joseph Rank could also be mean. One day at one of his mills he asked for a flour sample. The employee given the task of preparing it wrapped it up in two new sheets of brown paper with two lengths of string because it was for the boss. Old Joseph roundly rebuked him. 'You use one piece of paper and one piece of string—how do you think I made my millions?!' Memos sent between managers in the firm were written first one way across the page and then the other, which made reading difficult but saved on stationery costs.

Like his son Arthur, Joseph was not an easy man to have in the boardroom because any decision he made had the 'divine' stamp of authority and was therefore rendered unarguable. Divine guidance was frequently sought in the privacy of his office where Joseph would go down on his knees to pray for heavenly help on points of detail in the firm's policy. Later he would openly admit to his colleagues that he had been divinely guided towards a profit-making decision.

He was a very private man and showed none of his sons' tendencies to house parties or having a good time. Nor did Joseph Rank believe in giving out money unnecessarily. Alfred Beck remembers a conversation with Joseph Rank when he was treasurer of the Tooting Mission while he was having sandwiches in the vestry with Joseph, his mentor. He was reporting a balance in hand to the annual gift day and inquired, 'Mr Rank, have you possibly overlooked your usual subscription?' 'No,' said Joseph. 'The funds don't need it, Alf!'

Joseph Rank could also be an enormously generous man with his money and had a sympathetic side to his nature which occasionally showed itself to his employees. One of them whose wife was taken seriously ill, went to Joseph to ask for a loan of £50 to pay for his wife's treatment. Joseph said, 'No, I won't lend you £50.' The man turned to walk out of the office. Rank waited for him to open the door before saying, 'I'll *give* you £50.'

He was well known for donating vast amounts of money to various charities even though he tried to give anonymously. He gave more than £300,000 to the city of Hull alone. He was determined to devote a high proportion of his wealth to religious and philanthropic works, and it would be hard to number the causes he rescued. Another minister described him as the most generous and deeply spiritual layman he had ever met. Joseph Rank gave very large sums to the Methodist church. Ever since the inspiration he received from the early days when he used to hear sermons given by the lay preachers in Hull, Joseph held local preachers in great admiration. It was in 1933 that he gave £40,000 to the welfare of an association designed to look after retired preachers: 'There is no need to say anything about it to anybody. I don't want my name to appear in connection with it. Simply regard it as a gift from an appreciative friend of local preachers.' Four years later another sum of £25,000 was added.

Other recipients of his spontaneous generosity were The Wesley Deaconess Order and the Wesley Memorial Church at Epworth in Lincolnshire. He also gave £25,000 to the Commemoration Fund when the Methodist churches united. Various hospitals received funds, as did the Methodist War Emergency Fund. All these gifts were eclipsed by the amounts he gave in his support of missionary organizations. His first wife was very enthusiastic about missionary work and at one stage of his life he seriously considered taking up the vocation. The work of overseas missionaries fascinated him, and he gave with warmth and affection, wishing to know about how the money was being spent and in some way share the burden of alleviating suffering. R.G. Burnett writes: 'He wanted to be sure that it would, above all else, commend to others the Saviour who meant so much to him.'[11]

In one of his public speeches Joseph Rank remarked: 'I have found as much or more real joy in handing out as I have ever found in raking in.' This is an honest reflection on the fact that his money-making did bring him happiness and he was a big enough character not to deny this. After all, he had spent his entire life making sure that a transaction in business would only be made if and when it made a profit for the business.

Alongside all his giving, his business was booming and expanding. His Premier Mills at Victoria Docks, Silvertown in London were opened in 1922 and were proclaimed the biggest in Britain. The flour made there provided bread for 1.8 million people every day. Other impressive mills included the Atlantic Mills at the Barry Docks near Cardiff and then, later, the works at Birkenhead; all were outward symbols of a thriving industry. On 17 November 1933, the company was reorganised into Ranks Limited and it was front-page news around the world. R.G. Burnett writes: 'The boy who had swept the floor of his father's mill at Hull was now the head of the largest firm of flour millers and grain importers in Great Britain, and his fame had spread over every continent.'[12] Joseph Rank was Chairman and the managing directors included his two sons, James Voase Rank and Joseph Arthur Rank, and his son-in-law, Sidney Bruce Askew.

Joseph Rank shunned the publicity associated with the launching of the company. Newspapers called him 'the mighty miller of Hull'. When Sir John Ellerman died in 1933, it was said that Joseph Rank took his place as the richest man in England, but Rank's office issued a statement which gave some food for thought: 'We repudiate any statement that Mr Rank is the richest man. What makes a man rich? It is impossible to say who is the richest man.'

On his eightieth birthday, Joseph Rank was showered with praise and recognition but, true to form, his essentially humble nature and down-to-earth personality would not let such tributes go to his head. A great honour for him at this time was the decision to confer upon him the Freedom of Kingston-upon-Hull. In replying to the Mayor of the City Council, who gave him a silver windmill-shaped casket, Joseph Rank said,

'I claim no credit for success in life. I have but used one gift of common sense and I have always been supported by loyal and devoted fellow workers in my business. I have followed the rule of John Wesley—"Gain all you can, save all you can, give all you can,"—and I have found more joy in giving than in getting.'

In spite of the social status which Joseph Rank automatically acquired with his wealth, what mystified his colleagues was that he spent his spare time superintending a Sunday school and visiting poor children in their homes. In 1910, when he first became a Sunday school superintendent, he had over 1,200 pupils under his charge each week. He was also a circuit steward and class leader. 'His great humility made us all feel proud of him,' explained one of the ministers.

As the years went by Joseph's sons and son-in-law were given more and more of the responsibilities of the business. They had all been trained under Joseph Rank and he had guided them throughout their lives. As the younger generation took on more so Joseph gave more time and energy to his religious and charitable work. Joseph also had more time for his beloved cricket. Every August, he travelled to Scarborough for the cricket festival or, if in London, he would go to Lords. Joseph was also a great animal lover. He loved horses and dogs and if ever he was not found in his office he was almost always to be found in his stables and kennels, discussing the finer points of horsemanship with those exercising the horses and looking after the dogs. It is not, therefore, surprising that his children inherited this love of animals. His son, James, showed an interest in the turf and, surprisingly, Joseph approved, although he was less keen on the gambling associated with it, and he especially objected to the press confusing their names and was angry when a headline read: 'The millionaire Methodist racehorse owner'.

Joseph 'enjoyed' his love of horses, but he never let any such passion become more important than his work. Arthur, and his brothers and sisters, were greatly influenced by their father and mother who both worked very hard physically and mentally. Whether the sole aim for all this industry was in order to make money, or whether it was a puritanical streak in Joseph's character, the result was that hard work was the norm in the Rank household and Arthur, throughout his life, proved that he had an innate and enormous capacity for it. The remarkable achievements of his father were hard to live up to, but Arthur never shirked from doing just this.

J. Arthur Rank had tremendous respect for his father. The effect Joseph had on his son's life is incalculable. In a crisis Arthur would always ask himself what his father would have said and done. He was just as religious as his father, if not more so, especially towards the end of his life, but he always had a slightly more broad-minded approach. His father's faith though, had a great impact on him and it was particularly influential on the way he meshed his business and religious goals. When he was sixty he said to John Davis, his closest business partner, that on the centenary of Ranks the millers in 1975, he would return to Hull and tell the people there of his father's great achievements, of his faith and his ambitions and would pay tribute to him. Unfortunately, due to his own death in 1972, he was unable to carry out his promise.

In 1941 the Clarence Mills were destroyed in an air raid on Hull and not only was the great production capacity of the mills lost for a time but, as a contemporary commentator put it, 'the physical roots of a century's industrial tradition were disturbed.' Nearing the end of his life, Joseph Rank viewed the wreckage of the mills and said 'Some of my life-work seems to be going away fast'. R.G. Burnett says that he gave no sign of his sadness. He asked whether they had got the horses out in time and then said 'What's done can't be undone. It's no good thinking about the past. It's the future that matters. A few bombs can't destroy our work. After the war we shall build new and better mills.'[13] New mills were built on the site but they did not come into production until 1952.

When in the early 1900s Joseph Rank moved the family down to Bushey Down, Tooting in London, he and his wife had to find a Methodist church to attend. They first attended the Upper Tooting Mission but Joseph found it too 'high' Wesleyan for him; he preferred church worship to be of the most bare and basic kind. Walking in Tooting Broadway in the early 1900s he heard some people attacking the gospel, which angered him. This event, coupled with his conviction that the working classes wanted a straightforward, simple service with no frills, led to him building a new church: Tooting Central Hall. It opened on 10 November 1910 and was one of the greatest moments in Joseph's life. It was popular with working men and their families, with as many as 1,700 attending. So Annie and Joseph worshipped in the church he had built where, although a millionaire, he became Sunday school superintendent. This entailed him going to church every Sunday afternoon and staying on until the evening service. Towards the end of his life he worshipped at Redhill Central Hall where eyewitnesses described him as an austere, frightening man who didn't mix with the ordinary people in the pews.

Joseph Rank had a problem with anything other than the simplest forms of Methodism. The Rev. C. Leonard Tudor (later General Secretary of the Methodist Home Mission Department) was a young minister in Northampton at Park Avenue church and he wrote to Joseph asking for money to help with the building. The letter came back saying that if the building had a spire he would not contribute to it. Tudor replied, 'It has a spire and you can keep your money!' To which Joseph replied, 'Good for you, here's a cheque.' Joseph liked domes, wasn't keen on spires, but admired confidence above both. There is no doubt that Joseph's money, and later his son Arthur's, has had a massive impact on the Methodist Church but it is debatable whether the effect was a good one. As we shall see later, controversy surrounded Arthur's relationship with the Methodists, but the main legacy left by Joseph was in the form of his Central Halls which have become quite a burden to the Methodist establishment of today. What he wanted to do most was to preach the gospel to the poor and those outside the churches. The Rev. Dr Kingsley Lloyd comments:

> He thought this was a great way forward, to get in the crowds and preach the gospel to the working classes.

What Joseph desired was well-designed community halls rather than more traditional church buildings. These were to act as a half-way house for those who found going into a church intimidating. Fifty such halls were built by the time of his death. Joseph had a great vision for them but it is one that has never really been fulfilled. One can sit now in a half empty hall and think how marvellous it must have been when they were full every Sunday, but in the majority of cases they never were. Joseph, through the Joseph Rank Benevolent Trust, would only give money for the building of the halls if they were furnished with seating for 1,000 or more. There are several which have 1001 seats—unfortunately, they couldn't be filled then and they certainly can't be now. But Joseph believed God had told him to build them and there was no argument. Some believe that if he had been a little bit more open to guidance from other quarters other than his direct 'hotline' to the Almighty, more good might have been done. The Methodist church would have been very different materially but more advanced spiritually.

Annie died from a stroke, like her sister, in 1940 and Joseph's faith helped him through this bereavement as it did through his first.

> Religion did for him what wealth could never have done. It gave him serenity and peace; it saved him from disillusionment and cynicism. A well-known scholar and preacher who had no predilection in his favour—who, indeed had been criticized by him and had in turn criticized his critic—described him as one of the few rich men likely to enter the Kingdom of Heaven'.[14]

Joseph himself died in Reigate on 13 November 1943, aged 89. He left £1 million to Methodist charities. Long before his death he cannily gave his stock in his flour mills to his sons and their four sisters, leaving a taxable estate of only £70,000 and all his offspring millionaires in their own right. But his legacy, especially to his youngest son Arthur, was far greater than money. He had passed on his faith and confidence that anything was possible with God and, crucially, that God and business could be happy bedfellows. Hard work, a loving family home and total integrity were also high in the pecking order of imperatives for his youngest son's life plan. J. Arthur Rank lived his life and conducted his business very much along his father's guidelines.

Tributes were paid to Joseph throughout the press and the radio. The BBC announcement of his death was heard by one grandson in a German prisoner-of-war camp. Joseph Rank's body was laid in the family grave at Sutton, Surrey. Memorial services were held simultaneously at Wesley's Chapel, London and in Belfast, Cardiff, Edinburgh, Hull and Liverpool.

The *Methodist Recorder* obituary on 18 November 1943 referred to his:

> ... exceptional business ability .. by his integrity,
> diligence prudence, courage and simple living, [he]
> built up a milling business from small beginnings to
> one of the largest organizations of its kind in the world.
> In him was 'a well of water springing up to eternal life'
> which infused itself into everything he undertook... His
> was the path of the upright, and it shone more and
> more unto the perfect day into which it cannot be
> doubted he has at last entered—the joy of his Lord.
> For if the Lord knew how hard it is for those that have,
> or that trust in riches to enter into the kingdom of
> heaven, what joy there must be in his presence at the
> arrival of one who did not indeed abandon his wealth,
> but, steadfastly using it to high ends, was kept during a
> long life by the power of God through faith unto a full
> salvation.

Joseph Rank died one of the richest men in England.

2 ARTHUR RANK'S EARLY YEARS

High is the rank we now possess; but higher we shall rise;
though what we shall hereafter be is hid from mortal eyes.
SCOTTISH PARAPHRASES (1781)

Joseph Arthur Rank was born in Hull on 22 December 1888 while his parents were at Willersley House, Pearson Park. His father maintained for many years that he was born on 23 December and that was when he always celebrated his birthday until a business deal required the production of his birth certificate and the real date came to light. J. Arthur was the youngest son of Joseph's seven children—three sons and four daughters. Family life was dominated by Christianity. Just as his father's mills shut down on Saturday nights, neither was work done in the house on the Sabbath. On Sundays the children would gather and sing the children's hymn and read from the Bible, and the family joined the congregation at Queens Road Methodist Church in Hull where Arthur eventually started to teach at the Sunday school and was appointed joint superintendent. From that day he was hardly ever absent from Sunday school for the next fifty years. Of the sons, Rowland was the clever one but Arthur was quick, incisive and a bit of a 'know-all'. He could always do things better than his brothers and was often showing them how, until one day they hit him with a tennis racket and broke his nose.

Isolated incidents aside, the childhood of Joseph's children seems idyllic. There appeared to be almost no disharmony in the home. Both parents stayed very much in love throughout their life and the large family home was run on a strict but simple routine. Although wealthy, they never allowed themselves to be tempted by luxury and found contentment in the unpretentious pleasures of a very ordinary family with children's games, home-made bread and cakes and rambles in the countryside. For all seven children the strongest memory was going to church four times every Sunday: Sunday school was followed by the eleven o'clock service, then another stint of Sunday school in the afternoon before the evening service. Church-going not only became a natural part of their lives, but its importance was stressed by the fact that their father, who suffered a great deal from lameness in his feet, often hobbled in great pain to church and back, saying that 'the Lord's work must be done'.[1]

Arthur was sent to The Leys, a Methodist boarding school in Cambridge, with his brother Rowland. This is quite surprising since Joseph Rank didn't really believe in formal education, saying 'I didn't have much myself, and I haven't done so badly'.[2] (The eldest son, James, went to Hymer's College.) Rowland excelled but Arthur was not very happy. He was in School House from 1901 (third term) to 1906 (first term) and he was promoted only one grade in these five years. Although not unheard of at that time, this does not show a very advanced academic potential. Arthur's father Joseph, like his father before him, was never very impressed with his son's intelligence and used to say to him, 'you're a dunce at school and the only way you'll get on is in the mill.' So Arthur, like Joseph, started at the bottom and worked his way up. This probably explains Rank's oft-quoted sayings: 'It's better to be born lucky than clever' and 'The cheapest thing to buy in the world is brains'. Throughout his life, in certain company, Arthur would repeat that his father used to say he was a dunce. This must have left a mark on him and given him something to prove. In contrast to his lack of success in the classroom he was quite good at lacrosse, playing in the second team most of the time, but also playing in the first team on occasion. One of his teachers, a certain W.H. Balgarnie (James Hilton's role model for Mr Chips) remembered Arthur as 'a very small boy at the bottom of the school... a merry, irresponsible boy, amiable and popular, and enjoying life after his kind'. Arthur did enjoy life. From an early age to the grave, he would find fun in almost everything he did. His humour was never subtle and could err on the cruel side; he enjoyed jokes of the practical kind. During a school holiday, reunited with his eldest brother James, he emptied a sack of flour over James' head. He left school at seventeen and went straight into his father's mill, where his first job was to sweep the floors. There followed six months in the London office, then six months' attendance at the Mark Lane corn market. He worked his apprenticeship with W. Looker of Exchange Roller Mills, Luton, returning to his father's business in London for eighteen months, and working in all stages of the milling business.

Education for all Joseph's children stopped after they left school. None went on to university, as it was presumed that, for the boys at least, when they left school in their teens they would enter at the bottom of the ladder in the family flour business. Arthur might well have regretted the fact that he did not have three years' further study at university after school. A little more knowledge of literature, the arts and university life would have stood him in better stead for some of the situations in which he would later find himself. On one occasion when Arthur was talking about one of his religious film scripts, somebody asked him if he had written the script. 'No, when I was eighteen I was only taught to sweep floors and carry sacks of flour on my back... ' However, as Alan Wood pointed out, at least Arthur was not tainted by the upper-class belief that 'no real gentleman works'.[3]

After his training, Arthur's first real job for his father's firm involved him being sent to Hull, where he spent a year in charge of the newly built D Mill. During this time he had to live in digs on his own. This is where, it is said, he relinquished for a while all the deep-seated family traditions that had become so entrenched. For instance, he stopped going to church on Sundays and, it is said, he had his first cigarette, which almost caused him to be sick, on top of a bus. He did hold out on a bribe from his father not to smoke before he was twenty-one and received £250 as a result. At the Hull mill, Arthur worked from five in the morning until eight at night, spending eighteen months working his way around the mill in every job. He returned to London and lived with his parents again and joined the Premier Mills. So keen and hard-working was Arthur that when there was a strike and every ship at the London docks was behind with its unloading, he personally unloaded the stocks of Russian wheat bound for the Premier Mills. He had already learnt that swallowing black treacle counteracted any irritation caused in the throat by the dust from the wheat.

When war broke out in 1914, Rowland and Arthur went into the forces. Arthur joined up in an ambulance unit and reported to Edgware Railway Station in November 1914. Among those reporting for duty was Roy Hake, later Lt Col. R.J.V. Hake and a director of Rank's Religious Films Ltd. By that winter they were out in France. At first Arthur drove an old Panhard taxi converted into an ambulance, then he was promoted to sergeant and was in charge of about twenty ambulances. Stationed around Ypres, Salient and the Somme he became a gunner and then a signalling expert in the gunners and a deputy-lieutenant. Those who were with Arthur in the war remembered him as being a very popular member of the sergeants' mess. He was always a teetotaller, which seemed odd to most people, but he was not such a 'goody-goody' that he never used bad language. It was during the war that Hake and Arthur had an argument about drink. Hake said that he would never come to visit Rank if he would not allow alcoholic drinks in his home after he was married. The outcome was that Arthur, although remaining a teetotaller throughout his life, did always offer and serve alcohol to visitors at his home.[4]

There are some instances recorded in war-time which give colour to Arthur's character. On one night in particular, whilst billeted in a warehouse, Arthur, dressed only in a vest and underpants, danced and played the mouth organ and accordion. During the second winter of the war, he was part of a theatrical group that went round entertaining troops. They put on Pinero's *Dandy Dick* and it is well remembered how Arthur took the female part 'with such zest and enjoyment' that one gunner came up and said he reminded him 'of his old woman'.[5] These incidents had no specific bearing on the rest of his life, except it shows his continued sense of fun, and a tendency to behave outrageously.

While on leave from his duties in 1915 he joined the board of Joseph Rank Ltd but it wasn't until 1917 that he was finally withdrawn from the army and had to organize women's labour in the mills.

In October 1917 he married Laura Ellen Marshall, the eldest daughter of Sir Horace Brooks Marshall. This was to be the most important and longest-lasting relationship of his life and was a very happy marriage (Chapter 7 deals with this in more detail). It was at this time that Arthur was initiated as a freemason into Lodge No. 2729 in Streatham. He was introduced to freemasonry by his father-in-law to be whom he admired greatly. Marshall had been a senior founder of the Lodge at Streatham in 1898. After his initiation on 4 October 1917 he went through his second and third degrees on 6 December 1917 and 3 January 1918 respectively. He remained a member there all his life but never attended again after the death of Lord Marshall in 1936. And, as he never took office of any sort in the lodge, he may have stopped attending even earlier.

Although there is now perceived to be a conflict between Christianity and freemasonry, at the time there was no question of young men, and especially those in business, joining a lodge. In 1923 he had also been a petitioner (founding member) of Lodge No. 4520, the Old Leysian (based on his old school), which was consecrated on 22 February 1923. He resigned from this Lodge in 1952. After some investigation into his Masonic activities I can only conclude that they can't have meant that much to him. I have been informed that he didn't get the spiritual satisfaction he was hoping for, which might have accounted for his non-attendance. It is not possible to conclude whether his Masonic links affected his employment decisions in his business life. In any event, he kept paying his subscriptions at Streatham until the time of his death and thereby maintained some regular contact with the Lodge. One close relative speculates that he may have regretted joining the organization. Certainly it was only on rare occasions that he subscribed to Masonic charities, though in some instances of individual need of a member or their dependants he could be very generous.

When he was thirty-one his father gave him £1 million, saying 'there won't be any more when I'm gone' (though he was not ungenerous with his sons while he was still alive). It was decided that James, as the eldest son, would take over the family business. Both the other brothers were given shares in Joseph Rank Ltd. Rowland acquired a firm called Mark Mayhew Ltd, near Battersea Bridge, so that he could try out his own ideas. It was an archaic establishment and soon had to be pulled down. Sir Alfred Gelder, Rank's architect, rebuilt it and after Rowland's war service he returned to the newly built mill and became a miller in his own right. Later, when Rowland wanted to visit his father or brothers at Baltic House, he made an appointment as an individual miller, rather than just calling as a member of the family.

Meanwhile, Arthur went into a firm called Peterkin's Self Raising Flour, which also dealt in jams and pastries. This was to turn into one of the few outright failures in his life. He made a complete hash of the business. Whether, unlike his father, he did not have the guts to sack some of the staff who were not pulling their weight, or whether it was because the firm was given to him by his father to run, thereby depriving him of any will to succeed, is not clear. The end result was that he gradually sold out and returned to the family firm. Joseph was cross with his son but he allowed Arthur back into the family business. While his eldest brother James, looked after the wheat buying and the commercial side of the business, Arthur looked after the milling side. Rowland's business did somewhat better. He set up Associated London Flour Mills in competition with his father and brothers.

The three Rank brothers were very different, and quite competitive. Only Arthur inherited his father's faith and his teetotalism and, probably as a result of this, he was Joseph's favourite. Rowland, the most intelligent of the three, was also the most idle. Like the others, he shared their father's love for animals. He redesigned part of Aldwick Place in Bognor Regis for breeding racehorses and greyhounds, and his father enjoyed visiting there. In 1937, his greyhound 'Rotten Row' won the Waterloo Cup, and he kept vintage brandy that could only be matched by the cellars of the Prince of Wales. Rowland does not seem to have figured significantly in the life of his brother, and he died aged 54 in 1939 from the after-effects of being gassed in the First World War.

The eldest brother James (Jimmy) became a *bon viveur* and is described as blunt and cheery. He freely pursued his passion for racehorses, the gambling side of which did not impress his father. He became a successful breeder and eventually England's biggest racehorse owner and was given the great honour of being elected to the Jockey Club on the same day as Sir Winston Churchill. He bought Druids Lodge—the famous racing establishment in Wiltshire—in 1934 and, as well as horses, he also bred Wolfhounds and Great Danes. His wife was described by the *Sunday Express* as 'the most spectacularly successful woman punter the racecourses have ever seen'. Despite their different approaches to life James looked out for his youngest brother's welfare and when, aged 44 in 1933, Arthur lay ill with a burst appendix, James came to see him in Reigate and demanded that King George V's doctor, Lord Dawson of Penn, should attend him.

The job of a flour miller seems uninspiring to the outsider and one might conclude that none but a very dull person would take up such an occupation. However fair or unfair this perception is, there was undoubtedly a certain intellectual dullness about J. Arthur Rank that seemed to permeate his character. He achieved a remarkable amount in his life: he amassed wealth; he moved in a world steeped in glamour and excitement as well as holding a very powerful position in the City; yet, in spite of it all, he managed to remain largely untouched by it. Rank was, in many ways, very ordinary and uncreative in the artistic sense. People have thrown in so many conflicting testimonies of his character and behaviour that it is important to hold up the placard 'paradox' at this stage. The curious mixture of dullness and charm, sacred and profane, frugality and extravagance, sociability and seclusion at the heart of this unusual man may hold the reason why he was later driven to challenge the movie industry.

Unlike his two brothers, Arthur found that his Christian faith was increasingly important to him. From 1919 he was a regular teacher in the Methodist Sunday school at Reigate. He had returned to the faith after his short spell reacting against it whilst working in Hull. His faith was not expressed in any overtly dramatic form at this stage of his life; it was just part of him which he practised whenever he felt he could. The absolute ordinariness of Arthur lay in contrast to his hidden strengths. From the outside he looked and acted as a 'rather dull flour miller, the dutiful younger son of a famous father, shy and silent'.[6]

But in one respect Arthur was very different from his father—he had the ability to compartmentalize his life. He could be at a Methodist prayer meeting for an hour and then appear the life and soul of a party straight afterwards. He had the gift of allowing himself to concentrate so hard on what he was doing that he could switch from activity to activity, mentally and physically, without any trace of forgetfulness, awkwardness or irritation. Without this exceptional ability it would have been impossible for him to have done all he did and still have a happy marriage and active leisure life. Unlike his father, he didn't let his stress get to him outside the office or boardroom and when it came to relaxation he enjoyed himself immensely, which must have helped to keep his colossal responsibilities in perspective. Yet by the age of forty, Rank's life hadn't really found its true expression. He had achieved nothing on his own and, dominated by his father, whom he still called 'Sir', there was no obvious way forward in the milling business. A bored, slightly dull miller, with large financial reserves, a tendency to enjoy risk taking and an evangelical zeal, Rank was ready for something completely different.

3 THE RELIGIOUS FILM SOCIETY

O that the world might taste and see
The riches of his grace!
The arms of love that compass me
Would all mankind embrace.

CHARLES WESLEY

Say the name of J. Arthur Rank, and everyone thinks of the
movies. Those magic words 'J. Arthur Rank presents...' and the
man with the gong whet the appetite for the exciting, familiar
darkness of the cinema. But not everyone is aware that Rank's
extraordinary foray into the movie world came about as a direct
result of his evangelical Christian faith.

By 1930, aged forty-one, Rank was a solid citizen of
considerable wealth and a comfortable social position, living in
a smart house in Reigate. He had a reliable and secure job in
the family firm, but with his father safely in charge of the
family firm and an elder brother waiting to assume control, he
was at least subconsciously looking for a way to prove himself,
especially after his failure at Peterkins Flour. He had been a
governor at his old school, The Leys (1919-28), Honorary
Treasurer of the Leysian Mission, Deputy Lieutenant of the
City of London (1923) and President of the National Sunday
School Union (1929). He enjoyed his cigarettes (an expensive
brand), cards, shooting partridges and a round of golf, but life
was becoming a bit too unchallenging to occupy his energies.
It might even have been said that he was bored.

Rank's new interest rose out of the need to redesign an old one: Christianity.

He had always been certain that his job as a Christian was to pass on the message of his faith, but now he became convinced that its great truths should be portrayed in film. Young people were a great concern of his. Rank had been a Sunday school teacher all his adult life and he was to remain one for the rest of it. He had become dissatisfied with the primitive teaching techniques of the day—dull pictures and scripture recitation. Long and dusty sermons were not good enough, in his mind, for the communication of the gospel. It is said that his first inspiration to make films came during one such long and dull sermon. He thought it would be better if he could bring the Christian faith to life in moving pictures and show them to the children in his Sunday school.

After one such church session, Arthur said to his friend Hake, 'I have been listening to forty minutes of drivel.' His desire to counteract this waste of time led him to start a popular Sunday evening service in a school. He asked his secretary to find some religious films that he could show. Initially she couldn't find any but eventually some primitive pictures were found and he started to show them in the evening services with singing and band music completing the entertainment. This was to be the beginning of a whole new stage of his life.

Rank was not the first to think of teaching children about the Christian faith using film. The Rev. F.W. Chudleigh had started 'cinema services' for children, and children's cinema clubs had been open in the East End of London since the start of the decade. The Rev. Thomas Tiplady also predated Rank in using films for religious purposes. Others had observed, as Rank did later, 'Children can't sit still to be taught by word of mouth. But they will sit still and concentrate if they can identify themselves with the adventures of characters on a screen... if they are interesting enough.' Maybe Rank would not have come to this conclusion had he actually been any good as a Sunday school teacher but the truth is that he failed to communicate with his pupils and, although they loved him as a person, they did not find him easy to listen to.

However Rank reached this conclusion, the idea of showing films in church was an extraordinary thing to do since many religious people of his day, including some in his own church, thought films were nothing less than 'the devil's own work'. These first films would only have been silent pictures of general interest—for example, a primitive camera showed pictures of Jerusalem. Generally they would have been very simply made films and easily rented for a few shillings. Even so, Rank saw the excitement on the faces of the children and became hooked on this new means of communication, realizing what a dramatic means it could be to spread the Christian message. In addition, he quickly saw that this exciting new medium would be a powerful force in society, as well as a way of publicizing his own beliefs and principles and the British way of life of which he was so proud. It is not clear where his desire for mass communication came from, but it was to be with him for the rest of his life. Within ten years of this first enthusiasm he was to own studios, cinemas and distribution rights worth £50 million and have influence in every branch of the business.[1]

It is reported that Rank's first idea for making religious films was to film a good preacher and then distribute his sermon throughout Methodist churches. Rank obviously didn't share his father's high regard for the quality of local preaching. At least this way, Rank believed, the punters in the pews could be guaranteed to hear a good sermon. There was, however, an in-built resistance to films of any kind among the churches and the thought of replacing a live minister with a screen and a projector was unthinkable unless you had Rank's vision and enthusiasm. Seeing that there were not going to be any takers for his filmed sermons, he adopted another approach and decided to tell stories using film.

In 1932 Walter Knights was an organizing secretary of Methodist Publications Ltd, which was one of Rank's companies (perhaps an early indication of Rank's media interests), in the section dealing with church magazines. One of the newspapers he looked after was *The Methodist Times*, edited by R.G. Burnett.

At the time the paper was conducting a campaign against films in the cinema. Rank's father-in-law's business, Horace Marshall and Sons, Newspaper and Periodical Distributors, was based in the same building. Although Rank was primarily concerned with milling, he did have some interest in his father-in-law's business and was a frequent caller. He established a firm friendship with Dr Benjamin Gregory who was Ministerial Editor of *The Methodist Times*. Gregory became Rank's right-hand man, involved with everything Rank was doing at that stage, and was connected with film work right up to his death. One Saturday afternoon, Knights had a call from Dr Gregory saying that Arthur Rank wanted a chat. He recalled:

> He [Rank] came on the phone and said, 'I would like you to be interested in films.' I said 'I never go. Neither have I the time or the interest. I don't know anything about films or their making. As for religious films,' I said, 'there aren't any.' He said, 'Ah, but there will be one day.' To my surprise I said, 'Well, I'm very happy with what I do at present and I will be reluctant to stop. Haven't you made a mistake?' He said, 'Come to my office on Monday morning at 9.30.'

Knights went to Leadenhall Street, the headquarters of Joseph Rank Ltd, and there Rank told him about a company of men called the Guilds of Light who had been meeting. Originally set up to counteract the mainstream cinema, which it feared and loathed, the society, which had R.G. Burnett (biographer of Joseph Rank) on the committee, was quick to condemn the commercial film industry. The industry was described as 'the greatest crime-producing agency of this generation'.[2]

The chairman of the Guilds of Light was Thomas Marks, a barrister from the Ealing Methodist Circuit. Other members included the Rev. Callan Young, a Congregational minister, and Mr Bradbrook who was Secretary of the Religious Tract Society, in whose office they used to meet. They had approached Rank about a certain project which he hadn't time to investigate, so he asked Knights to go along and meet them. Initially, they were interested in finding out whether films could be used in church work. They were aware that the amount of material was very limited and mostly silent. Eventually Rank came to a meeting and they talked about making a film using his money. In this way, in 1933, the Religious Film Society came into being.

Knights had also visited the Lambeth Mission where the Rev. Thomas Tiplady (a Yorkshireman like Rank), had been running his film service since 1928. The Ideal, Lambeth was a church which had been converted to run as a commercial cinema on weekdays. Tiplady had seen the potential of film for reaching non-churchgoers long before Rank and had had considerable success. He had had to ensure the place was fireproof before he could open it as a cinema and some of the money, £2,000, had come from Joseph Rank.

Tiplady had already been fighting Rank's battle with the Methodist Church, which strongly disapproved of his ideas. *The Methodist Times*, which had been supporting the 'Clean Film Campaign', launched an outright attack under the heading, 'Sex, Drink and Gangster Films in Methodist Mission Hall.' Tiplady had said they were over-reacting and that most films were not bad. A reporter went to visit the Ideal on a weekday when Tiplady was showing a sex-triangle drama called *The Tarnished Lady* and noticed that although the pulpit was faintly visible in the gloaming he could not see the cross. 'Perhaps it was as well,' wrote the reporter, 'that the cross remained hidden. It was an immense opportunity. What did he give them? Two or three hymns composed by himself, half a dozen slides illustrating the story of David and a silent film depicting the adventures of a gang of Mexican robbers. There was no evangelistic appeal whatsoever' (*The Methodist Times*, 18 February 1932).

But Tiplady was attracting full houses of young people and, with the help of films to illustrate his moral and religious teaching, and the first use of a projector and screen to teach people hymns and prayers, he was carrying out his ministry. 'Every Sunday night for thirteen years a long queue waited outside the church for the doors to open and they filled every seat. It began at 6.45 p.m. and we did not close until 10.00 p.m.' Tiplady had done a lot of Rank's groundwork in making films acceptable to the Methodist Church at large. He had a regular feature in *The Methodist Recorder* and on 11 February 1932 he wrote words which summed up a lot of Rank's thinking: 'The cinema is the greatest invention since the printing press and the Church must put aside all moral, intellectual and artistic snobbery and, either directly or indirectly, bring this invention into the service of Christ.' Tiplady received requests for advice about using films for religious and educational purposes and a year before the Religious Film Society was founded, he was proposing a national organization to distribute films of a religious nature. In March of the same year he wrote in *The Methodist Recorder*:

> We have not adopted the cinema. We have allowed the
> world to capture it. In the Bible and in *Pilgrim's
> Progress* we have material for a hundred films. The
> church's blindness to the possibilities of the cinema is a
> tragedy of the first magnitude. Some day churches will
> awake. I prophesy that within fifty years every church
> will install in its Sunday school a cinema machine. Our
> great preachers will make 'talkies', and preach in a
> hundred churches at one and the same time, and our
> finest choirs will be heard on the 'talkies' in our most
> out-of-the-way village churches...

In a sense, with the millions of pounds Rank was about to spend, he was right. As a result of Knights' visit to Lambeth, Tiplady came to the Guilds of Light. Soon afterwards, it changed its name to the Religious Film Society.

Rank's interest in cinema was solely, at this stage, to promote the religious message with stories and pictures of an excellent quality. He realized that the films shown in churches and halls needed to be of the same high quality as those made at ordinary cinemas, or people would not bother to watch them. He strongly believed God had given him the job of making good-quality religious films.

Rank did not share with the original Guilds of Light their complete antipathy to the movie business. He was not a cinema goer and he was not out to get Hollywood. He merely wanted to promote Christianity through good films. Indeed, Hollywood had not ignored religion as a source of good stories. As McNab points out in his book *J. Arthur Rank and the British Film Industry*, religion had produced some of the greatest American box office successes, such as *Four Horsemen of the Apocalypse*, De Mille's *The Ten Commandments* and *King of Kings*; all these films had had considerable appeal and financial success. R.G. Burnett and his colleagues, however, thought that US producers had 'caricatured and misrepresented' religion.[3]

The newly formed Religious Film Society couldn't decide on their first story until Rank produced a book from his briefcase called *Lax of Poplar*. For a man of no known literary talent he rather surprisingly announced, 'Here is your story and if no one else can write the script, I'll write the script.' Everyone was stunned by this sudden exclamation and, no doubt, bowled over by his confidence. At the next meeting they decided that it should be made.

W.H. Lax was a famous Methodist evangelist, one of the most important preachers of his day and three times Mayor of Poplar in London's East End, where he had a mission to the poor. Rank agreed to fund the project but there was an early hitch. The star of the show, Lax himself, flatly refused to co-operate. He said he couldn't face his congregation if he got mixed up with films, and he added, 'Mr Rank, what you have proposed to me I could not possibly tell my wife.' Rank turned to him and said, 'Mr Lax, I want you to go home and pray about this. We want you in this film—we can't make it without you... now I want you to go home and come back in a month's time.'

A month later and Knights remembers a very different Mr Lax.

> He came in quite joyfully and brimming with
> enthusiasm he said, 'I'll make the film, I can see the
> possibilities. Yes, Mr Rank, I'll make that film. I can see
> myself preaching to people who I've never seen or am
> likely to see. I'll make that film!'

So, in 1934, the first of Rank's religious films, called *Mastership*,[4] was made within a week at Merton Park Studios. It was not unintentional that the star was a Methodist minister; this would help it to find favour in the sceptical Methodist churches, most of which thought the movies a corrupt force.

It told the story of a squabbling East London family who were all brought to salvation by Mr Lax's preaching. It also dealt with the evils of alcohol abuse. At the end of the short but emotive film, the evangelist leans towards the camera to drive the message home:

> Is there anything more sad than the sight of a human
> being mastered by a vice?... There is nothing more
> joyful than to see that individual conquer his vice and
> surrender his life to the mastery of Christ.

The film lasted twenty minutes and cost £2,700. It was directed by Aveling Ginever who ran a small film company called Gee Films. It was described as 'avowedly a cinema sermon which could be incorporated in any religious service of any denomination.'[5] Lax turned out to be a very good actor and was appreciated in the studios. The film premièred at the Polytechnic on Regent Street and the Archbishop of Canterbury was invited. After that, it was decided that Knights should go around the churches with the film to try and interest them in it. This was the humble start of J. Arthur Rank as a film distributor.

The use of the new medium and the heart-rending strength of the message had a powerful effect on many audiences. On one occasion, in a miners' club in South Yorkshire, the film was greeted with a long, stunned silence. The local pastor eventually stood up at the front and said in suitably hushed tones, 'You have seen the challenge. Who is your master? Do you want drink or do you want Christ? If any of you are prepared to accept Christ, stand up now.' Twenty-four men, with tears in their eyes, rose to their feet. Knights remembered it as a moving experience—'they were tough boys'. Furthermore, when a copy was sent to missionaries in China and the Far East, six Chinese Communists who saw it became converted to Christianity. No doubt Rank's heart glowed when such reports came back to him, even though later on he himself was to describe the film as 'lousy—there is no other word for it'. Made purely as an evangelistic enterprise, *Mastership* was never shown commercially.

The film saw the end of the brief working relationship between Rank and its director, Aveling Ginever. They went their separate ways mainly due to their different views of theology. Ginever had made an earlier film *In Our Time* on the theme of Christ dying for all, whether believers or not. Arthur did not like this idea; he believed that only those who personally trusted Christ received the benefits of his death.

Inasmuch (1934), Rank's second religious film, was based on the life of St Francis of Assisi, and the part of the abbess in the film was played by none other than Greer Garson in her first screen role. Filmed at Merton Park Studios where *Mastership* had been made, it was directed by Alec Saville. Donald Wolfit played St Francis but, in spite of his presence, much of the acting and technical production of the film fell well below the standards of the day.

Rank was concerned about the quality of his religious films, and within a couple of years had taken important steps to ensure that films of a far superior quality could be produced on a permanent basis. With this in mind he arranged for his next two religious film productions to be made using the superior facilities at the Rock Studios, Elstree, and 1935 saw the release of films on two very different religious subjects. The first was an adaptation of a story by Canon S.N Sedgwick of the last days of the life of Christ as seen through the eyes of Barabbas. Although hampered with a very stilted script and hammy acting this was technically much superior to either of his previous productions.

One problem with producing films based directly on gospel events was that the scripts were always written in 'Authorised Version' language, a style which persisted until the end of the 1940s. The intention was to avoid giving offence to sensitive Christians who believed that Jesus really spoke in the style of the King James Bible translation. While this was acceptable some of the time, its use for the entire dialogue often led to stilted and slow delivery from the actors. In *Barabbas* this was not improved by the self-conscious acting of Torin Thatcher who plays the leading role and of Christine Silver who plays his mother. In one scene she visits her son in prison and Barabbas describes how he is likely to suffer death by crucifixion. All his mother can muster by way of consolation is the immortal line: 'There, there, Barabbas.'

Torin Thatcher also appeared in the second film made at the Rock Studios later that year, which was in every respect a much better production, by far the most intelligent and professionally made story commissioned by the Religious Film Society up to that date. Titled *The Common Round* it ran for just over half an hour and was clearly influenced by the success earlier that year of Alexander Korda's production *Sanders of the River*, an Edgar Wallace drama set deep in the African jungle. In Rank's film Torin Thatcher plays a missionary in a similar remote African district who has to fight plague and prejudice. He is helped in this by the faith in Christ that was instilled in him by his old headmaster Dr Pike. The climax of the film shows the rescue of his mission by an aviator who turns out to be an old school chum. The freshness of the script and the story stems from the fact that it was not tied down to previous religious experience by being based either on an actual biblical story or on the life and work of a well-known preacher or saint. The cast of the film also included the Black actor Robert Adams and the character actor George Zucco, playing the part of the missionary's old headmaster, who was later to find fame in Hollywood. The film was directed by Stephen Harrison, who eventually moved from film to television and became a pioneer of television drama. Both he and James Sloan (usually credited as Jas B. Sloan), the director of *Barabbas*, were to work with Rank on his most ambitious production *Turn of the Tide* (1935) which became J. Arthur Rank's first feature film (of which more in the next chapter).

Although Rank was paying for all these films, he had no knowledge of how they were made and he wasn't too interested in finding out. Eric Cross who was the cameraman on *Mastership* remembers seeing a man stray on to the set and have a look at his camera. Cross said, 'I'm sorry I must ask you to leave, you're mucking around with the equipment—are you involved with the production?' A shamefaced Rank apologized for being in the way and then got out of it.

Meanwhile, Walter Knights took Rank's religious films all round the country, into prisons and youth clubs, schools and women's meetings. Once he even took some to Chequers at the request of the Colonial Minister, who was entertaining heads of various colonies. As more films became available, the approach was more organized. Knights would get a directory of all the ministers in any given area or town and invite them to a showing. He met thousands of ministers that way and the word about Rank's religious films spread. Rank underwrote all this activity very heavily. Once, when things weren't going so well, his small team told him so and said that all his money was going down the drain. Rank didn't look at it like that. 'We are buying experience, and experience can be very costly at times. Carry on, you're all doing your best.' The only times he complained was when, in his view, things weren't going quickly enough: 'We must get out to where the people are,' or when he felt people were not trying. 'I can't' was not acceptable to Rank unless 'I've tried' preceded it.

Up to this time the Religious Film Society had been forced to hire commercial studio space either at Merton Park or Elstree to make their productions. In effect these were 'sponsored' films in which the Religious Film Society footed the bill while the actual production of the film was undertaken by a professional film company. With the success of his films so far Rank now realized that more films could be made economically if he owned his own studios to make them. With this in mind the Religious Film Society adapted an old cinema in Gypsy Hill, Upper Norwood for the production of their future films. Mrs Rank opened the new studios in mid-1937 at a ceremony which included a dedication by the Bishop of Lichfield.

A set had already been built for their ambitious first production from the Norwood Studios: a forty-minute biography of the great Christian scholar and translator, William Tyndale. The film was written, and the studio scenes were directed, by a newcomer to the Religious Films unit, Lawrence Barrett. The film was notable for the fact that extensive location photography took place in Hamburg, Cologne and Antwerp on the exact locations which were associated with Tyndale's life. The film now has a historical value, as large sections of the medieval areas of Hamburg and Cologne featured were destroyed by bombing in the Second World War. The part of Tyndale was played by Alan Wheatley. Barrett was to remain author and scriptwriter of many Religious Film productions for the next thirty years.

The Norwood Studios, while giving Rank unlimited time, and therefore the ability to produce more films more quickly, had their drawbacks. Owing to their limited size they were not ideal for the production of biblical stories which occasionally required large sets. Director Jas B. Sloan complained that camera movements were severely hampered by lack of space. The sound system also left a lot to be desired, particularly when films were later released on 16mm and shown in church halls with poor acoustics. Even so, several short biblical films were completed, including *Fishers of Men* and *Who Then Can Be Saved?* (both 1938), the latter being photographed by Eric Cross who had filmed *Mastership*. The part of the rich young ruler was taken by John Laurie, who was to appear regularly in British films over the next forty years. The most ambitious story to be filmed at the Norwood Studios was an adaptation by Lawrence Barrett of a play entitled *The Proconsul* which told the story of the persecution of the churches in the third century.

It was during this pre-war period of production at the Norwood Studios that an affiliate company was set up to handle the distribution of films throughout the network of churches and schools that Rank had established. This company was Religious Films Ltd and it was RFL, as it was affectionately known, that continued the effective distribution of 16mm religious films until long after Rank's death in 1972.

While all this was going on Rank's interest in commercial film productions was growing. He had already established British National Films Ltd in 1935 with Lady Yule and John Corfield. The following year Rank set up Pinewood Studios with Henry Boot from Boots the Chemist. At his eightieth birthday dinner Rank remembered:

We needed millions to keep it working. So we went to a certain bank (which I don't like—I won't mention its name) and they said, 'That's alright, but just as a matter of form, it'll have to go before the board.' But the board turned it down. I said to Lord Portal (who'd suggested this bank) 'This is a lousy bank if you ask me—I'm going to my bank' and I just said 'Look, I want this money, it'll be alright, I've never let you down yet,' and they said, 'You can have it with pleasure.'

It was Pinewood Studios that became the real rival to Alexander Korda's magnificent studios at Denham. Here Rank reestablished his relationship with Norman Walker, who had directed *Turn of the Tide*, and was busy in secular film production. Rank invited him to form a new production company with Dr Gregory (former editor of the *Methodist Times*) and Roy Hake (later Colonel Hake and Rank's land agent) who was a friend of Rank's from the First World War. It was Rank's intention that this company, GHW Productions—named after the initials of its directors—would produce religious films good enough to be shown in commercial cinemas. They did not need to confine themselves to biblical stories but would produce ordinary feature films with a religious slant, however veiled, as well as documentary and factual films which would be suitable for use within Rank's cinema circuits and also in churches via Rank's new 16mm distribution company, Religious Films Ltd.

In order to show the films, churches needed to be provided with equipment. This too was financed by Rank, and it was Walter Knights who was placed in charge of the Methodist Cinema Committee, a scheme by which a church participating in regular screenings would be allowed to hire a 16mm sound projector for £20 a year. The projector would be shared by a Methodist local group or circuit of churches, with each film being lent for a month. Walter Knights would personally visit the churches to demonstrate how to work the machinery, and also how the films should be used. Rank's cinema circuit had something in common with the Methodist circuit system, in which preachers circulated between different churches each week. Knights looks back:

It was hard to keep pace with the demand. On one
tour I visited twenty-one towns in succession and slept
in twenty-one different beds!

It was often possible to use a local cinema in the mornings for
a couple of hours to show the local clergy what was on offer. But
after the initial introduction the films were shown anywhere that
would have them: youth clubs, women's meetings, schools... There
were also special 'film missions' with a week of film services. In this
way, and thanks in no small measure to the extraordinary efforts of
Walter Knights on Rank's behalf, a very large number of films were
shown to a very large number of people.

The new company wanted a new image for their films, so
all the films made by GHW began with 'A GHW Production' on
the opening title card. GHW began its production schedule
with a series of well-made films on the life of St Paul, with Neal
Arden playing the title role. The production quality was on a
much higher level than anything which could be achieved at the
Norwood Studios, although only two of the series of five films
were made at the new Pinewood studios. When space allowed,
however, and the large sound stages at Pinewood could be made
available, as in the case of *The Way of Salvation*, it really showed,
and Norman Walker delighted in the excellent facilities
available to him. Walker was well known for his location work,
and in 1939 he managed to take a unit to the south of France
for exterior shots for *The First Easter*. Later that year, just before
the outbreak of the Second World War, he completed much
outstanding work in the fjords of Norway for a contemporary
story dealing with the problem of seemingly unanswered
prayer, entitled *Beyond Our Horizon*. This last film was widely
distributed as a supporting film through the cinemas which
Rank by now controlled (see the next chapter) and also on
16mm through Religious Films Ltd.

But how were all these films being received? Knights recalls:

I was often invited to a 'house party' and at one I took
along a film we had just made at Norwood called
Fishers of Men (1937). At this party were the local clergy,

and local people, shopkeepers and so on and the bank manager. The hostess was a wealthy lady and believed in the idea of religious films. After showing the picture the local vicar slaughtered it and said it shouldn't have been made or shown—it wasn't good enough. Others added their disgust and I had an uncomfortable time. But when everyone thought that the discussion was over the bank manager stood up and said 'I go to the cinema once a week and tonight I've seen a film I've never seen the like of before. It said something to me that no other film has said, and I want to pay tribute to those responsible for the production. I feel I owe it a great deal, I hope you understand that this film came here tonight especially for me.' Then he sat down. Everyone was very quiet, then the hostess asked me if I would close the discussion. I thanked her but said that the last speaker had made a fitting close. It is plainly evident that the religious film is one man's meat and another man's poison. It is strange how reaction differs, you find some helped and some want to complain, many wanted the endings altered.

In 1938 the presence of the experienced Tiplady on the board of The Religious Film Society finally resulted in a film based on his work in Lambeth Mission. It was called *A Prodigal Son* and was a modern version of the great Bible story. It ran for twenty-two minutes and was directed by Jas B Sloan. The Rev. Tiplady himself appeared in the film, which was partly shot in Lambeth, including his 'down-and-out' club. Tiplady wasn't totally impressed by it: 'The film lacks balance, some parts being over-emphasized,' but he concluded that it was 'specially useful for mission work'.

During the build-up to the war there was increasing public pressure for cinemas to open on Sundays. This was something with which Rank's religious beliefs must have struggled, but once again he was able to seize the opportunity for his mission. He went with a young John Davis, later to become increasingly influential in Rank's business matters, and Earl St John, both directors at Odeon cinemas, to visit the Religious Film Society studios at Norwood. Rank's concern was how to use this new situation to the best Christian advantage. It was decided that the Religious Film Society should make a series of three-minute 'shorts' under the overall title of *A Thought for the Day*, well produced and not too preachy. But, despite Rank's decision to use Sunday opening to Christian advantage, the religious hierarchy were still unconvinced it was a good idea. He must, by now, have been used to their raised eyebrows, but showing films on the Sabbath was really going a bit too far. Rank, however, was completely determined to take the gospel to where the people were going to be on a Sunday. There would be thousands of service personnel on the streets on the Sabbath with nowhere to go except the cinema. So he set about his lobbying with his usual commitment and confidence, and put his case before the top brass in the Church of England. During one of these confrontations a very senior cleric summed up their fears:

> But Mr Rank, we know there's going to be a war. And
> supposing a soldier is asked what his religion is, he
> might not say C of E, RC or OD, he might say Odeon
> or Gaumont!

Of course, it was far from Rank's intention to turn the cinema-going population away from religion. In the event, over 300 religious 'shorts' were made and were shown throughout Rank's screen network, with a new one being shown every three weeks. Any clergyman who was anyone made a recording (even Donald Soper, who was quite opposed to Rank's methods and theology) and in pride of place just before the main feature, it was bound to have an impact. Some shot from the hip:

> Whenever you're prompted to do a kindly action,
> remember the slogan 'Do it now!' I knew a man once
> who used to say 'I try to live so that when I die even
> the undertaker will be sorry.' Remember the lines,

'I shall pass through this world but once, any good therefore I can do or any kindness I can show to any human being let me do it now. Let me not defer or neglect because I shall not pass this way again.' I don't know who wrote those lines but he was wise and his advice is never more needed than today.

If there were no filmed 'thought', a local minister would be asked to come on stage in front of the screen and give one in person. This practice continued on Good Fridays for many years. The Rev. Dr John Tudor remembers getting cat-called and booed, but really loved it. Most ministers, including the Rev. Dr Kenneth Greet, found these ventures into cinema evangelism 'very worthwhile'. Again, Lord Soper, disapproving though he was of Rank, did not miss out on this opportunity.[7]

I remember going on the stage. I was able to interest them and I took the opportunity to apologize for interrupting their innocent pleasure. But having been given the opportunity I wasn't going to turn it down. It was tolerated with a certain amount of agreement.

Derek Greeves, another minister, used to have to go to preach at the Odeon, Marble Arch, which he found a harrowing experience. He knew he'd failed to crack it when a couple on the back row went into a passionate clinch at the start of his talk and were still at it when he had finished.

Rank was never one for letters if a 'face-to-face' opportunity to discuss an issue was an option. He did make exception on religious matters and when dealing with cranks. A favourite complaint was that Rank showed films on a Sunday. To one such he replied:

You quote me from the Old Testament—I would refer you to the New Testament and Christ's teaching on the use of the Sabbath Day.

You rather infer in your letter that I am the type of person that is out to gain the whole world and have no concern about my soul. I can only say to this that I think it is a very unfair thing to infer without having any knowledge of me whatsoever, but for your information there is no danger of this, for I am glad to say I have a personal experience of Christ's power in my life, and His guidance in my daily living.

Coming to the question of the opening of cinemas... I am glad to say that recently, through co-operation with Church Leaders, it has been generally agreed throughout the trade that cinemas will not open until after Sunday school hours, and as more and more Leaders of Churches become convinced of the value of the opening of cinemas on a Sunday, and the good they can do, the more quickly will the programmes improve.

The justification for the opening of cinemas on a Sunday is very definite and there is conclusive proof that this is so, viz, the prevention of evil. From Court Missionaries and Chief Constables evidence is forthcoming that where the cinemas are open on a Sunday much drinking in public-houses is prevented; young people are kept off the streets and prevented from getting into trouble, which can have an effect on the whole of their lives.

In the cinemas that I control which are open on a Sunday, in nearly every performance a special film of about three minutes is shown, called *A Thought for the Day*, and in this three-minute short, the audience's thoughts are directed to higher things.

I am hoping, as the years go by, that this experiment, which has now become a permanent feature, will be developed, and will make it impossible for anybody going into the cinemas that I control on a Sunday not to have their thoughts directed to God; and eventually a film will be evolved which will enable them to worship God on the Sabbath Day.

I hope that my above remarks will be of help to you to understand the position a little more clearly.

All good wishes, Yours sincerely, J. Arthur Rank.[8]

The idea behind the 'religious shorts' was that they didn't preach or dictate but that they told a true story. Although it is inconceivable to imagine them being tolerated today, they did have an effect on some people at the time. And it was always Rank's philosophy that if one person's life had been changed then the whole enterprise was worthwhile. His religious film company received a letter from one older lady who had seen the first 'religious short' they made. Walter Knights kept the letter:

> Dear Sir, I was in your cinema last Sunday night and at the end of a newsreel there was short picture and it said that of all the people who are in trouble one of them might be your neighbour. I had fallen out with my neighbour, in fact we hadn't spoken for years but after seeing this picture I had an urge to go and knock on her door and I didn't want to go and knock on her door. But by late afternoon I could resist it no longer and I went and did so. When she saw me she beckoned me to come in and she burst out crying. She said, 'You're the only person who's come near. I received this telegram this morning, my son has been killed at the front'.

When the letter had been read to him Rank said, 'How much did you say this film cost? Well, this letter has paid every penny of it!'

Before the war there had been talks aimed at amalgamating the Religious Film Society with the Christian Cinema Council, an organization set up by the Anglican Church. The Christian Cinema Council's secretary, Mr Baxter, died suddenly in 1939 and the job was advertised. There were eighty applicants and the successful candidate was Noel Evans, a barrister from Gray's Inn who at the time was working for the Monmouthshire County Council. When he got the job he had no knowledge of films or film equipment but he was to play a significant role in the later history of Religious Films Ltd. At the outbreak of war Pinewood Studios were requisitioned and all production went to the Denham Studios which Rank took over from Korda who had hit financial problems and gone to the States.

Shortly after war broke out, a bomb hit the building in Holborn, where the Religious Film Society was based, and the offices were moved to Dunstable. In the provinces, Knights carried on showing his films in the Bedfordshire villages where people were happier to go than the towns, which were too risky. The RAF Chaplaincy department made an arrangement with an annual fee for their chaplains to hire films to show to their men, and Knights and his colleagues were often dispatching films in aircraft to various far-away places. In addition, Knights was approached by the public relations officer of a large manufacturer in Dunstable, who asked if a short selection of films could be put together to show to the workers during their lunch hour—the night shift lunch hour. That meant showings that started at midnight and went on until 1.30a.m. After a time the day-shift workers wanted films too, so the programme was repeated at midday. Soon there were requests for longer films, whether this was because the films were good or because the workforce thought this was a good ruse I don't know.

The films were given more respect than other war-time entertainment. In one venue, Knights and his team were setting up the equipment and noticed the stage was filthy and the back wall smeared with food. It was explained that Will Hay had been entertaining there the night before. Nothing like that happened to the Religious Film Society. But with Rank's energy behind them the films went everywhere. They were particularly popular in the air-raid shelters. A leading Methodist preacher, Dr Sangster, asked for them to be shown in the basement of the Central Hall Westminster, and they were also taken to underground offices along Millbank.

The war slowed down production but some quality pictures were made. *The Man at the Gate* (1940)—Rank's favourite religious film—tells the story of an embittered mother who has lost two sons at sea and is in danger of losing a third as well as her husband. She finds her faith by listening to George VI's famous 1939 Christmas

Broadcast which quoted from the hitherto little-known poem 'The Man at the Gate of the Year' by M. Louise Haskins. This went on general release and had a good reception. As was now the custom this film was directed by Norman Walker with Jas B. Sloan as production supervisor and Eric Cross (of *Mastership* fame) back as director of photography. The cast included William Freshman, Hubert Harven and Harven's wife Mary Jerrold, and the leading role was taken by Wilfred Lawson in the first of three films that he made for GHW Productions Ltd.

With the income and confidence derived from *The Man at the Gate* GHW Productions went on to produce their first full-length feature, again starring Wilfred Lawson, with Betty Stopfield as his leading lady. *Hard Steel* (1941) tells the story of a steelworks foreman who allows ambition to destroy his relationships with family and workmates. With the help of his wife and a lay preacher friend, he recognizes his mistakes and makes a new start. With a strong script, good production values and location work in a Midlands steelworks, this film conveyed its message effectively. It also contributed to the kind of British productions of the day considered most suitable for the war effort. It received full theatrical distribution and was favourably received.

If *Hard Steel* and *The Man at the Gate* could be described as quasi-religious films, perhaps more moral than spiritual, there was no mistaking *The Great Mr Handel*. Rank must have thought that with the success of his last two ventures this next one would really secure a place in the mainstream cinemas for religious films. In the end, making films showing the greatness of the British way of life was always going to be second best for him to making overtly religious films and getting them critically accepted and box-office-friendly. This film came about as his control of the British movie industry grew (more of which in the next chapter) and his confidence must have been running at an all-time high. *The Great Mr Handel* tells the story of the composition of 'The Messiah' and Handel's later years in London. It was Norman Walker, a knowledgeable and enthusiastic music lover, who persuaded Rank that there would be an audience for a film about Handel's great work. It was, after all, a favourite among all major choral societies and 1942 marked the bicentenary of the first performance. It was with this in mind that Rank consented to the film's production and moreover agreed that it should be photographed in Technicolor. Photographed by Jack Cardiff and Claude Friese-Greene and using lavish set designs by art director Sidney Gausden, the film attained a very high level of production with Handel's music arranged specially by Ernest Irving, from Ealing Studios. With Wilfred Lawson in the title role and Elizabeth Allan as his leading lady, the film contains a good balance between storyline and music. *The Great Mr Handel* was a landmark in film history, being the first colour film shot with 'character lighting' instead of the flat overall light previously demanded by Technicolor. However, filming in Technicolor was to have its problems, particularly during wartime, due to the precarious quality of the film stock available.

Technical advances meant that you could have your rushes developed overnight, see your day's work the next morning, check you were happy and then carry on. After the first day's shooting of this film they discovered that all the men had green eyebrows, so they had to start again. No expense was spared to make this, probably the finest of Rank's overtly religious films. But, with limited love interest and with a heavy emphasis on Handel's Lutheran spirituality, the result was empty seats in the cinemas and low returns at the box office.

Lady Rank was critical of it. She thought it wasn't relaxed enough and that it was too much like a stage play (in fact, it had begun life as a radio play by L. Du Garde Peach). Indeed, she was quite critical of a lot of Rank's beloved religious films. She voiced what many others thought as well—that even though the films were coming out new, they already looked old-fashioned. We need to remember today, however, that then as now, a film on the life of Handel would be regarded as 'art house' material—sincerely made, but unlikely to appeal to the wide general audience who were looking for escapist entertainment during the dark war years.[9]

Meanwhile, Rank had been looking at the whole state of the cinema industry—not just the making of films, but their distribution. What had started as a hobby had now become a business; a deep-felt mission had become a passion.

4 RANK'S TAKEOVER OF THE BRITISH FILM INDUSTRY

Faith, mighty faith, the promise sees,
And looks to that alone,
Laughs at impossibilities,
And cries: 'It shall be done!'
CHARLES WESLEY

To gamble when it is of little consequence whether a few thousand is lost or gained is probably not a true description of the word 'gamble', but it could be said that Joseph Rank was a gambler in the way he bought and sold wheat in order to make profit. It was a precarious business, although he had a special gift for 'getting it right'. Some of Joseph's children seem to have inherited this bold streak. Both Arthur's brothers went in for racing—horses and dogs—and Arthur, instead of continuing his settled, prosperous and secure work in the family business, with a hobby of making religious films, decided to chance it in the world of commercial cinema.

Although Rank's burning desire was to spread the gospel, his business sense told him that he was never going to get his overtly evangelistic films shown in the main cinema networks. So, while continuing to make his hard-core conversion pictures, Rank also started to make films with a more broadly-based appeal that kept a strong moral and wholesome story-line, which he hoped would influence people subconsciously into good living.

J. Arthur Rank possessed the stability and backing, both financial and spiritual, that allowed him, without undue effort, to take on this bizarre 'gamble'. When Joseph Rank heard that Arthur was going into the movie business he was very shocked. He was highly suspicious of the whole venture, and was mainly worried that Arthur would lose all his money. He also told Arthur, 'If you go into the film industry, you'll lose any reputation for honesty you've got.' Rank was later to recall his father's words and claimed confidently that he hadn't lost any of his integrity. It is perhaps significant that such was the dominance of Joseph over his son, that Arthur's film empire didn't really get going until after his father's death in 1943.

Arthur had been brought up by his father to act always with the brain of a businessman, so it came naturally and automatically to him to try to gain financially. While it would be unthinkable for him not to be considering financial gain, this would not be his sole reason for doing business. Indeed, it is well documented that Arthur firmly believed that God called him to the movies. In an interview with *The Methodist Recorder* on 26 March 1942, Arthur said:

> When I got into this business in all its sides and branches
> I realized the great possibilities for making entertainment
> films with a message that would not merely please the eye
> and stimulate the imagination but would also become a
> help in the serious matters of the daily lives of film-goers.
> I could relate to you some of my various adventures and
> experiences in the larger film world and you would not
> only be astonished, but it would, I think, be as plain to
> you as it is to me that I was being led by God.

Rank knew that films were the most powerful suggestive medium there was and he said, 'It should not be used to debase human values but to help men and women make this world a better place to live in.'

One journalist, perhaps uncharitably, concluded in *The Daily Herald* of 15 July 1948 that Rank had got involved in the movie industry because he was a man of inherited wealth and 'people like that are often driven into strange activities to prove that they are not just a rich man's son.'

I don't think there is any doubt that Rank's genuine conviction was of a God-given 'mission'. Although he used to answer questions concerning his motives for entering the world of films by saying it was a help for the country, or that films could do wonders for the export trade or raise national prestige, those who worked closest to him knew it was his firm belief in God which led him in that direction. The difficulty he had in persuading journalists that God had led him into films can easily be imagined. Fleet Street was uncomfortable with his real reasons, and Arthur was hurt and upset by the criticisms they wrote about his motives. He showed typical naivety in the way he expected journalists to see eye to eye with him and support him. Alan Wood describes how Arthur had commented on one article by saying: 'I don't believe he would have written like that if he had stopped to think that Jesus Christ might have been looking over his shoulder.'[2]

The key to the whole of J. Arthur Rank's career was his religion. His Methodism was not an insignificant eccentricity, it was the grounding of all his actions and decisions, although it may not always have been obvious. His ability to compartmentalize his life allowed him to change his whole manner if the situation so required. Consequently some have criticized him for not being sincere in his religion. This ability to change from the sacred to the mundane was part of his character, however, for both were important to him. Geoffrey Macnab describes Arthur's endeavour to become involved in films as 'a curious collision between business and missionary enthusiasm, a mixture of prudence and recklessness'.[3] This 'curious collision', within nine years (1935-44), made J. Arthur Rank the most influential figure in the British film industry.

So it was that the more publicly known motivation for Rank's entry into movies was his desire to communicate British values and the British way of life across the world. This was no mean ambition, given the domination of American films at the box office. No one knew it at the time, but Rank was to be responsible for the making of many great films of the forties that gave the British movie industry its 'golden years': *Oliver Twist*, *Henry V*, *The Red Shoes*,

Hamlet, Odd Man Out, Blithe Spirit, Brief Encounter and *Great Expectations*, to name but a few.

Although Rank offered his wholehearted financial and moral support to build a great industry, making sure it was equipped with the most modern technology, and although he created a world marketing organization and was willing to give producers and directors great freedom of action, many people both within and outside the industry did not take his intentions or his efforts seriously. They either doubted his sincerity or took advantage of his honesty for their own benefit. Some were also very critical of the virtual monopoly he was able to create. But the fact that Rank was so 'safe', financially, meant that he was able to give freedom to his creative workforce that no other situation would have been able to. Of course, with such a free rein to operate how they chose, there were some failures. Rank would remark, 'The trouble really was that I didn't know anything about producing films. I only took it on because there was nobody else to do the job.'

The first of Rank's more commercially acceptable films was *Turn of the Tide* (1935). It came about through a challenge in the *Evening News*, responding to a *Methodist Times* assault on the low moral standard of the films of the day. A reporter on the London paper challenged R.G. Burnett, the editor, saying, 'It's all very well finding fault, but why don't you produce a film that would be suitable for family showing?' The reporter even suggested the text they could use—*Three Fevers* by Leo Walmsley. Rank accepted the challenge on Burnett's behalf and, finding that he wasn't alone in wanting to raise the standard of British movies and present a good image of Britain to the world, he set up a modest company, British National Films, with another rich Methodist, Lady Yule. Lady Yule was the widow of Sir David Yule, a Calcutta jute magnate, who had died leaving her a fortune. They made a formidable team and added respectability to the venture. However, for Lady Yule, dabbling in films was a hobby and something she did not take that seriously. It is said that she was not at all interested in whether profits were made or not and it is claimed that at board meetings, whenever finance was mentioned, she started to yawn or lit a cigarette. John Corfield, who had introduced Rank to Lady Yule, became the producer of this first film. Norman Walker was hired to direct this glossy production of Leo Walmsley's novel which was to become Rank's first feature film. The cast included Geraldine Fitzgerald, Wilfred Lawson, John Garrick and Moore Marriott.[4]

Rank was hoping that *Turn of the Tide* would become a commercial success and break in to the American market, which dominated cinema. The film was beautifully shot against the North Yorkshire countryside around Robin Hood Bay and Whitby. It was well directed by Norman Walker, winning third place in an international film exhibition in Venice. David Lean, at the time a film editor on newsreels for Gaumont-British, was brought in to help edit some of the storm sequences. Unfortunately the film failed to recover its costs, although it was widely shown as a supporting picture in smaller cinemas. The owners of the big cinema chains at the time apparently laughed in Rank's face when he suggested they should show it as a main feature. They wanted more sexy stuff. This just wasn't box office; it was a good ordinary story about two fishing families. There appeared to be a concerted effort 'to keep this miller out of Wardour Street'. Rank was piqued that a good picture, made in England and internationally acclaimed, wasn't considered attractive enough by the distributors whose opinion he did not respect. 'I decided that the film business had got into the hands of the wrong people,' he said.[5]

Turn of the Tide had cost him £30,000 and he only got £18,000 back. Rank was the kind of man who never let disappointment get him down and he saw this not as a failure but as an opportunity. He saw that distribution was as important as production, and it made him look more closely at the box office. *Turn of the Tide* became rather an aptly named film as Rank learnt the crucial lesson that there's no point in making a product if you don't have a shop to sell it in.

It was at about this time, while he was still looking at distribution and ticket sales and deciding whether to gamble some of his money and energy on developing them, that Lord Portal and

Japhets the bankers helped him to make his decision. The British motion picture industry was in a mess and they told him that he was the man to clean it up.

Lord Portal was a trouble-shooter for the Conservative party. The Board of Trade, who commissioned him, wanted something done about British movies before the industry collapsed.[6] Lord Portal had been Chairman of the 1936 Berlin Olympics and Macnab writes: 'Lofty Olympian ideals, religious fervour and patriotism seemed to propel these two forward in their bid to rescue that endangered species, the British film.'[7]

The movie industry was a dangerous area for careless investment: the Prudential Assurance Company had lost £10 million backing productions and funding studios. At the time, 80 per cent of movie screens were showing US films and this fact was held largely responsible for the ailing industry. In 1927 the government had introduced film quotas to cut down on US imports and encourage more British production. However, US pictures had continued to dominate, with 5,000 cinemas and a weekly audience of 20 million largely dependent on them. Before the war US producers were earning £50 million a year from British cinema-goers.

This pattern had been broken by a film called *The Private Life of Henry VIII* (1933) with Charles Laughton, made by Alexander Korda for his own company, London Film Productions, United Artists in Britain. It was good box office in Britain but also did rather well in the States. It was soon realized that this was a way forward—to make big money in America which had 65 per cent of the world's market, and use the profits to make bigger and better British movies which could in turn earn more on the international market. This idea was put to Rank by Lord Portal but at the time, quite wisely, Rank and Japhets were unhappy about such a risky investment and preferred to concentrate on better distribution of British films in Britain.

C.M. Woolf, who had the best knowledge of the British movie business, had the same idea. He had been responsible for building up the Gaumont-British chain. In 1935 he resigned from Gaumont to form General Film Distributors Ltd (GFD) in which Rank and Portal invested. Rank had been warned off Woolf as a slightly dodgy character, but Rank rather liked him and decided to put his trust in him because he knew so little about the movie business and Woolf knew everything.

It is reported that Rank asked Woolf if he was prepared to sort out his reputation and 'go straight', to which he replied that he wouldn't let Rank down. After three months, Rank received a furious letter from a business associate saying that Woolf had double-crossed him. Woolf was duly summoned to Leadenhall Street, where Rank reminded him of his promise to be honest and Woolf declared that he had been. When Rank showed him the letter Woolf said that Rank should be aware of what this man had done to him. Rank pointed out that he had a different understanding of integrity—'It doesn't matter what anybody does, you've got to go straight!' From that time on C.M. Woolf never again let Rank down, and Arthur was lucky to have him as a partner and constant help. The two men were often seen together and a deep and lasting friendship developed between them. Rank always wore the watch which C.M. Woolf left him in his will when he died in 1942.[8]

Rank also went for finance to his friends in the City and support was pledged from among others Lord Luke (of Bovril), Lord Lindenberg (of Japhets), and Sir Edward Mountain (of Eagle Star Insurance). Never before had a film enterprise had such backers. It was a start, but with the Americans distributing most of the films in Britain, there was a long way to go. By now Rank thought he could win the battle to save the British movie industry. Portal then withdrew, having done the job he had been asked to do by the Board of Trade.

Under the guidance of C.M. Woolf and with Japhets' and other bankers' money Rank tried out a few productions and acquired a few cinemas. He set up General Cinema Finance Corporation in 1936 as a holding company to control the empire he was about to build. On Woolf's advice, Rank bought a stake in Universal Pictures which, at the time, had annual deficits of around $1 million. They needed someone to buy a 25 per cent interest for $2 million, which Rank was able to do through the General Cinema Finance Corporation. This involved an agreement to distribute its product in Britain and to distribute and produce its British newsreel. This was a good strategic and financial move and Rank profited from Universal's turn in fortunes over the next few years. Rank's deal was very much from his father's business textbook—'Buy up, or into, what other men have begun.'

Rank now had the opportunity to buy into the 300-strong Odeon chain of cinemas which had been built by Oscar Deutsch. Deutsch was a metal merchant and speculator from Holland who had put two or three mortgages on one cinema and used the profits to build another one. The first Odeon (Oscar Deutsch Entertains Our Nation) was built in 1930 in Birmingham. Deutsch's wife had been responsible for the interiors of his cinemas and between them they really changed the feel of 'going to the pictures'. His cinemas were large, seating an audience of two thousand, but the comfort, ambience and lighting were appealing and the public responded. But Deutsch had become heavily over-committed financially, through bad advice, and Rank had helped him out of various difficult financial tangles. During 1940-41 Deutsch and the Ostrer brothers of Gaumont-British were negotiating with Rank about bringing all their interests together. They used to meet in large motor cars in the park with drawn curtains to discuss the deals. Deutsch was suffering from a malignant disease and when he died on 6 December 1941 Rank got total control of the Odeon chain. By 1944 it was earning $1 million after tax. After Deutsch's death, Rank agreed to pay his widow a very substantial annual sum of money for the duration of her life.

Gaumont-British was also struggling financially. They had 275 cinemas in addition to several production companies and a television company. The company was first offered to John Maxwell, who owned the Associated British Picture Corporation and Associated British Cinema Ltd (ABC), with some 400 cinemas. But Rank outsmarted him and ended up in control of Gaumont-British whose assets amounted to $80 million.[9]

Rank now controlled two of the three big cinema chains and some production companies. He then persuaded Korda and Prudential Assurance to add to his Pinewood studios, which he had established in 1936, and build him new studios at Denham, which were to be the best in Britain. The Pinewood and Denham studios, along with the Gaumont deal, made up practically the entire modern studio space in the country. Korda was then persuaded to sell Rank a print laboratory, also at Denham, and Rank bought out another company which sold about 90 per cent of equipment and furnishings for British cinemas, including cameras, lenses, projectors, sound systems, screens and even chairs. Rank had turned himself into seller and buyer.

It took Rank nine years to complete the 'rationalization' of the British movie industry.

Rank was in control of the British film industry at the time of the movies' greatest boom. The war years proved a great boost for British films. In spite of the fact that resources were strained and many of the technicians and workers were called up, films somehow became a focal point for people to gather, feel patriotic and also be diverted from the endless news of war. Sir Anthony Havelock-Allan, a British producer, recalls:

> American pictures were slightly out of tune, not so
> many, not so good, not containing the kinds of names
> that took people into the cinema. Because the country
> was feeling patriotic... things about English people, that
> were funny about them or dramatic about them, they
> wanted to see them... If there had been stronger
> competition, maybe they wouldn't have... it was a very
> good period, when the odds weren't against us... [10]

Swept along by his own patriotism and the encouragement of the government, Rank carried on making films throughout the war, seeing his productions as a highly important part of the war effort and a contribution to national morale.

Macnab quotes a letter from a Mr T.H. Martin who wrote to *Picturegoer* praising British films:

We are sick and tired of having American films (chiefly second rate) rammed down our throats, and please don't say: 'Do you have to go? There's plenty else to do'. They may be slick of production and technically sound, but they are filled with Oomph-oozing women, their bodies covered or uncovered so as to stimulate the sexual rather than the artistic senses; not forgetting the immaculate negro either depravedly drooling inarticulate dirges or attempting to knock seven hells out of a valuable piano.

Imagine, therefore, what refreshing contrasts are provided by British films, full as they invariably are, of superb acting by people full of character, and in which one can almost exist, so realistically and vividly are they portrayed.[11]

Not everyone agreed with this outpouring of patriotism. Those who showed the films were not always so keen on British films. Macnab quotes that Mr Greenhalgh, chairman of the Bolton branch of the Cinematograph Exhibitors Association, was unhappy with the quota system which demanded that 15 per cent of his time on screen had to be given to British films.

I see no reason why I should bolster up incompetence by being forced to give 15 per cent of my screen time for British films on which I know I shall lose money. The British public, in the main, does not like them, and shows its dislike at the box office as my records prove. Those people who claim to like British films are those who only see the much boosted films and their views do not represent the views of our patrons as a whole.[12]

However, US films still dominated British screens, mainly because there were many more US films. In 1944, only thirty-eight British features were released.

In a very short time Rank was right at the centre of the British film industry. Macnab speaks of 'a general state of amazement' at

Rank's achievement and states that although Arthur frequently referred to his doing what God was bidding him to do, some critics were more inclined to put his rise in the film industry down to luck—for instance, a number of deaths of top people in the industry had allowed Rank to gain power. In an astute summing up of Rank's drive, Macnab describes it as a combination of 'that war in his psyche between business and benevolence'. He sees Rank as both an evangelist and a businessman—one who had enthusiasm for communicating a message, and the capitalist knowhow to gain the power to do so: 'both wolf and lamb'.[13]

Many people were mystified by Rank's swift acquisition of so much of the film industry. He had extremely limited knowledge of film production and he was not particularly creative. What was more, he was not artistically or aesthetically appreciative of the medium. Macnab tells us that it was his policy never to judge or pass comment on any films made under his auspices, commenting that he was not qualified to make such a judgment about something he knew so little about. Culture of any kind was not his strong point.

Nevertheless, towards the end of the Second World War, Rank was in the position to make the big pictures Lord Portal had wanted years before. He could put Britain firmly on the movie map. Rank's name was almost synonymous with films and his trade mark of a man banging a gong, first seen after the war, which was actually taken from General Film Distributors, was instantly recognizable.[14]

But amidst all this enormous power playing, Rank remained the businessman who could still get into trouble on the sets of his movies. Alan Wood's book has a story similar to Eric Cross' during the filming of *Mastership*. When Jessie Matthews was making *Climbing High* at Pinewood, she apparently noticed a tall, dark man standing watching at the back. She asked the assistant director if he could ask him to leave. Afterwards the assistant director said: 'It was quite all right. He couldn't have been nicer about it. I asked if he wanted anything, and he said there was nothing in particular, and he went without any trouble at all. He seemed rather a decent

73

chap.' Jessie Matthews asked if he knew his name: 'Yes, I think it was Rank, or something like that... '.[15]

Rank's motive by this time can no longer be seen as being as single-minded as at first. It had all become too complicated. With so many creative and business minds involved, a broader definition of his vision is required. R.J. Minney writes in *Talking of Films*:

> ... Rank, by drawing so much of the film business into his own net, was trying to keep the British film industry speaking with one voice—solidarity.'[16]

But for some, this was worrying. How could an industry of such diversity be forced under one umbrella? Minney goes on:

> ... because of the war and the shortage of films there was an eagerness to make more British pictures, but the opportunity was no longer available to newcomers; for now Rank had control not only of the greater part of the means of film production but also of two important circuits for showing these pictures... However laudable Rank's aim, nobody can possibly view without concern and even alarm the bringing under one individual control of so many studios, so many stars, so many technicians and so many cinemas.

Minney then draws a parallel with the outcry there would be if more than three newspapers were in the control of one man. Granted, he was writing long before the advent of Rupert Murdoch and somehow one feels that Rank's influence on his media was somewhat less directive and more benign.

Michael Balcon of Ealing Studios was one of Rank's critics. He was a socialist and he was frustrated because some of his films, including J.B. Priestley's *They Came to a City*, were not shown anywhere, despite all his efforts. His complaints led to a campaign against Rank through the Cinematograph Films Council, a body set up to advise the President of the Board of Trade. Eventually a government committee, under Mr Albert Palache, was appointed to report on any monopolistic tendencies in the film industry.

Rank refuted such suspicions, and put them down to a certain amount of jealousy in some parts of the movie industry. He was well defended in the House of Lords. Lord Brabazon said: 'It is highly inadvisable at present when a man like Mr Rank has engaged to fight the US films, to worry him with pinpricks.'

At the time, Hugh Dalton, President of the Board of Trade, was putting a friendly check on Rank's business movements and Rank did not buy anything else big in Britain, but in November 1944 he acquired half of the Canadian Odeon chain and laid plans for a 2,000-seater in Cairo and other cinemas in South Africa and Palestine. He also branched out into a new style of film-making, as a young Bob Monkhouse recalls:

> I... got myself a job with a new enterprise by the flour
> magnate turned movie mogul, J. Arthur Rank. He was
> setting up a cartoon film studio intended to rival
> Disney and had poached one of their top executives to
> run it, a steely-eyed Californian named David Hand.
> With him from Hollywood came legendary storyboard
> creator, Ralph Wright and one of Tom and Jerry's
> principal animators, Ray Patterson. From these men, I
> and forty others, were to learn the wonders of Walt.[17]

As well as cartoons Rank also hired the famous American director Wesley Ruggles to work on a musical, *London Town*, for the US market.

The main thrust of the Palache Report, set up to monitor monopolies in the film industry, was that a strong British film industry depended on a safeguarded independent production base. Macnab continues:

> The report posits an antinomy, monopoly v.
> independence, which itself harks back to the British-
> realism/Hollywood-whimsy opposition which some of the
> 'quality' critics sought to draw. Monopoly is associated
> with big business, inertia, a lack of creative imagination: it
> is the force for the bad. Independence, by contrast, is
> linked with flair, imagination and integrity. Independent
> producers are the Davids to Rank's Goliath.[18]

Except that, in this case, God was on the side of Goliath.

The Board of Trade stressed that, 'By independent, we have in mind both freedom from foreign domination and freedom from dominating British control.'[19]

Rank, however, because he owned studios, cinemas and a lot of money, could allow his producers to sustain losses without the problems they would entail had there not been the backing of the newly formed Rank Organisation and its resources. The result was that Rank's producers were far more creative and adventurous than any independent producer could be. Rank may have been the one controlling the money and not himself a very creative person, but because of the sheer volume of money, he was able to allow a free rein to his producers.

Although Rank was criticized for monopolizing the film industry, he always argued that he was no bigger than any of the main Hollywood companies with whom he was in competition. 'The Americans are tough, but so am I, and I have learnt quite a lot about the ways and methods of the trade.'

Rank's early encounters with the film industry had not left him favourably impressed with the personnel. Most of them did not meet his high moral standards of conduct and integrity. Hollywood stars' off-screen antics were often more lurid and better gossip fodder than their on-screen personas. He particularly didn't want any scandal or bad behaviour from his stars and so, towards the end of the war, his famous Charm School was established, where his actors and actresses were groomed for stardom. Acting and drama lessons were held in the Pinewood studios. Despite it being 'his' charm school, Rank's involvement was minimal, for it was run by managers and directors. Many famous names passed through it, including Joan Collins, Dirk Bogarde, Diana Dors, Patricia Roc and Honor Blackman. The charm school idea has been criticized in various ways but by none more acerbically than Ken Russell:

> ... Around this time British films were very high on
> charm. Officers in the forces had it to a man and no

one living in the West End was ever without it.
Commuters north of the Thames sometimes had it
while the unfortunates south of the river seldom had it.
People from the East End never had it. J. Arthur Rank,
the film and flour mogul, dreamed of making a fortune
by exporting it on celluloid and opened a charm school
for that very purpose. As long as the encyclopaedia of
cockney rhyming slang exists, J. Arthur will be fondly
remembered... [20]

When Rank had found someone he could trust he put all his
faith in them, even to the extent of allowing them to write their
own contracts. Sir John Mills found himself in this position and
was struck dumb. He recalled in a BBC Radio 4 interview in 1990:

Rank came into my dressing room at Denham Studios
and said that he'd been thinking about signing me up
under contract. I suggested that he should talk to my
agent but he said 'No, we like each other and trust
each other and I want to make the deal with you.' I
pointed out that this was rather unusual but he
insisted. 'I'm very keen to have you. There's a piece of
paper, here's a pen and now you write the deal.' That's
the sort of man he was.

Rank sought out young British film-makers including
Ronald Neame, David Lean and Anthony Havelock-Allan and
they formed a company called Cineguild which worked under
his banner. Other names associated with it form a complete cast
list for the story of British cinema: Laurence Olivier, (*Henry V*
and *Hamlet*), Michael Powell and Emeric Pressburger (*The Red
Shoes* and *Life and Death of Colonel Blimp*), Frank Launder and
Sidney Gilliat (comedies including *St Trinian's*). Together they
formed a roster of producers and directors all working
independently and who, having gained Rank's trust, could then
do what they wanted. Although they certainly did not share in
Rank's evangelical zeal for the gospel, it is true to say that while
Rank was able to exercise his authority, not a single film made

had any immorality or allowed bad to triumph over good.

In 1945 Rank felt ready to take on the Americans on their own turf. He admired their technical expertise—and he wanted a slice of the US market. He began preparing the ground with an article in the *Imperial Review*. In it he commented that the Americans were receiving $80 million a year from Britain and this meant they could produce big-budget pictures. He said Britain could not allow such a sum of money to leave the country without 'some corresponding sum from the other side of the ledger'—by which he meant the exhibition of British films in the States. This was to be a recurring theme in Rank's pronouncements about the British movie industry right up to his final years. The article concluded with the threat that if British producers could not get their films shown in America, then the British government should restrict the number of US pictures allowed in Britain. It's worth bearing in mind that this was not merely Rank the businessman; it was also Rank the British propagandist who was worried about the influence of US standards and life-styles. He felt he had a God-given mission to put a good British way of life on to the big screen and to counterbalance the mores of Hollywood. A journalist asked Rank about his ambitions to break into the US market:

> He opened his silver cigarette-case. In it were cork-tipped cigarettes and ordinary ones. He said: 'If a man is used to an ordinary cigarette it takes time to break the habit and change him over to cork-tipped. What I am trying to do is change the American cinema-goer. It takes a lot of time and it needs a lot of films—inserted one by one into programmes. But it can be done. It must be done.' Doing it lost him £6,000,000 in four and a half years.

There was no doubt that making films was a very expensive business and the constant outpouring of money, although apparently freely undertaken, did cost Rank some pain.

They were making *The Red Shoes* and I had a bit of a
fight with them about what the budget should be but
they agreed in the end. John Davis and I then went off
on a business trip. We hadn't been away long when we
heard, from our colleagues who we'd left behind, that
the picture was going over budget. That wasn't
anything new! We agreed to paying more money
because they had to finish it. You see once they started,
unless they finished it then you'd poured your money
down the drain. And so they'd always got you in the
palm of their hands.[21]

In fact *The Red Shoes* went £300,000 over budget, but in the
end did make money.

So the man who declared that his interest in movies
started because, 'I believed it offered tremendous
potentialities as an instructional force for the Methodist
church' was about to start on a business trip to the States, and
was ready to take on the full might of Hollywood. Following
the article in the *Imperial Review*, and only just after the end of
the war, he arranged his visit to the States with the
government's blessing. It was perceived by the Americans that
it was on the government's behalf. By this time Rank owned
about 60 per cent of the British film industry. He was rich and
could take chances. He had some good movie product on the
shelf with international appeal and he was eager to compete
with Hollywood. But a look at the facts had convinced him
that it was a good risk; good enough for a man who goes
through life telling himself, 'I always win my bets'.

A *Fortune Magazine* article from October 1945 recorded the
historic visit. Under the headline 'Movie Missionary' the piece
began: 'Britain's J. Arthur Rank, millionaire miller and
Methodist movie magnate, is out to give Hollywood some
"healthy competition".' To give the article a context the author
quoted *The London Morning Post* of 1923 which really summed
up Rank's whole fear concerning the US movie industry and
explains why he felt his trip was necessary.

If the US abolished its diplomatic and consular services, kept its ships in harbours and its tourists at home and retired from the world's markets, its citizens, its towns, its countryside, its roads, motor cars and counting houses would still be familiar to the uttermost corners of the world... The film is to America what the flag once was to Britain. By its means, Uncle Sam may hope some day, if it's not checked in time, to Americanise the world.

The *Fortune* article goes on to describe how a Yorkshireman who taught a Methodist Sunday-school class had come over 'to check at least some of Hollywood's influence... Arthur Rank is tall, broad-shouldered, physically agile and fifty-seven. His shrewd brown eyes are set close to a long, hawk like nose, and his forehead is ridged with wrinkles that come from intensive scrutiny of the motives and manoeuvrability of men.'

Rank had two main aims: one was to use US know-how to build up a good technical production base in Britain, as well as borrowing some acting talent; his second aim was to set up adequate distribution and exhibition of his pictures in the US so that he could share in that great market. He had some useful weapons: the Americans' fear of the quota system the British government might impose if he didn't get his way; his unlimited credit; and the fact that he was worth being nice to since he had 600 screens to fill back home.

Rank knew the frustrations: it was hard to get the Americans to show any of his films. When he took over the highly acclaimed *The Red Shoes*, he actually had to hire a theatre in Boston for the première because no one would show it for him in New York.

Rank did not travel alone. He took with him a crack team: a lawyer, George Woodham Smith, who was an intimate with Conservative party theoreticians; an accountant, Barrington Gain, substituting for Leslie Farrow, one of Rank's most trusted advisers, who had stayed at home because he couldn't stand Hollywood; John Davis, his right-hand man (see Chapter 6); and a new acquisition—Justus Lawrence, once a PR man from Samuel Goldwyn, who had met Rank while doing Army PR in

London. It was Lawrence who advised Rank on how to conduct himself in the States. He banned any talk of British Government reprisals if the US cinemas wouldn't show Rank's pictures. Instead, Rank concentrated on his product, saying that he knew it had not been good in the past but now US screens would be proud to show his films. He spent many long hours on this mission, often having to endure much that was contrary to his nature and his background. He was told it was necessary to achieve his objective, so he did what he had to—attending huge press conferences, large dinners and glitzy cocktail parties.

While he was away Rank missed England terribly. He kept his watch on British time and was often wondering what was going on back home. He would turn to John Davis and say, 'John, I know exactly what Nell [his wife] is doing now, I can see her do it.' She was always in his mind. But, despite his home-sickness he performed very well, adapting himself to each situation. He visited some flour mills and became the humble miller who had accidentally fallen into the movie world. With Methodist ministers he was the simple non-conformist, and with the more friendly producers he played the part of the rustic Yorkshireman and even sang a few notes hopelessly out of tune. In tougher moments of negotiation he pointed out that he was personally opposed to the quotas threatened by the British government, but as President of the British Producers Association he had to defend their stand in supporting quotas. But he was so well spoken and so apparently kind that even delivering the bad news didn't enrage his audience.

Rank was frequently a diplomatic triumph. He appeased the anti-British Bertie McCormick from Chicago by saying how surprised he was to see that Chicago was so beautiful when, if the movies were anything to go, by he'd expected it to be full of gangster-lined streets. In fact, Chicago attracted Rank more than Hollywood. On another occasion when he was asked to name his favourite film he chose *The House of Rothschild* because in it the father instructs his sons 'to walk the earth with dignity'. There was enough similarity with Rank's father to make the choice perfectly believable and at the same time it showed that he was not blind to the wisdom of a cultured and great Jewish household. When he was confronted with a tricky question at a press conference he would adopt the familiar technique: he would get out his cigarette case and there would be an awful fumbling to get the cigarette out and then to get it alight. He would then be able to deliver a reply to floor the most cynical hack.

His teetotalism was well known and respected by his hosts. One night, Rank and his team were invited to dinner at Mary Pickford's beautiful home in California. Trays of drinks started to appear—lemon juice, tomato juice but, to the consternation of Rank's colleagues, no alcohol. When they went through to dinner there was an array of wine glasses which were duly filled with fresh water for the duration of the meal. After dinner Buddy Rogers, Mary's husband, leant across to John Davis and inquired if he was teetotal. On discovering he wanted a proper drink they went downstairs to a bar where alcohol was freely imbibed. On the way back to their hotel Rank commented that it had been quite a party and seemed oblivious to the fact that the earlier teetotal atmosphere had been in deference to him. But no matter what time he got back from the various parties to which he'd been invited and no matter how much drink his colleagues had consumed, he always gathered his team together to plan the next day.

While in the States Rank teamed up with the ambitious David O. Selznick to form a company called Selznick International Pictures of England Ltd for the co-production of big budget films in Britain. Rank was to be Chairman of the Board and own half the stock, while Selznick would provide the production, directors and stars. Rank even managed to bring in his passion for religious films by nearly securing as the first picture the story of *Mary Magdelene* starring Ingrid Bergman and Joseph Cotten. The budget was to be $5 million, compared to *Gone with the Wind* which cost $3,800,000. Unfortunately the film was never made. He also induced RKO into co-production based in Britain, and achieved another first by being able to offer US stars proper Hollywood rates to act in British films. He even secured the Winter Gardens in New York as a screen to debut his films in the States and began predicting that he would be able to gross some $15 million a year from his films being shown over there.

Although they were impressed by Rank, the Americans were not that worried. They still saw him as a newcomer with no knowledge of film-making and they reckoned it would take him another twenty years to achieve their know-how. He was liked personally, but seen as a bit of a novelty. He alarmed a few big studio executives by calling a halt to a meeting so that he could write postcards to his Sunday-school class. He also traumatized various Hollywood party-givers, including Jack Warner, when they sent out invitations saying 'from 7.00 p.m. till late' to discover the Yorkshireman on their doorstep at 7.00 p.m. prompt, ready for his Canada Dry with lime juice while Mr Warner was still in his dressing-gown.

Rank discovered that a lot of the British films were being held up for all kinds of reasons, but essentially it was a stalling position in order to 'keep our pictures off American screens'. Rank also realized that, as he said subsequently back in Britain, 'Film people here have not a very high opinion of the intelligence of American audiences. I have. If Shakespeare is done properly, as in the case of *Henry V*, they will like it'. And he learnt that the stars he was using needed to be glamorized for the US market and that they all spoke too fast for the Americans to understand.

Rank was deeply impressed by the up-to-date equipment which was found in all Hollywood studios and remarked that the British technicians must be far cleverer than their Hollywood counterparts because they had to deal with such antiquated equipment.

After his visit, Rank reflected that Americans and Britons do not understand each other. He was also a bit bewildered by the sheer size of the place. He wrote to one of his US colleagues just before he left after his six-week stay:

In my heart I have a great desire to co-operate with our American friends. I believe we can give more to the world if we work together than if we each go our own way. Whatever rebuffs I get, I shall stick to this policy and return to the charge again and again.[22]

He said much later in his life,

We don't understand [Americans] and they don't
understand us and that's why I've always got on with
Americans because I know they don't understand me
and I don't understand them. How and why they made
me a life member of the Motion Picture Industry of
America?—I couldn't believe it. They said I had done
something to help the Hollywood producers to raise
the standard of films—whether they meant it or not I
can't tell you!

But Rank's US trip laid the foundations for a 'special
relationship' with the States. He said that they never broke a
promise to him and he had a strong belief that together the UK
and the US were a world dominating partnership. He recalled
going racing with Harry Warner and put all the dollars he had
on him on a horse bred by Louis B. Mayer which was the
product of a British mare and an American stallion. His host
asked him why he was risking the bet on this horse. 'We stood
alone because we had Winston Churchill. His breeding was
American and British. You know America and Britain together,
nothing can stand against us. And the horse came up and I had
dollars to roll around in my pocket.'

But the acid test was whether British movies were going to
be good enough to be screened in the States. They had
produced little enough before but Rank had *Henry V* on its way,
as well as *Blithe Spirit* and *Caesar and Cleopatra*, starring Vivien
Leigh.

His films were by no means sure-fire successes, and *Caesar
and Cleopatra*, based on Shaw's play, was a case in point. It was
hugely expensive and, although it is somewhat legendary now,
it was a flop at the time. Alan Wood quotes Rank as saying that
Caesar and Cleopatra 'might have made quite a good script if
there had been a little love interest put into it'.[23] He had
apparently asked George Bernard Shaw if this could happen,
but he rejected the idea. This film, Alan Wood says, caused the
greatest amount of attention and fuss of all the Rank films.

Shooting began at Denham on 12 June 1944. Although Shaw was eighty-eight, he became deeply involved in all the costumes and extras, and was immensely fussy that everything should look just right. He often enclosed water colour drawings to illustrate the shade of colour required for a moustache or a piece of costume. The costs of the film grew and grew and Shaw was heard to comment: 'I pity poor Rank. The film will cost him a million.' Later, he was apparently to write to the producer, Gabriel Pascal, about Rank: 'He shocks me by his utter indifference to the cost... The result justifies him. The man is a genius: that is all I have to say about him.'[24]

This was an example of Rank's role as a financier. Shaw was the greatest living writer and Rank felt it important to film a play chosen by Shaw and use a director approved of by Shaw. With amazing courage, Rank had backed the film, in spite of it being war-time and in spite of endless problems (one setback was Vivien Leigh's pregnancy—all the sequences of filming had to be changed—followed by her miscarriage when all the work had to be delayed six weeks).

The film was generally criticized or, as Alan Wood puts it, classed as 'a glorious failure'. The failure, it was generally agreed, was due to keeping strictly to Shaw's original script and not deviating or adjusting the story at all for the purpose of the film. When Rank was asked how he felt about this he remained absolutely silent.

That Christmas, after returning from his successful trip to the States, Rank invited all the film critics to a lunch at the Dorchester, where the menu consisted of lobsters, turkey and ice-cream. On the bottom of each menu was inscribed: 'Ah, well—A Happy Christmas, anyway.' And in his speech, he said: 'I am only doing this job because no one else will. All my group are willing to learn. We can take criticism, and welcome it. I wish you real success and happiness in criticism in 1946.'[25]

5 THE DECLINE OF FILMS

Though waves and storms go o'er my head,
Though strength, and health, and friends be gone,
Though joys be withered all and dead,
Though every comfort be withdrawn,
On this my steadfast soul relies—
Father, thy mercy never dies!
ROTHE TRANSLATED BY JOHN WESLEY

After the war Rank was truly a public figure. It is unusual for the men behind the men who make the stars to come into the public consciousness, but Rank was seen as a dramatic personality even though he himself was not at all dramatic. It was the sheer breadth, size, motivation and contrariness of the man that made him fascinating. As Rank's empire and importance grew, and he was receiving descriptions like 'a phenomenon of our times' from journalists, he presented an increasing number of profile writers in the press with the problem of trying to sum him up for their readers. Interviewers had to find out how this respectable, quiet, unimaginative businessman and Sunday school teacher could have ended up hobnobbing in a mink and orchid world with dazzling actresses and the *glitterati* of Hollywood. The most famous press comment about him came from *Time* magazine which, while explaining his bizarre route into movies said that there was 'Methodism in his madness'. Victor Thompson, writing in 1948, described it thus: 'Since Alice fell down the rabbit hole and found herself in Wonderland there can have been few stranger translations than his.'

One journalist reported in 1946 that writers all over the world were vying with each other to find a clue to Rank's personality and concluded that he seemed to defy the scrutiny of the sketch writer. Rank's face and imposing figure were certainly well known since he was often seen on newsreels—greeting dignitaries at premières of his new films, for example. It was hard for him to remain private when he was so involved in a public business. But neither was he too shy of his face being known judging by the large portraits of himself that hung in his many offices. He had a tendency to switch between a handlebar and a toothbrush moustache and a Canadian writer observed that 'his large face reveals so little of brilliance that many people feel his bland expression is a mask'. His appearance was also described as a 'good-tempered de Gaulle'. None failed to remark on his Sunday school teaching, his Yorkshire background or his kindliness. Nor did they ignore the presence of John Davis, instrumental in establishing the Rank Organisation (see the next chapter for his influence on Rank's business).

Before Rank's empire got so big he used to see almost anyone who wanted to talk to him—at times some of his executives despaired—but after the war he realized that he had to devolve a lot of his power and most of it went straight to Davis. Davis handled all his incoming mail, passing only a small proportion on to Rank; he also looked after his interviews and appointments. Rank was aware that he was a limited public speaker and not a good broadcaster (which explains why there is no record of his voice in the BBC sound archive). He was much more effective in dealing with small groups.

A *Yorkshire Post* profile of 5 December 1946 had nothing but admiration for his rigid and cherished loyalty to his religious and moral principles. The journalist concerned summed up:

> I think that Rank's main problem is his lack of intimate
> knowledge of the film medium; his main strength is
> that he is a good man, sincerely and humbly anxious to
> promote higher standards and better living.

In April 1947 the very first world convention of the Rank Organisation was held in the Dorchester Hotel in London. The Organisation's various activities in all aspects of the motion picture industry, from film-making and distribution through to cinema ownership and furnishings, was now truly a global enterprise. The delegates, who came from all over the world including Australia and New Zealand, Hong Kong and Canada, were given the slogan 'Faith, Thrift and Honest Toil'. Rank announced that he wished to have more competition. 'We in this country know what is meant by cricket. We see a side playing together as a team. Individuals get rid of their ego—and ego is a danger in the film industry. We will have to work as a team if we are to compete successfully... We are something like the British Commonwealth of Nations. We are not bound by contracts, but there is that spirit which is growing—as we are growing—which will enable us to fulfil what is expected of us.' One delegate from Australia said that he had travelled 13,000 miles and it had all been worthwhile because of listening to Mr Rank.

At this time the London headquarters was moved to 38 South Street. Alan Wood describes it: 'The visitor found himself stepping on a black marble front hall, inlaid with silver, with a log fire burning in the great hearth, a tapestry on the wall, and a black marble staircase leading up to Rank's enormous room on the first floor.'[1] Rank never used the lift but instead used the extra time to walk down the stairs composing his thoughts and saying a prayer before going outside. Arthur's brother James, came to visit him there and remarked: 'Arthur, this isn't the sort of office you were brought up to... '

Rank's daughter Shelagh had married an American, Fred Packard, in 1945 and they lived in Hollywood. Following his successful trip to the States in 1945, Rank took his wife with him on his next visit in 1947 so that she could see their grandchild. This time a big fuss was made of Rank by the Americans. The tour was made in grand style in a private air-conditioned railway coach and once again the journalists were straining for similes. *Time* magazine wrote: 'He resembles General de Gaulle, except that he does not share the look of a supercilious camel.' *Life* wrote: 'He has a nose of generous size which terminates in a soft downward curve, so that in profile Rank looks rather like a hungry anteater snuffing at an ants' nest.'

The *Times Herald* wrote:

> Tall. Heavy. His solemn cloud-capped nose gangling just above a changeable moustache. Used to the manipulation of men and money and power, but nervous—constantly crossing his long legs—constantly smoking cigarettes—mumbling a little and picking his words with great care when confronted by questioners anxious to learn his plans...

One American reporter asked Rank, 'Is it true, Mr Rank, that you're dumb?' After a long pause, at length Rank's reply came: 'No, just dull'.[2]

Whilst in Hollywood, Rank heard reports that the post-war Labour government in Britain were planning measures that would effectively end the golden age of British movies, which had recently included *The Way to the Stars* (1945) and perhaps James Mason's finest performance in *Odd Man Out* (1946). It was now 1947: films were at the peak of their importance in British life, and a third of the population were going to the pictures at least once a week. With Dalton as Chancellor of the Exchequer and Cripps at the Board of Trade, a plan had been drawn up to impose a 25 per cent *ad valorem* tax on all US films coming to Britain. On his return Rank went to see the Home Secretary, Herbert Morrison, to express his horror at the idea. 'I do know something about Americans. I know that they'll be bloody mad with you. Perhaps you'll save sixteen million dollars; but you'll have to spend sixty million getting back the goodwill you'll lose.'[3]

Indeed, the Americans did take notice and voluntarily decided to freeze part of their dollar earnings in Britain. Rank was told of this in a 3 a.m. phone call from the States, after which he apparently turned over and went to sleep, a much more peaceful man.

Then, as part of Hugh Dalton's 1947 summer package as Chancellor of the Exchequer, it was decided, for no apparent reason, that instead of a 25 per cent tax, a 75 per cent levy was to be placed on imported US films. The theory was that this tax on US films would be given to the British movie industry. Rank had become suspicious of what was happening so he had sent John Davis to investigate. Davis remembers:

> I went and sat outside the Cabinet Office for a whole day, trying to see anybody who would see me. At the end of the day they said, 'You can go home now. We've settled it' and we discovered later that they had introduced the 75 per cent *ad valorem* duty.

This tax on profits provoked great anger in the Americans and they were especially angry with Rank, because they had believed that, as he was trying to do the best for British films, he had had the backing of the British Government on his visit to the States. They then concluded that Rank must have known before his trip that the tax was imminent, and therefore that he had double-crossed them. Of course, they were wrong. But nothing could be more offensive to Rank than for people to think he had broken his word. In addition, all his hard work building up good relations with the US movie-makers had been wasted. According to Wood, he felt as if his work had been thrown away—the 'sweat and perspiration' had been for nothing.[4]

The immediate result of the tax was a trade war. Hollywood refused to export any of its productions to Britain. This spelt immediate disaster to distributors and cinema owners (of which Rank was the biggest) since they were heavily dependent on the regular showing of US films. What the politicians seem to have forgotten was that British film production depended for its finance on the proceeds of showing Hollywood's pictures. The cinemas were in the impossible position of not being able to afford *not* to show US films. Dalton's intention as Chancellor had been to save £57 million of the £70 million per annum which had been crossing the Atlantic. But because of the boycott, the tax backfired. Desperate British cinema owners and distributors began to re-screen stockpiled US movies which still had to be paid for, so the dollar drain was added to and not reduced. Consequently, as Harold Wilson pointed out, 'We were actually paying out $50 million for the privilege of seeing *Hellzapoppin'* for the third time and *Ben-Hur* for the twenty-third.'[5]

John Davies recalls:

Then Sir Stafford Cripps and Harold Wilson (now at
the Board of Trade) came along to see Arthur and I
was there too, and they said, 'This is a serious problem
for England and we need your help to increase your
production of good British movies.' Now, if anyone
said to Arthur that they needed his help in the national
interest, they were home and dry because he believed
in England. And I said, 'What happens when the *ad
valorem* duty is taken off?' They said, 'We'll look after
you.' So J. Arthur set a programme for forty-seven
films at a cost of £9,250,000.

Meanwhile, on the other side of the Atlantic, the Americans
weren't going to take this lying down. They didn't want to go
through any intermediary like the 'two-faced' Rank, so they sent
over a top man from their organization and he was seen by the
British Government. This 'top man' was Eric Johnson,
Hollywood's chief administrator. Thus an agreement was signed in
March 1948, ending the 75 per cent levy. This was agreed without
any consultation with the Rank Organisation or the British film
industry. The result was that a large backlog of the best US films
came and flooded the market and the Rank Organisation lost £20
million. There was no stopping the British public from going to see
the newly available Hollywood imports because they had been
starved of them.

The dollar problem, however, remained. Harold Wilson tried
to combat it with a new policy which at the same time, he believed,
would help the British film industry. He announced that the quota
of British-made films should be raised from 30 to 45 per cent. This
was a good idea in principle but in practice, although there were
more British movies screened than ever before or since, there was
a significant fall in quality. The Rank Organisation was already
over-committed and the rest of the industry was too enfeebled and
apathetic to meet the demand. So, apart from a few quality films
such as *Black Narcissus* (1947), poor films were produced to fill
screens and cut losses while stockpiled Hollywood pictures

continued to be shown. By 1948 Rank had made some extremely bad films. 'Our plans to meet an unexpected and critical situation were too ambitious... We made demands on the creative talent in the industry that were beyond its resources... As a result we spread our production capacity, in which I still have unshaken faith, too thinly over the films we made.'[6]

The Rank Organisation had promised forty-seven feature films but soon abandoned this target in favour of producing a smaller number of prestige movies in order to recoup cash from the US market. They were to include *Oliver Twist*, *Hamlet*, *The Red Shoes*, *Scott of the Antarctic* and *Saraband for Dead Lovers*, all produced in 1948. Wilson was forced to back down and the ambitious quota figure of 45 per cent was back to its original level of 30 per cent by 1950.

Rank was deeply hurt by all this since his integrity had been brought into question through all these political manoeuvrings and, although innocent of any shenanigans, he wanted an explanation. He invited Harold Wilson round to lunch at the Dorchester, and asked him to justify going back on his agreement. Wilson's response to Rank's challenge was simply, 'Oh, Mr Rank, but that was only a piece of paper.'

Rank was so outraged by this dishonesty and double-dealing that he never again worked directly with any Labour politician. This whole affair scotched any hopes of getting special promotion for Rank films in the States, and was responsible for Rank's films never really taking off there. Wilson also did his best to end Rank's stranglehold over the film industry by setting up the National Film Finance Corporation in 1948, with funds to subsidize independent producers. As one account puts it, 'new-style socialism was in collision with old-style capitalism.'

Rank decided to put his money into big films to attract box-office success. He was well known for giving his film producers enormous freedom to experiment, in the belief that creative people needed the room to make mistakes. But his lavish and expensive productions merely added fuel to Wilson's campaign against him. As President of the Board of Trade Wilson commented in the House of Commons: 'Pandering to artistic perfection... [interruption]... The Right Hon. Gentleman knows what I mean... We have all known of films in the making of which thousands of pounds were spent in order to try to get one particular scene just right... one particular scene, which, in the end, has not appeared in the finished film... '

Wilson continued his undermining of Rank's empire on a visit to the States in November 1949, when he said, 'It would be a great mistake to regard J. Arthur Rank as the British Film Industry.' He admitted that Rank had done fine work but also said that he wanted to discuss the 'problem' of Rank in a debate in the House of Commons when he got home.

Rank would have had very little truck with the Labour Party at the best of times, so these blows hardly damaged a blossoming friendship. His grandson Fred Packard puts Rank in a political context:

> Grandpa was right of centre, very anti-Labour. Like a lot of religious people he believed in the freedom of the individual. He was anti-Catholic, especially having seen their ultra-right stance before the war when the Catholics stood with Nazis. Grandpa believed in the individual's ability to create his own destiny, and that falls easier into the Conservative camp. Tony Blair was not the leader of the Labour Party when Grandpa was around, and the old-style Labour was anathema to him.

Rank was a great fan of Churchill, and liked to pronounce words in the same way he did. He supported most traditional Conservative policies—for example, he thought opposition to apartheid in South Africa counter-productive, which was to bring him into conflict with certain parts of the Methodist Church.

Because of all these events, Rank was to turn down an offered peerage from the Labour regime. He waited until 1957 when he was offered another one by Macmillan. (When his father Joseph Rank had been offered titles, he had declined them, saying, 'I'm Joe Rank and everybody knows me as I am.' Arthur's brother Jimmy also declined offered titles.)

Rank did try to bridge some of the divide between himself and the Labour Party by employing, as his public relations expert, a Mr Sydney Wynne, son-in-law of Ernest Bevin. He also had on his staff a Mr Victor Finney, formerly a close associate of Lloyd George. But, despite his endeavours, the mutual misunderstanding between Rank and the Socialists persisted.

He did, however, have one left-wing bent and that was his absolute opposition to capital punishment. He was convinced that only God had the right to take a human life. He had sorted out his position in case he was called on to vote on the issue in the House of Lords after he'd accepted his peerage in 1957. His tendency was to forgive—except, it seems anyone who broke faith with him, especially Labour politicians.

From this point in 1948, Rank started losing money. The *ad valorem* tax had taken its toll and in addition the Government had introduced an Entertainment Tax. Since the late 1930s, Rank's commercial films had made good money. Now the Rank Organisation was in crisis. Rank's only comment to his shareholders on being £13,589,858 in the red was that 'my colleagues and I are not unmindful of the desirability, as soon as practicable, of rearranging on a longer-term basis a substantial portion of this credit'.[7]

After the crisis it was necessary for Rank and Davis to secure the services of a new financial consultant. They approached an acccountant called Ronnie Leech. There were those who tried to stop him, saying that he shouldn't get involved in Rank's mess and with that 'awful man Davis', but he ignored the advice and Davis was later to comment that when Rank persuaded Leech to join it was the best day's work Rank ever did for the Organisation. Leech remembers his first impressions of Rank as a 'kindly, modest and totally relaxed man. Later on I also discovered he was a very determined man who likes to have his own way.'

This was a really tough time for Rank. Later Davis recalled how he dealt with it.

As you can imagine, in a crisis such as this and in an industry such as the film industry which is always in the public eye and involved in politics, there were many cross-currents at work. This was when Arthur showed his great courage and loyalty and secured the greatest benefit from his Christian faith. It didn't matter what happened, he was never annoyed and sometimes sorrowful when somebody did him a dirty trick. But his loyalty to those working around him was profound, particularly to myself.

In 1949 the Rank Organisation's Annual General Meeting announced an overdraft of £17 million. Rank went to his bankers and addressed the Board of the bank, asking for the money. 'Tell me, Mr Rank, why do you want to borrow £1 million?' he was asked. 'Frankly, Mr Martin, to lose it. If I don't get these films made and shown they will be dead money. At least if they're shown we'll get something back.'

The story of Rank's massive overdraft was widely reported. Apparently someone approached Rank around this time and asked, 'Can you sleep at night?' 'Yes,' replied Rank. 'I have no difficulty in sleeping.' The man went on, 'Well, if my company owed £17 million I wouldn't be able to sleep.' Rank said, 'It's quite all right owing £17 million, if you've got £60 million to pay it with!' Rank's film assets alone, if realized, would probably have raised this sum—and Rank's milling empire even more. In the world of the seriously rich, such debts were only a mild inconvenience.

But it was not only the conflict with Hollywood that had caused the losses. The Government's Entertainment Tax was seen by most people in the movie business to be partly, if not largely, responsible for the troubles affecting Rank. This tax was levied at the box office—the Government gained about 33 per cent of the entrance fee. While Rank was criticized by politicians and shareholders for his extravagance in production the fact was that in 1949 the Entertainment Tax was taking 4d in every shilling, whereas the film producers were only getting 2¹/₂d—less than 25 per cent. Many felt that it was intolerable that an industry to which so much importance was attached at the time should be taxed almost out of existence. Not only that—there were anomalies. For example, the stage play *A Streetcar Named Desire* was exempt on the grounds that it was educational and yet *Henry V* was taxed some £400,000. Successive Chancellors regarded the film industry as a cow to be endlessly milked.

Rank declared at a shareholders' meeting that without some relief of the Tax there was a grave danger that the regular production of British films would cease. In 1948 he had lost £4,650,000 on film production. Out of the £27.5 million paid in admissions, the Government had taken £10.5 million. Rank said, 'Too much of the industry's life blood is being drained out of the box office.' Unless the Government announced tax alleviation by the following June, 'We may then have to make the unwelcome decision that production must cease.'

Even the unions sympathized with Rank. In November 1949, 120 cine-technicians had to be made redundant, most of them at the Denham studios. Tom O'Brien MP, who was General Secretary of the National Association of Theatrical and Kinematograph Employees acknowledged that, 'Mr Rank has no more money to make pictures: therefore he has to limit the production schedule he now has... I agree with Mr Rank that he has lost enough for one man for the time being.'

The rebuilding period, in which the Rank Organisation branched out further into the leisure industry, was a time of great stress and strain. Rank and his wife were determined to make the Rank Organisation successful again and to keep the Americans away from it. They gave the controlling interest in the Rank Organisation to a charitable trust (later to be known as The Rank Foundation) which would secure it against a US take-over. Rank and his wife retained no financial or voting interest. The control of the voting power of the group was now vested in a company limited by guarantee and without share capital whose main object was to support and encourage the British film industry. As a result of this reorganization, the control and operation of the company would not be affected by

Rank's death and the control was firmly established in British hands for the future. By Rank's eightieth birthday, the shares were worth £40 million.

The publicity surrounding Rank's failures and the high-profile crisis, as well as his success, once more caused inevitable interest in the man behind it all. This was something abhorrent to Rank, who found all the publicity highly embarrassing. He said that once when he met the Queen at a function he was shaking from head to toe: the public side of the business was one of the jobs he hated most. In earlier days his daughters had laughed at his discomfort as photographers made him walk around the grounds of Pinewood Studios with a clutch of starlets on each arm. Shelagh commented:

> His toes were probably curling at such times—not my father's line of country at all.

His awkwardness was understandable. During his early successes in the film world, he was seen as a bit of a misfit—a Yorkshire miller in the glamorous world of the movie business. Before his involvement with films, no one in the media had shown the slightest interest in him. After the war, though, the articles came thick and fast. He remarked to a journalist how uncomfortable he found the exposure and especially how much his wife disliked it, 'You see, we never realized what we were in for.'

Rank was also learning that journalists were not to be trusted and he became very careful what he said in interviews. He would take an inordinate length of time to answer questions and one writer commented that even in answering 'I don't think so,' you could almost play gramophone records between the words.

In an interview with the *Daily Mail*, he was posed a question about his current production list:

> Sitting against the dark green brocade of his high-backed Jacobean chair, with the window light behind him, he posed a very good profile as he gazed upward at the far-off ceiling. This was not the avowed and

proud Methodist considering the Kingdom of Heaven.
This was him trying to find the right word. So
conscious is he of the risk now of using the wrong
word, the loose statement, that he will suddenly say,
Yorkshire fashion, after a series of entirely non-
committal remarks, 'You know, the trouble with me is
I'm too open-gobbed.'[8]

The same article by Reginald Pound paid Rank an
immense compliment:

What I had not realized before and can now affirm is
that J. Arthur Rank's wealth and influence are not
what make him essentially interesting to know. If he
were stripped of them he would still be worth writing
about.

Another journalist who interviewed him in 1948 was Victor
Thompson. He commented that it was his Sunday school
teaching that was the real key to the man's character:

He seems to remember all the time that it is easier for a
camel to pass through the eye of a needle than for a
rich man to enter the Kingdom of Heaven. But he
seems to be quietly confident that a man who can
transform the British film industry ought to be able to
negotiate satisfactorily with St Peter.[9]

While the public eye scrutinized the paradox of Rank's
character, his capacity for hard work remained boundless in his
task of building up the British film industry. He was being
attacked from all angles.

The US motion picture industry was at the height of its world
power. Two of Rank's US partners—United Artists and Twentieth
Century-Fox—were both convinced, for some reason which Rank
never understood, that their shareholdings gave them the right to
control the management of Odeon and Gaumont. They went to
considerable lengths to prove their point of view, engaging many
high-powered lawyers in the States and in England. But there was

good will. Twentieth Century-Fox, while protecting their interests, did everything they could to help Rank in his ambition to secure a strong British film industry and these protracted negotiations resulted in a long and successful partnership between the two companies.

These were trying times but Rank never lost his patience and would spend hours talking and negotiating, motivated by a desire to convince the Americans that it was in their interests as well as his own that his films were shown in their country. Eventually United Artists sold their interests in Odeon to the Schlesingers of South Africa. In fact, they offered it to Rank, but at the time he didn't have the money. The Schlesingers, like United Artists, then displayed the same conviction that they had control over Odeon: once again, Rank and Davis had to disillusion them.

After a while Rank was in a position to buy them out. Davis, sometimes regarded as the 'brains' behind Rank's successes, suggested that one of the trusts created by the Rank Organisation should carry out the transaction. However, the trustees in question were not used to such unorthodox behaviour and were reluctant to make the deal. It was left to Davis to convince them of the need to borrow the money from the bank and eventually, because Rank was firmly in favour of the proposal, the trustees agreed to approach the bank, who then lent the money because of their confidence in Rank. Rank and Davis looked back with some laughter at this situation because they knew that the only reason the trustees had agreed to the proposal was because they were sure that Davis would fail in his attempt to persuade the bank to lend the money. Despite the very risky business of film production, Rank had a remarkably confident, almost bullish attitude to borrowing money from banks. John Davis recalls another meeting with the bankers to secure a loan, which illustrates Rank's irresistible style:

> Our side consisted of Arthur, Watmore, the then senior
> partner of Peats, Ronnie Leech and I. By accident or by
> design a very great banker, the late Mr Eric Smith, came
> into the general manager's room and asked how we were

getting on. It became clear to him why the meeting was taking place. In a nutshell, we were anxious to complete the large production programme which was certain to lose money because of the changed conditions. Mr Smith turned to Arthur and said, 'Can you tell me, Mr Rank, why we should lend money for you to finish this programme when you already owe us a vast sum and you yourself say that you know you will lose much of this additional borrowing?' Out came the cigarette box, the fumbling, and then Arthur turned to the eminent banker. 'But Mr Smith, it is your business to lend money.' After a deadly silence which I thought would never end, we were granted the loan.

As the next chapter shows, Davis had considerable influence in Rank's business. During the crisis in 1947 the Rank Organisation accounts made very depressing reading. Davis suggested to Rank that since he always protested that he wasn't in the movie business to make money, he could make a donation to the funds. Rank coughed up £1 million of his own money. Despite the apparent financial difficulties of the Rank Organisation, Rank was never going to be a poor man. His father had died one of the richest men in England, and the family coffers were deep. Rank's milling activities earned him money throughout his film career, so this kind of loan, although serious, was not going to leave the Ranks without food.

Perhaps surprisingly for one so publicly reticent and, at times, blunt, Rank was also by reputation a brilliant chairman at shareholders' meetings. At times he needed to be. One board member described him as 'simply wonderful', probably because when the going was tough Rank had a great ability to defuse the situation by giving a reply quite unrelated to the question posed so that the shareholder, baffled, would thank him profusely for his words and sit down. But Rank's 'I'm not in it for profit' attitude, coupled with the extraordinary amount of money that was being spent on lavish productions, understandably raised questions with the shareholders. It was hard for them to be satisfied with being part of Rank's dream of what he called 'prestige' movies, and his mission of raising the intelligence of the British people and their moral values. At the time R.J. Minney wrote in his book *Talking of Films*:

> Public appreciation can of course be influenced and trained; but I contest the claim to restrict the use of the word 'prestige' to films of limited appeal. The word cannot be monopolised and narrowed in this manner. To that word no one can be said to have the sole right. There is no reason why it should be used as a pall to be drawn reverently over the dead face of a film that has failed commercially. Prestige has nothing whatever to do with cost.

After all the trouble over the *ad valorem* tax and the subsequent power struggles some people thought Rank didn't like the Americans but in fact he had great admiration for them. In retrospect, he said that they had always been kind to him. His view was that the Americans were dominating the film industry and so were portraying the American way of life. He commented: 'I don't want to see that, I want the British way of life shown as well'—not 'instead of' but 'as well as'. Americans still held him in high regard: he was given an honorary degree from the University of Boston in 1948, and became only the second person, along with Bob Hope, to be made a life member of the American Motion Picture Industry. Occasionally US producers would find themselves invited down for a weekend at his home in Reigate or later in Sutton Scotney. One such was awe-struck by the way Rank's home life was so unsophisticated and different from the world of Wardour Street:

> He begged my pardon and said he was going off to Sunday school to teach. That came after I found him making his own breakfast because he didn't want to give the servants too much work on the Sabbath.

J. Arthur Rank has never been without his critics. When he first went into the movie business some regarded him as a bit of an amateur. But Rank was fully conscious of his limitations—he simply ensured that he was surrounded by people who did know what was going on. Criticism of his artistic ineptitude has continued to the present day. Ken Russell, who doesn't have a good word to say for Rank, writes:

> ... when I suggested to Harry Saltzman, co-producer of the Bond films, that we do a picture on Nijinsky he snapped back, 'What film on a dancer ever made money?' I couldn't tell him. I doubt if *The Red Shoes* did. Rumour says that its financier, J. Arthur Rank, hated the film and buried it. Thus passed away the first art film in the history of the British cinema.[10]

Rank came in for other strong criticism. Among those who were quite vitriolic about him was James Mason, who had built himself a reputation as a result of being in Rank films. When he established himself in the United States at the end of 1946, he denounced Rank:

> Arthur Rank is the worst thing that has happened to the British film industry. He has no apparent talent for cinemas or showmanship. He surrounds himself with a lot of quaint folk who know nothing about the creative side of film-making. The result is that creative artists are mishandled.[11]

J. Arthur Rank replied saying:

> Mr Mason is an actor, not a businessman. We are trying to do the best we can for British film-making. Mr Mason has appeared successfully in many of our films. I hope he will appear again.

And he did, in 1962.

Rank's 'hotline to the Almighty' also earned him some enemies. Sidney Cole, a former Vice-President of the Association of Cine-Technicians, observed: 'He assumed that he was more acquainted with God than other people were, which is always a doubtful proposition.'

At times it must have seemed to Rank that everyone was out to get him. But he had an unerring ability to win people round when he met them. One of Arthur's main critics was Lord Beaverbrook, owner of the *Daily Express*, *Sunday Express* and *Evening Standard*. This was probably due to the fact that Beaverbrook was a friend of Isadore Ostrer, of Gainsborough Films, whom Rank had eventually bought up. On their first meeting, when Rank was taken to dinner with Lord Beaverbrook, the whole evening was a disaster, as Rank was polite but dumbstruck. Subsequent meetings grew warmer and eventually Beaverbrook only had praise for Rank, although for some years his papers still criticized some of Rank's public actions.

Brendan Bracken, Chairman of *The Financial Times* and director of *The Economist*, was also a critic of Rank's, as were the Labour papers, the *Daily Herald* and the *Tribune*. Some of the criticism was that Rank was still taking on too many films from Hollywood. Mr Frederick Mullally, Assistant Editor of the *Tribune* (and author of a pamphlet entitled *Film, An Alternative to Rank*), said that Rank 'draws his best and most stable profits from the exhibition in this country of American-made films'. Rank was also criticized for 'expanding British production too much and too fast [and]... meeting production losses out of his exhibitions profits'.[12]

Rank was always heard to say about criticism: 'We must learn to live above it.'

But, on the whole, the creative people he employed—the producers and directors, actors and writers—defended him stoutly because he gave them a free hand. Although he was supposed to read all the scripts before production, he really didn't interfere with their creative designs. Even extravagant eccentrics like Gabriel Pascal were allowed to plan productions in their own way. Actress Jean Simmons described Rank as 'just like a favourite uncle' and Trevor Howard said he was 'absolutely charming'. David Lean said he was 'a man whom you could trust'.

Rank wanted his films to be good box office, but he also wanted them to be good for the people who came to see them. There was never any gratuitous violence. There was never a film of which he would disapprove or not want to go and see himself. Even his staunchest critics had to admire what Rank had achieved with the British film industry. Lord Soper admits that: 'As a film magnate, his influence was good rather than bad.'

George Elvin, General Secretary of the Association of Cine-Technicians, said in tribute to Rank that he and his union would always be grateful for the 'tremendous pioneering work of Lord Rank in developing the British film industry, particularly on the production side. Naturally, we have had differences from time to time but they never became acrimonious.'

Rank's memory of his relationship with Elvin and the other big union bosses, Tom O'Brian and Mr Bushby, was not quite so glowing. On one occasion these three had a difference of opinion and they asked Rank in to arbitrate. In his speech on his eightieth birthday, Rank recalled:

> Talk about fireworks, talk about sparks flying. I said to Mr Bushby, 'You know I don't know much about the film industry, I've had no training for it whatsoever. I started sweeping floors in a mill and I know something about Trade Union principles and you're going against them.' He said, 'Mr Rank, when I fight I've got no principles!' 'Well,' I said, 'You go down to the Odeon at Marble Arch and you have the best lunch you can get there and settle the thing between you and I'll be here when you get back.' When they got back they were able to tell me, 'It's all right. We've agreed about everything.'

In one industrial dispute at the Teddington studios there was a meeting with the unions, to which Rank was invited. While the union leader was talking, there were shouts from the members saying, 'Sit down, comrade! Sit down. We want to hear what Rank's got to say!' And with his common sense and diplomacy, a settlement was reached with good will on all sides.

Despite the troubles at the Rank Organisation in the late forties its dominance of the British movie industry was still strong. It became very difficult, if not impossible, for an independent producer to make a film because Rank's studio commitments were so vast that there was never any studio space available. In 1948 he came under fire from smaller independent cinema owners, who accused him of acting dictatorially and wielding near-monopoly powers. The fact that he had the majority of British cinemas and the ABC chain had the rest meant that a producer had no hope of making his film unless Rank or ABC liked it, because without the big screens to show it on it would never make money. Rank publicly declared himself opposed to monopoly, believing that fair competition kept everyone's effort at a maximum, but perhaps the frustration of those outside his sphere is understandable. In fact, the only real monopoly as Rank saw it had been that of the Americans dominating Wardour Street and British Cinema Screens from 1920 onwards.

If it was a monopoly that Rank was running, then it was a very 'hands-off' one. John Davis comes to his defence:

> He never used his power incorrectly. He didn't want
> power, he wanted to see the British way of life projected
> all round the world. He relied on the likes of David Lean,
> Michael Powell and Carol Reed to make good films. He
> didn't want to see the script. We saw every film he made,
> but he never made any comment to the people who made
> them. When we saw Laurence Olivier's *Hamlet*, Arthur as
> usual didn't pass any comment [apparently he just said,
> 'Thank you very much, Sir Laurence'] and Larry took
> exception to this and never really forgave him. It wasn't
> that he didn't like the film—he just didn't think it was for
> him to make comment, and he didn't know how to phrase
> his congratulations.

Why could he not have said something at this screening to the assembled company? The truth was that Arthur was very pleased with and proud of the film but had not been brought up to be articulate about artistic matters or to be verbally effusive. His complete lack of understanding of the vulnerability and insecurity of the artistic temperament led many people to criticize him: where he saw no need to bolster morale, his creative employees took this as a cold rebuff. Alan Wood supports

Arthur in the way he did comment on *Hamlet* on this occasion. He writes: 'Would it not be unpardonable impertinence for him to offer any praise or criticism to the great Olivier, on what was an obvious masterpiece of Shakespearean interpretation?... Who was Rank to presume to pass judgement on a great work of art?'[13]

John Davis comments:

> His main motivation for all his involvement was a love
> of England and projecting the British way of life. He
> thought we were a great country. He knew nothing
> about films. He talked far more about technical
> equipment. Some say he was taken for a ride by some
> film makers. That's a bit strong, but some did take
> advantage of his integrity. He always expected
> everyone else to have the same integrity that he had
> but that was not always necessarily so.

Alan Wood also points to the gullible nature of J. Arthur Rank, especially within the rather overpowering and glamorous world of films. Sometimes his trust was abused. His wish to help the film industry whilst remaining ignorant of all the processes involved led him to lay himself open to abuse. At meetings he was heard to say: 'I know I have no talent for making films; but I can help you get what money you want.'[14] Alan Wood goes on to write: 'The film sharks basking round the tables there passed a smile of rich content and pleasant anticipation.' They were not all honest.

What caused most grief from those in the industry was that the Rank Organisation had so much power and boundless facilities, and yet the screens were dominated by foreign films. After the war eight out of ten films watched in Britain were from Hollywood. Ralph Bond was a leading documentary producer, Vice President of the Association of Cine-Technicians and Chairman of its Executive Committee. In 1946 he wrote a pamphlet, *The Future of British Films*, in which he said:

> An art that is capable of appealing to the great mass of
> mankind is something to be reckoned with. No country
> can afford to ignore its implications, and no country with

any pride in its own traditions and culture can be satisfied when the majority of films shown in its cinemas come from abroad... Domination of 80 per cent cannot be justified... A country without its own films is like a country without its own art and literature. The fact has to be faced that the British film industry has always been in an inferior position to Hollywood, when by every test of merit and skill and resourcefulness it should at least be able to compete with Hollywood on equal terms.

Despite all Rank's efforts, the British film industry was not competing, and has not ever competed, on equal terms. Some have wanted to put the blame for this failure at Rank's door. R.J. Minney, in *Talking of Films*, perceived that the Rank Organisation had become top heavy and too costly for the whole empire (as Rank himself referred to it); the vast organizations of control were still controlled from the top office:

As a result, thousands of pounds are put on the cost of every film. It is no longer possible to make a picture at a moderate cost. Not satisfied with this needless inflation the Rank Organisation has been recklessly lavish on its production, spending far above the possibility of return from the market within its own domination. Films, to be commercially successful, should cost at most £200,000. Rank films of late have been costing £300–£400,000; *Henry V*, £500,000; *Men of Two Worlds*, £600,000; *A Matter of Life and Death*, more than £650,000; *London Town*, £1,000,000; and *Caesar and Cleopatra*, £1,300,000. Hollywood, despite a far wider assured market, rarely indulges in such extravagance.'

The Rank Organisation was regarding high-budget Technicolor films, such as *Scott of the Antarctic* and *A Matter of Life and Death*, as a short cut to the US screens, but Minney for one was very worried that it would be the British tax-payer who would foot the bill for the losses. I'm not sure whether he knew just how rich Rank was, nor could he have predicted the guile of John Davis at the

Rank Organisation for finding other ways to make money. But Minney, as a film expert of the day, concluded that the British movie industry in 1947 was on the threshold of a big boom—and since Rank wasn't achieving major success, the Government should intervene and let someone else have a go.

It has become the norm in histories of the British film industry to dismiss Rank as an ignorant miller who should have kept his nose out of movies, but the truth is that without Rank's enthusiasm and investment, the British film industry might have well have collapsed in the 1940s. Through his virtual monopoly he had brought about peace between the sellers and producers who were tearing the industry apart, and he came close to creating a market for British films in the United States. This is something no one else has achieved, before or since. The integrated company, the Rank Organisation, he had set up had, in many ways, succeeded in bringing together the competing demands of 'art' and 'business'.

As the years passed, the running of the Rank Organisation increasingly became the job of John Davis. The movies began to reflect less of Rank's original vision and more of a big organization's need to make money (see next chapter). It was John Davis' job to get British films shown in different countries and he came to the conclusion that the only way to get British films shown was to buy cinemas in those countries. And this they did—including those in Canada, Australia, New Zealand, Jamaica and throughout the Caribbean.

Because of the high importance Rank gave to distributing his films around the world, he employed Air Commodore F.M.F. West VC, CBE, MC to take over from Teddy Carr of Eagle-Lion Distributors. Rank said, 'You never know what's going to happen in the film business. But I believe it's a great task. I wouldn't advise you to leave the RAF if I didn't believe that showing British films to the world is a job of great national importance.' After West had been doing the job for a while, he exclaimed: 'I've flown more since I joined the Rank Organisation than I ever did in the Air Force.' His job was opening cinemas around the world and dubbing films into the various languages concerned. There was great expansion abroad and gradually the Rank Organisation was to diversify into all sorts of other areas to make money—advertising, all kinds of leisure facilities, motorway service stations and latterly casinos, which really would have upset the Methodist Conference and might have been too much for Rank himself.

The attraction of the world of cinema for J. Arthur Rank has been endlessly debated. Why did he chose films? Why not another industry? Some have come to the conclusion that because he was forbidden trips to the theatre and cinema by his very strict father, both these forms of entertainment took on a veneer of glamour—the excitement of dabbling in something which was hitherto denied him must have given him a thrill. Someone else with an equally puritanical upbringing as far as entertainment was concerned was David Lean, who established himself as one of the greatest British directors. He was brought up as a Quaker and was forbidden to attend theatre or cinema.

The world of cinema was steeped in the usual worries and fluctuations of any business and this undoubtedly attracted J. Arthur Rank, whose second nature was doing business. However, the difference in the film industry is the addition of the passions and creative energies of the producers, directors and all the various personnel needed in getting together a successful film. As Carol Reed, one of the great British directors who worked for J. Arthur Rank, said:

> When a picture is absolutely finished and there is
> nothing more you can do about it, it is like falling out
> of love... Making a picture is all work and worry and
> fear and panic. But not making a picture is worse.
> There is no happiness in this business.[15]

R.J. Minney, while acknowledging that Rank had succeeded to some degree in 'raising the tone of British films', also suggests that '... one must not overlook those excellent pre-war films, *The 39 Steps*, *The Stars Look Down*, *Pygmalion* and *The Scarlet Pimpernel* made earlier by the British film industry.'[16] Rank had not been behind every great British film.

After the Second World War, one of Rank's chief rivals said, 'Had it not been for Rank there would be no British film industry today.' The director Alexander Korda said: 'Any who deny what Arthur has done—they know nothing. His role and his courage were enormous, holding up the film industry when there was nobody else to do it. A very great and noble role, not for any pounds he might get out of it, but because of the devotion to British films which anyone who comes into them invariably gets.'[17]

Rank was determined to make the British film industry a power in itself, respected throughout the world, and in this he was successful. He had become Britain's chief distributor and one of the world's major producers of motion pictures. How and why he reached where he did are not necessarily complicated questions. He was, after all, his father's son, and enjoyed the processes of business: starting companies, expanding them, taking over other people's business, and exploiting their hard work. Add this to his profound Christian faith and strong patriotism, and you find a man with the vision of using cinema for the good of the nation's soul and its reputation abroad, and a man who can bring it about.

6 RANK AND DAVIS

*Why hast thou cast our lot
In the same age and place,
And why together brought
To see each other's face... ?*

CHARLES WESLEY

It seems clear that Rank did not make his mark in business by
his intellect. He was street-wise and astute rather than clever.
He had a phenomenal memory and a good business brain
coupled with a keen awareness of how to build up a company.
He also had an overdeveloped competitive instinct—essential to
his success—and a tremendous self-confidence, or confidence in
God, which made him irresistible at board meetings. A simpler
way of explaining his phenomenal success is that he worked
very hard. He had to.

I heard various versions of his schedule, some of which
seemed to include very little sleep. He told a reporter in 1943:
'I do not take holidays. In normal times I take a fortnight's rest
each year. Then I'm fit to go on working all day and night if
necessary.'[1] On a working day he would start at about 7a.m. with
a cup of tea in bed, plus the financial papers. He would reach
the office about 8a.m. so that he could do some quiet work for
half an hour before it opened. His office day began at 8.30a.m.
and any executives arriving late at the South Street
Headquarters would be reprimanded and told, 'These hours
wouldn't do in Yorkshire'. Lunch and dinner were considered

as extra opportunities for business meetings. No time was wasted. Indeed, Rank did not believe in wasteful extravagance of any kind and was always as dedicated to turning off electric lights as he was to lowering old-style film-makers' expense accounts. After the war, when all his businesses were booming, he would work an eighteen-hour day, leaving some of his younger staff exhausted. And because he never drank alcohol, his brain was always fully alert and he would work late into the evenings and the night when other minds might not be quite so sharp.

Rank met John Davis in the late 1930s, and by 1944 had made him managing director of the Rank Organisation. Davis, an accountant, had started as a junior working for Associated Electrical Industries. One of their investments was in a company in which Oscar Deutsch—of Odeon fame—was involved. Deutsch was impressed by Davis and, when they needed a new man for Odeon Theatres, appointed him as chief accountant. When Davis began, he discovered that although the company had been trading for six months there were no accounts at all. After endeavouring to make some order out of the chaos, he produced a report stating that the company, although only small at this stage, needed £2 million on capital account, £500,000 of which was needed for the Odeon, Leicester Square.

Davis' report came only two months after a public statement had declared that Odeon Theatres were fully financed. As a result, the report caused a little excitement and Oscar Deutsch summoned him to the Dorchester where he was lunching with Rank. This was to be the first time that Davis met Rank. He remembers seeing Rank standing by the reception in the hotel: 'I don't know why, but I thought I'd rather have him as a friend than anything else.'

Davis met Rank again when Rank had agreed to put up money for Odeon Theatres Ltd with Hill and Mountain as joint financiers. On the death of Oscar Deutsch in 1941 Davis began to wonder about his own position. At that time the National Provincial Bank had its war-time headquarters at East Cheam and on 10 December 1941 Rank took Davis down to see the manager. On the way back Davis dropped several hints to start a conversation about his future but Rank assumed his periodic deafness. It wasn't until they had arrived back at the Dorchester that Rank said to Davis, 'Oh, by the way, John. The bank manager agrees with me that you should be joint managing director. I'll deal with it at the board next week.'

Davis remembers:

> Rank took a liking to me. I suspect that the reason was that most people were in films for their own ends, or that was how it seemed, and I was a young man wanting to do a job of work. In fact I needed a job. I was always a hard worker and if Rank wanted anything I produced it for him the next morning. That was how our relationship began, as employer and employee, and we gradually drew closer together. I could also understand mechanized accounting.
>
> We were not workaholics. We just enjoyed what we did, though I admit we did work very long hours. We both had a suite in the Dorchester—I had been bombed out of my Chelsea flat. We had breakfast together, all day together and then dinner together with someone else present.

Recognizable by the red carnation in his buttonhole, Davis was known to be a clever accountant. For many years he was Rank's right-hand man. Some said he was a hatchet man. He himself recalled:

> A lot of people got fed up with me. I was always regarded as the 'no' man, which wasn't true. I was trying to keep things on the straight and narrow.

Some said that Rank took on Davis because he realized that he did not have the sort of temperament to be absolutely ruthless in his business dealings, and because of this Rank retained his popularity. Others said Rank could be as tough as anyone. Certainly Davis did not see himself as others did:

I never regarded myself as a hatchet man. I came into the company, the figures were in chaos and I had to sort it out. Coming into an organization that was financially and operationally in a mess—anyone charged with the responsibility of trying to put things right was not going to have a popular life. I got involved with Anthony Havelock-Allan, Ronald Neame and a few others and they were good film-makers so it wasn't a problem for them. Some may have thought me a hatchet man but that was because they were not good film-makers.

Despite his protestations there were rumours of a London club composed entirely of managers whose common bond was that they had been sacked by Davis. It was said that half the heads of British industry had been under him at one time or another and been fired.

His and Rank's was a curious relationship. Davis enjoyed luxury and relished his position of wealth and power. He was married several times and had a glamorous life-style, in contrast to Rank's. In 1962 *The Financial Times* described him as, 'A tough Churchillian... [who] fits the film czar part to perfection.' They were very different in their approach to many things. For example, Miss Gookey, who worked as Rank's secretary at the Rank Organisation, remembers that Rank himself rarely dictated letters: he much preferred to do business by talking things through with people. Rank very rarely wrote anything down, necessary letters were short and to the point, and most of his deals were sealed by his word, not his signature. Conversely, John Davis would come in and start dictating letters at great speed from 7.30a.m. and then perhaps dictate all day.

Sir John Davis was a good chairman, but could be rather brusque in his dealings with people and very demanding in what he expected from the executives and staff in general. Lord Rank, on the other hand, had a calm and quiet personality, and was never prone to outbursts if anything went wrong. He was always very kind to me.

Despite their differences in personality and lifestyle, Rank had a great admiration for Davis. His admiration would have been completely pragmatic, and he would have seen that his skills outweighed any criticisms of him as a person. Rank was never very judgmental of people anyway, and this gave their relationship the right conditions to flourish. In addition, the Rank Organisation was an incredibly complex structure that Davis had been instrumental in establishing so after a while there was no way that Rank could have run the business without him. Reflecting on their long association, Rank observed that Davis, after Rank retired, always got his own way in the Rank Organisation, and commented that it wasn't surprising, since he had brought him up to it.

Rank trusted him and Davis was loyal to Rank above all else. But despite the trust that Rank put in Davis, those with power in the City believed Rank and trusted him, an honour they would not give to Davis.

But they did disagree on certain things. Rank recalled what he described as his greatest joy when he was right and Davis had been wrong:

> I was a lone wolf on this particular film project [*The Kidnappers*]. Everybody said, 'You're just wasting your money.' John said, 'You're a blithering fool. I wouldn't make it at any price.' But it didn't cost a lot of money and it made a fortune.[2]

John Davis can be credited with a massive amount of Rank's success. After all, Rank could have fulfilled several of his ambitions in a far quieter way. He could have produced good religious films without taking over cinema chains and he could have boosted the standard of British movies without taking over almost the entire industry from lenses to chair production. *The Observer* newspaper asked how Rank could have spent the first forty-five years of his life in relative obscurity only to become such a colossal figure in such an alien and dramatic world.

The answer may be found not in Mr Rank himself but in his most intimate business associate Mr John Davis. This gentleman had all the sophistication and all the knowledge of the highways and byways of Filmland that Mr Rank lacked and still lacks. So intimate has their association been that Mr Rank is said to have been guided by him in all matters from high finance down to whom he should meet. Only by meeting Mr Davis is it possible to understand how Mr Rank, amiable, gauche and only of average imaginativeness ever came to stand before the public as a confused giant who was but yesterday proclaiming that British films labelled with 'J. Arthur Rank presents...' were about to conquer the markets of the world.[3]

Rank had a very idiosyncratic way of working. He always carried two or three briefcases around with him in which he kept virtually all the running papers of the Rank Organisation; these included hundreds of envelopes with notes on the back. He prided himself on being able immediately to lay hands on the appropriate piece of paper. Once a week he, John Davis, the lawyer Woodham-Smith and accountant Ronnie Leech would go through everything from 6.00p.m to 3.00a.m. or 4.00a.m. Rank was a methodical man and this used to make progress very slow, especially as he insisted on going through every note on the back of every envelope. This may be why he had to work such long hours. Whenever one back-of-an-envelope note was lost, no further discussion could take place until he had found it.

Rank had inherited from his father a precise memory for fact and detail. He was slow and painstaking when he read articles, books or legal documents, but the end result was that he could recall totally what he had read. He had a similar gift of being able to recall conversations with people. He preferred to do business face to face and he was one of those old-fashioned men who, when he shook hands, made a contract on which he would never retract. His word was his bond.

Of course there were always tough problems to be sorted out but, as Davis remembers, no matter how grim the situation or how hard the work, Rank always made it 'very great fun'. His enthusiasm for life, films and flour was quite schoolboyish. His biographer referred to his 'schoolboy habit' of dipping into a box of chocolates concealed in his desk. But Rank's approach to business was not immature. He was a determined man, and so was Davis. They both liked having their own way and sometimes this brought them into conflict. On such occasions Davis would retire behind the evening paper, not to read it (Leech pointed out to him on more than one occasion that it was upside down), but to hide until Rank noticed his withdrawal. His point made, a new approach was found, and eventually a joint decision arrived at.

Once Rank and Davis had a very knotty problem. At about 1.00a.m. they broke off and while John Davis and one or two others sat up all night to come up with a solution, Rank went to bed. When they came to breakfast at 8a.m. and told Rank of their success, he said, 'I knew you would, I prayed for you in the night.'

After the war, in order to cope with the enormous amount of work and the long hours, Rank cut down his travel time to and from Hampshire by taking a suite at the Dorchester Hotel. There was probably some arrangement with the Inland Revenue to make it a partial business expense. Rank used his Dorchester address for many important business meetings. Usually he would go up on Sunday evening and stay, often with his wife, through until Thursday when he would return home to Sutton Manor.

In 1952, at the peak of his power as Chairman of the Rank Organisation (which was Incorporated in 1946) and Joseph Rank Ltd, J. Arthur Rank had 65,000 employees. He was also closely associated with something like sixty-five companies. His film assets alone amounted to £70 million but, despite all this, he still had time for various Methodist committees, for his religious films and for his Sunday school class. Although an enormously wealthy film magnate, he was never too proud to be humble. He sometimes had real difficulty in knowing what exactly he had actually acquired. Someone remarked, 'I have seen him scratch his nose and screw up his eyes in thought while trying to recall the name of one of his own companies.'⁴ Even Rank's phenomenal memory could not instantly span his vast empire.

Rank had various business maxims that he adhered to and passed on to his family. He would say, 'Don't be greedy, take your profit and let somebody else have some,' and 'Never spend your capital!'. He maintained his integrity and he could see no need to be devious about anything. In all Rank's dealings his Christian beliefs were transparently displayed. He was a teetotaller in a world where alcohol passed for water and his meetings, even with hard-bitten associates, would frequently open in prayer. His certainty of God's presence with him gave him tremendous confidence in the boardroom but was somewhat frustrating to his colleagues. One member of the Rank Organisation was reported to have complained, 'You can't fight the chairman and God.'

Rank relied heavily on God's inspiration and he always consulted his Maker on every decision he ever made. And, when things went right, he counted it as a blessing from God. On one occasion at a Rank Films board meeting when new films for a series of documentaries were being considered, Rank stopped the discussion, looked around the room and said:

> Do you know, gentlemen, what's the most wonderful
> monument in London? [Long pause] Cleopatra's
> needle. And do you know why, gentlemen? [A further
> long pause] Because it is the only monument in
> London upon which the eyes of our Lord Jesus Christ
> have gazed.

Not necessarily historically accurate, perhaps, but a reminder to all, even in important meetings discussing film ideas and finance, that the Sunday school teacher was never far away. Rank was able to live in the two worlds and make them both work. It was his ability to compartmentalize his brain which was so useful when running a big organization, and was much admired by his colleagues. Rank applied his Christianity to every aspect of his life, including his business dealings. John Davis remembered that they never had a row, only disagreements, and never ended a day without saying 'Good-bye' and 'Godspeed'. Davis remembers also Rank's compassion and forgiveness when dealing with everyone, even those who had let him down.

> He'd listen to their explanation and say, 'Thank you
> very much.' And when they'd gone, he'd turn to me
> and say, 'I can't think, John, how unhappy that man
> must be.' That was where his religion came in, he
> never ever hated anybody. Rank honestly believed that
> you could make money honestly; if you stick to your
> standards you can win through.

But Rank had some unorthodox views of how to manage his enormous empire. In the early days of the Rank Organisation, he said to Davis, 'We don't really want a board. We just need the two of us—it makes a good board and there is less argument.' But it wasn't to be. Gradually Rank lost a good deal of his control of the Rank Organisation as he devoted time to Ranks Hovis McDougall (RHM) and the financial considerations at the Rank Organisation became more pressing than upholding Rank's standards. As Davis took over from Rank, the quality of the films changed. Rank didn't go to see films in the later years of his life, and he bemoaned the fact that they now had to have naked women in them but he acknowledged that, in order to make a successful film in the sixties, this had to happen.

> It was difficult. If we didn't think we should show a
> picture in our cinemas we couldn't say to the
> distributor, 'We're not going to show this film.' It's the
> only thing we weren't absolutely straight about. You
> see, the censor had given it a certificate and they would
> say, 'Who are you to say that the British public couldn't

see this picture?' And so all we could say was 'We're awfully sorry, you may be right but you take it somewhere else because we don't think it's entertainment. We don't think it's box office.' We tried to raise the standards of pictures.[5]

There was no doubt that Davis was a tough cookie and a very good business partner for Rank. But Rank had his own tough side and it would be completely misleading to think of him as a soft touch when it came to striking business deals. There is a story of one hapless, over-friendly businessman who was invited down to Sutton Manor to strike a deal. In the course of the negotiation apparently he asked Rank if he would mind if he called him Arthur. Rank said, 'Not at all,'—but it was later estimated that such impudence cost the man £100,000 on the deal.

Rank was also a firm but fair dealer when industrial relations were under pressure. Once when there was a dispute at one of his studios, a union representative came to see him at his Park Lane office, spoiling for a fight. He emerged ninety minutes later and remarked with astonishment and admiration, 'I can't understand that chap Rank. I've been with him arguing for an hour and a half, and he hasn't once lost his temper.'

On another occasion Rank showed a Solomonesque way of dealing with workers' problems. Walter Knights recalls:

We had a problem at the Norwood studios. The man appointed as director proved unsuitable; the staff asked me to go to Rank and ask for a replacement.
I discovered that the man frequently lost his temper and raged and stormed. I told Mr Rank, but he made no immediate comment. At the next meeting when both of us were present, Mr Rank called on me to state what I had told him about the unrest in the studio.
I did my best and said that there was an unanimous request for the man to be removed. The director then had to put his side of the case, and he quickly lost his temper, and thus gave the meeting the reasons for the complaint. That was how Rank worked.

Of course there were people other than Davis whom Rank trusted a great deal. One such was L.J. Williams, General Manager of the Westminster Bank when the Rank Organisation had a debt of £14 million. Later, he joined the board of RHM and became a director after he retired. As Rank's nephew Douglas Hutchinson, who was in the business, observed:

> Arthur had tremendous regard for L.J. He backed him
> when it must have been very hard to do so. He was a
> splendid little man and a great director of RHM. He
> hung on to Arthur's coat tails which not many could do
> and he had Arthur's attention. If L.J. thought
> something was bloody stupid, he would say so and
> Arthur would listen.

Other sound advisers were the large, genial American Earl St John, whom Rank had chosen to supervise his productions; he had a shrewd knowledge of public taste balanced with an eye for quality. Others he could depend on were his solicitor, Woodham Smith, who was instrumental in putting Rank's empire together, and Walter Clark, an accountant, who looked after all Rank's affairs.

The arrival of the fifties saw new vistas opening up for Rank and Davis. By then, film production had almost stopped, and the stages at the Denham Studios were being used as warehouses, while the Gate at Elstree was put on the market. Many theatres and cinemas were closing. Rank had made forty films in both 1949 and 1950, and he vowed never to do so again. 'We have learnt our lesson,' he said. Only twenty films were planned for 1951-52. With the Entertainment Tax biting deep into their profits, they experimented with using cinemas as theatres, as live acting attracted a much smaller tax levy. But the advent of television in particular was to be a major challenge.

Rank had a keen interest in the technology involved in television and made ambitious plans for setting up his own transmitters in order to televise sporting events and shows in his cinemas. Meanwhile, through his ownership of Metropolis and Bradford shares in Gaumont-British, Rank had a controlling interest in Baird Television. This company had been merged with Cinema Television Ltd in October 1940. It was generally considered, and confirmed by Asa Briggs' *The History of Broadcasting*, that J. Arthur Rank, although worried about the rapid development of television, was geared up to use it to his own advantage and, unlike many of his colleagues in cinema, felt that it could be of mutual benefit to both industries. He is quoted as saying in November 1950:

> It is definitely not my view that television will harm cinema. American experience is that, after the novelty period, it has helped other entertainments.[6]

Rank thought that television would complement cinema. He considered it would bring a more direct and urgent dimension to the big screens and thought of it more as a public, rather than private, occupation. However, the idea that his films might be shown on small television sets was less acceptable to him, because of the obvious need to make the pictures much smaller and thereby seemingly to spoil the main attraction of the film—the big screen. Although as early as 1949 he sold seventy-five of his films for showing on US television, including *Nicholas Nickleby*, *I Know where I'm Going* and *Waterloo Road*, he would still rather have the traffic going the other way. To this end, Rank made a deal with a Chicago-based company to manufacture large-screen television systems for commercial use in cinemas.

For a long time Rank was in negotiation with the BBC, hoping that he'd be allowed to re-transmit 'selected items from the BBC Television programme and special items from Pinewood Studios to C.M.A. cinemas in the West End'.[7] He did not get very far with this proposal: the BBC was not keen to enter into competition with film companies generally, nor was it deemed suitable to ally the BBC to someone like Rank. Although in theory the film companies would provide material for television consumption, in practical terms this was not popular because television editors would often make cuts in the films in order to suit the slots available to them. They frequently did this without giving overall consideration to the impact of the film.

Showing his inborn business mind, Rank, although pro-claiming he was not keen to promote or acknowledge the use of television sets for domestic use, nonetheless started selling them through his Bush Radio business. This was a very profitable sideline. It may or may not be correct to call this double standards; but, according to Olive Dodds, who was in charge of Rank's contract artists, none of the artists were allowed to work for television if they were on Rank's books.

Television in the end became a rival to the cinema industry. Young people in particular were attracted to the new medium and cinemas around the country felt the pinch. They began to close and, to combat the fall in numbers of young people, cinemas tried hard to entice families along. X-rated films were kept to a minimum, and the sale of confectionery and ice creams began. In November 1952, Rank was asked to appear in court because one of his West End cinemas had not paid its quota. It was revealed that he had made a profit of £1 million on sales of ice-cream in the previous year—another example of how Rank's business ability was always filling in the gaps made by inevitable social or economic developments.

In 1951 there were 800,000 television licences in Britain. By 1960 there were nearly 11 million. At the same time, over the same period, cinema attendances fell from 1,635 million to 501 million. Interestingly, an organization called FIDO (Film Industry Defence Organization) was set up to ensure that film producers did not support or sell their goods to television companies. Rank had refrained from getting too involved in business dealings with television because, as he pointed out, 'We are not going to increase the competition against ourselves'. So J. Arthur Rank supported FIDO, but later invested in Southern Television, recognizing that British films would not make a comeback.[8]

Rank consistently stated that he was not afraid of television, even when his audiences were falling. In 1955 he said: 'It all depends on the weather and the type of film. Television has little effect when a good picture is showing. It affects attendances a good deal when a poor film is shown.' Davis expressed a similar faith: 'We believe that people will want cinema entertainment over the years. The whole of our philosophy is based on the fact that people want to be entertained together in the mass.'

When his older brother, Jimmy Rank, died in 1952 Arthur went back to the flour-milling business full-time and John Davis effectively took over the Rank Organisation. Fortunately for the Rank Organisation, it had many other business interests, and under the heading 'manufacturing' were many smaller companies. The two most significant of these were Cinema-Television, which owned Bush Radio, and Rank Precision Industries, which made cameras and projectors for the amateur and professional, as well as lenses, dictating machines and sound equipment for cinemas and both film and television studios. By 1956 the trading profits from these smaller enterprises accounted for nearly a third of the total company profit of nearly £6,500,000. It was now this side of the company and not the films which was developing fast.

In the same year the Rank Organisation announced that it would be closing forty of its cinemas, and now it was beginning to see the potential of turning these buildings into entertainment centres of a different kind: dance halls, super-markets and, later, bingo halls—a decision which caused Rank some trouble with the Methodist Church. When making the announcement, Rank also stated that a further thirty-nine cinemas would be closed in the next few months.

The closures were easily explained: 184 of Rank's 570 cinemas had made a loss in the previous year. In 1956 cinema attendances were just over one thousand million, but had gone down dramatically to 915 million in 1957. 'I say with great regret that I believe that some hundreds of cinemas will close in this country in the next year,' said Rank. It is easy to imagine Rank's sadness—he had had such massive hopes for the British cinema, and he had put so much money into making it great. But even then the Rank Organisation was still rebuilding or reopening some cinemas after war damage, and it bought fourteen others in England and another twelve in Northern Ireland.

In September 1957 Rank hosted a lavish party at Pinewood to celebrate the twenty-first birthday of the studio complex. Five hundred guests, cocktails, champagne and show girls helped to mark this special occasion. The actresses Jill Ireland and Jill Dixon, both twenty-one, helped Norman Wisdom launch 500 balloons with messages giving prizes to their finders, and the party was graced with practically all of Rank's stars, old and new, including Belinda Lee, David McCallum, Dirk Bogarde, Kenneth Moore, Margaret Lockwood, Phyllis Calvert, John Mills, Michael Redgrave, Flora Robson and A.E. Matthews. But it would be misleading to suggest that Rank would have been chatting happily with these folk. I wrote to several of Rank's stars to ask them to contribute to this biography and most of them replied that they didn't know him at all and so had nothing to say.

A year earlier, away from the film business, seeds had been sown for a new enterprise which was to transform the fortunes of the Rank Organisation. Rank and Davis announced that they had joined the US Haloid company of Rochester, NY, in forming Rank Xerox. This company would develop the rights outside the United States and Canada of a new process of electronic printing—'xerography'—described in the report as 'the art of forming and utilising electrostatic charge patterns on an insulating or photo-conductive insulating surface'. 'The industrial applications of this art,' *The Times* observed, 'which is understood to cut out photographic developing and printing as a separate process, are thought to be very extensive.'

A newspaper article at the time said that this was a shrewd move by John Davis, and very little to do with Rank. Davis does not disagree:

> I created Rank Xerox. We had two factories in the
> north of England that had been making war
> equipment, which of course wasn't wanted any more.
> First I tried to sell them, but I couldn't. Then I said to
> the board, 'Find a product which will have a
> continuing demand' and they found a reference to
> Xerox, which was then known as Haloid. I met Joe

Wilson, the man behind it, and we took a liking to each other. I trusted him completely, for he was just an honest man trying to develop this business. I felt the same way as him, so we made a deal. He had the good idea; we knew all about the making of film equipment, had a worldwide organization and knew all the bankers. By the time I retired, it was worth £1,000 million a year.

But even if it was Davis' idea, it was still Rank's decision to invest the £300,000 in the project. There is no doubt that the acquisition of Xerox was a master stroke that saved the Rank Organisation from extinction. The Organisation was £18 million overdrawn at this stage, and the bank was on the verge of withdrawing their loan.

The decline in cinema attendances continued its alarming trend into 1958. A 24 per cent drop on the previous year took cinema attendances down to 755 million. By 1959 it was down still further to 625 million. Television and consumer spending patterns were blamed: gramophone records, dance halls and the demand for 'luxury' goods such as washing machines and motor cars were all affecting the spending power of the public. The Rank Organisation's profits were reduced from £1.8 million to just £223,000. Rank had confronted the problem

The industry is faced with serious decline in the availability of films which attract the public, even though the more limited number which are now being made available are attractive at the box office. In this country there are four main booking outlets: ABC, Gaumont, Odeon and Fox. Together these theatres need something in the order of 2,008 first feature films with high public acceptability a year. These films are not available and are not likely to become available in the foreseeable future. In fact the drastic cut in output of films from Hollywood is most disturbing.

Rank predicted more cinema closures and went on:

You seem to think I am nervous about this industry.
This group will win through. I am an optimist and I
have grounds for my optimism. I believe that the
industry is getting into a sounder position than it has
ever been before.

Not everyone was impressed with his confidence. George
Elvin, General Secretary of the Association of Cinematograph
and Television Technicians, deeply regretted the decision to
close a further eighty cinemas.

It is not a policy of rationalization. I feel it is hara-kiri.
The only way to get the public back to the cinemas is to
make films the public wants to see. Closing cinemas and
making fewer films is going the wrong way about it.[9]

What was in the minds of most of his members was not how to
make the next film at Pinewood, but whether or not they were still
going to be employed. In response, Rank said he was still committed
to making good pictures. The government's Entertainment Tax,
which resulted in the eventual bankruptcy of the film industry,
continued to damage Rank. Why no one in the government could
foresee the result of their actions was ascribed to ignorance. But as
Alan Wood points out in his book: 'There is always, it must be
confessed, a certain amount of virtuous pleasure and satisfaction to
be derived from seeing a very rich man come a cropper.'[10]

Rank was criticized in the *Evening Standard* for appearing
'gloomy'. In his reply he drew on his experience as chairman of
his father-in-law's firm, Horace Marshall & Son (distributor of
newspapers). 'I am in the wholesale newspaper distributing
business and I know that newspapers get from the wholesaler
between 50 and 65 per cent. I wonder if they would be gloomy
to wake up one morning and find that the Government had
reduced a return of 60 per cent to 13 per cent. The newspapers
would put up the black crepe down Fleet Street and they would
be screaming that the government was a robber.'

Austere measures were taken by the Rank Organisation in
order to cope with the losses. Top executives took a cut in salary.

The actor Alec Guinness remarked, 'At the end of my first year's contract with the Rank Organisation I was given a Christmas present of a leather wallet and a bowl of hydrangeas for my wife. At the end of the second year I got a cigarette lighter and a bowl of daffodils for my wife. At the end of the third year I got a letter of thanks from John Davis.'

During all the closing of studios and the business of cutting the losses it was tricky for Rank to get his PR right: on the one hand he was criticized for looking gloomy, which was bad for business confidence; on the other, he was criticized for appearing happy, which looked insensitive, as some of his staff were losing money, if not jobs. Rank was no doubt confident throughout. 'We're fighting back and we mean to go on fighting,' he declared. His inability to get it right was blamed on his political naivety.There was a little light on the horizon: Rank saw hope in the promise that the Entertainment Tax would be lifted in the April 1958 budget. He had been fighting it for ten years, but now conditions in the country were such that it could go. A *Sunday Times* reporter watched Rank as he sat and listened to the budget speech on 20 April 1958:

> Lord Rank's countenance is not, to say the least,
> mobile or demonstrative. But even his impassivity was
> unable entirely to conceal his feelings as he sat in the
> Peers Gallery during Mr Heathcoat Amory's budget
> speech. Not a flicker animated his face, but I fancied as
> time wore on and the Chancellor worked through a
> number of proposals without mentioning the cinema
> tax, Lord Rank's posture grew more hunched and
> glum. It was not until an hour and a half had passed,
> as Big Ben struck five, that he heard the fate of the
> industry he bestrides. He leant slightly forward,
> turning his head and putting up his hand to be sure
> that he caught every word. Then sitting back, he drew
> a forefinger slowly across his forehead. The involuntary
> gesture of relief spoke more than all the later
> comments of the industry's official spokesmen.

In 1960 some of the press were reporting the beginnings of a cinema revival and questioning the Rank Organisation's strategy: it had closed one quarter of its 600-plus screens. Davis rejected this: 'Far from having closed down too many, we have not closed enough.' He also refuted the idea that more people were going to see films. The change in the Entertainment Tax had helped profits to rise, but audiences were still declining by 2 per cent a year. Even with this slight turnaround in the takings, films which had cost Rank so much money were not going to rescue his fortunes. The real saviour of the Rank Organisation was photocopying and the deal Davis had struck securing the world rights outside of the Americas for Xerox. That deal could not have come at a more valuable time from the point of view of the company's liquidity.

It was after this that Rank really started to lose control of the Rank Organisation. He knew it was now safe in Davis' hands. Davis had by now become so powerful in his own right that it would have been impossible to have two such important people running it. But it was when Rank started to lose interest that the Rank Organisation started to lose some of Rank's character. When at his most powerful, Rank had barred 'X'-certificate films from his cinemas. He had always been against the 'X' certificate and was worried that the category might be misused 'to the detriment of screen entertainment.' Now they could be shown, although the Organisation would still ban a picture if it was unduly provocative or sensational. Of the sixteen directors, Rank's was only one vote. Fortunately, in the late fifties public opinion was on Rank's side. 'We are relieved to observe a public trend both in this country and overseas against the more unwholesome form of 'X' film' said *The Times* of 15 September 1960.

In the end, Xerox was to dwarf the rest of the company. It was to make Rank and his immediate family multi-millionaires. By comparison the other parts of the Rank Organisation were not doing much. At some point in the sixties the Xerox patent ran out and competition came into the copier market. The frailty of the Rank Organisation became apparent, and John Davis was ousted.[11]

In the cold light of history none would doubt Rank's reputation as an amazing and far-sighted businessman. He was a courageous industrialist, but not a Hanson or Weinstock. He didn't understand business enough to be able to strip one down and start again from scratch. He made his own astonishing confession of his inadequacies in his speech at the eightieth birthday dinner put on for him by the Rank Organisation:

> You've all been very kind to me and anyone can say
> what they like. I don't know anything about literature,
> I haven't got a scholastic mind, I know nothing about
> finance at all.

But perhaps Rank's overriding quality, in terms of business, was his confidence and the confidence he inspired in others. He said that confidence was the biggest money-maker in the world. He would point to the rarity of strikes, especially in the milling side of his business, and say that it was due to the confidence that the workers had in their management. Alongside his confidence was his optimism. 'Of course I'm an optimist. If you're guided to do something you can go at it, it doesn't matter what anyone says to you, you can. If I wanted to do something, I generally got what I wanted.' He admitted that he made mistakes but he thought that mistakes were crucial to development. 'If you are too frightened to make mistakes, you never get anywhere.'

His other great business commitment was to quality. He declared himself ignorant about marketing, nor did he like it, but he swore that 'a black cat with a label round its neck could sell something if it was quality.' When he was signing off at the end of a long spiel on how to succeed at business he said, 'You need to have integrity, brains and enthusiasm for work and you can set the Thames on fire.'

His main problem, some suggest, was that apart from Davis and Woodham Smith, Rank tended to surround himself with mediocre people. Rank would say that his father had a terrific ability to judge a person's character very quickly: 'He never made a mistake.' Rank envied this because it would take him two or three months before he could really figure someone out.

Integrity and sincerity was something Rank demanded from his own staff: 'I won't have any man working for me if he's not honest.' But he had to adopt a fail-safe system to help him in his character assessments. He would invite the person around to the Dorchester for lunch where they would meet his wife. 'Women have got very good intuition,' he'd say. When they left he would ask Nell whether she thought they were straight, and if she thought 'no,' that would be it as far as their future as a Rank business partner was concerned.

After Davis left, things were never the same at the Rank Organisation. The kinds of movies that were coming out were not like the ones Rank had been so proud of during the war years. Ethel, one of his sisters, criticized him, saying, 'I can't understand you, Arthur. A good Christian like you, how can you reconcile that?' He replied, 'Oh, you don't understand these things. You don't know what people want.'

The name Rank was appearing in all sorts of unlikely places as the Rank Organisation expanded to compensate the ailing movie industry. Developments included petrol stations and the move to more 'X-rated' movies. Some parts of the family remained uncomfortable with the exposure Rank was getting through the movie industry. His sister Ethel thought it vulgar that the family should be associated with all that tinsel. She thought the name was being cheapened by appearing on bingo halls and her outspoken criticism may have accounted for her never being invited to Drynachan (Rank's Scottish retreat) with her husband Jock. For Ethel, her brother had become too successful and she could be quite crotchety with him. Perhaps it was another time when his hotline to God was so sure that he could not believe he was in the wrong.

Davis, however, never lost faith in Rank:

He had a wonderful brain and I was the luckiest man alive to have met him when I was still a young man... Looking back, I was a brash young man. He placed his confidence and his loyalty in me and these have never wavered. Over the years a deep affection has grown up between us which has had a great influence on my life for the better. A relationship which I think is unique in business. Arthur has been a wonderful colleague and a wonderful friend and in many ways a second father.

Although not obviously a religious man through most of his life, towards the end Davis attended services at a London church. Maybe all those years of observing Rank's Christianity had finally got through to him.

On 6 June 1962 Rank announced that he would retire from his role as Chairman in the autumn of that year. He had been in charge since 1941, and was now to be the first life president of the Organisation. To mark the occasion of Davis succeeding him as Chairman Rank bought Dinah Sheridan, Davis' wife at the time, a diamond necklace. He commented that no man reaches such a position without a wife's support. To the newspapers he had now become 'legendary' and was often referred to as 'Uncle Arthur'.

One over-enthusiastic journalist had reported his retirement five years too early but quoted Rank then as saying, 'I believe the film business is a young man's business, so I'm making way for younger men'[12] At the real function in 1962 Rank wiped away tears of emotion as tributes were paid to him. In his speech he revealed: 'Do you know, when I left school they said I was the biggest nitwit that ever walked?' Control of the Rank Organisation was to be officially handed over to John Davis although he had actually been wielding supreme power for the past five years. Summing up his contribution to the British movie industry one newspaper said on the day after the announcement:

Despite his appalling virtues, Rank is an honest man who tried his best to put a British-made film into a cinema in every part of the world. His emblem, the man striking the gong, became known from Hong Kong to Hawaii.

From the moment Rank gave up the chairmanship he never interfered with Davis' running of the Rank Organisation, but neither did he lose interest. Even after he took over control at Ranks Hovis McDougall, there was never a day went by when he didn't contact Davis to see how things were going. The group was now back on its feet after the collapse of the movie industry. In the previous financial year it had had a trading profit of more than £8 million and was now worth £88 million.

On his retirement the Rank Organisation presented Arthur with a book. It contained 28,066 signatures of his employees. The inscription at the front read:

We who have been associated with you in the activities of the Rank Organisation record our gratitude and admiration for: The great contribution you have made over the years to the group which is proud to bear your name—and indeed to the British Film Industry as a whole. The ever present evidence of your kindliness and humanity and of your steadfast faith in the principles for which you stand. Your leadership and the unfailing support and encouragement you have always given your colleagues. TO YOU, ARTHUR, (as your friends who have signed this book affectionately address you) we say, 'for all this a most heartfelt thank you,' and we ask God's continued blessing on you and Lady Rank all your days.

At this time his cinema chain had been reduced to 374 screens and the only Rank studio was at Pinewood.

However, it was Rank who had created the Rank Organisation and, as the tributes flowed in at his eightieth birthday dinner held at the Dorchester, his achievement was fully acknowledged. Sir George Bolton, Chairman of the Bank of London and South America said, 'You must be very proud when you look back on the outstanding growth of the company you created. The Rank Organisation has earned the respect and admiration of the business and financial world.'

7 MRS RANK

Didst thou not make us one,
That we might one remain,
Together travel on,
And share our joy and pain,
Till all thy utmost goodness prove,
And rise renewed in perfect love?

CHARLES WESLEY

Everyone says that The Honourable Laura Ellen Rank, Nell, was a wonderful woman. She obviously had the measure of 'Arpie', her husband, and he would do very little without seeking her opinion. Of course, he also sought the Lord's advice but there was an understanding between them that Nell and the Lord didn't argue. Nell was also a very religious person, a lifelong Methodist and a cigarette-smoker.

Nell and Arthur met in London. Joseph Rank had moved his family from Hull to London, and they had started attending the Tooting Methodist Mission. The couple met at a function at the Savoy Hotel to celebrate the new Tooting Mission which Lady Marshall (Nell's mother) had been invited to open. Nell's father was Sir Horace Brooks Marshall (later Baron Marshall of Chipstead), a former Lord Mayor of London and Governor of Rank's old school, The Leys, in Cambridge. Horace Marshall and Sons had made their money as newspaper and periodical distributors based at Temple House. Lord Marshall was also a close friend of Joseph Rank. Nell and Arthur married on 18 October 1917. At the time it was a better match for Arthur than for Nell for, although the Ranks had money, Arthur was in the end the son of a miller, while she enjoyed a higher social status.

Nevertheless, Nell matched her husband in his unpretentiousness—you wouldn't know either of them had a penny, the way they presented themselves. He did wear expensive suits, but she had no interest in clothes whatsoever. She was more frail than he was and he looked after her very carefully. She was charming; she had an old-fashioned sense of values and principles, good moral ethics and wouldn't stand for any hanky-panky. Someone who remembers her attending church in Reigate described her as 'a shadowy figure who was very frightening'. Within her own family however she reportedly had a strong sense of humour. When Mrs Powell, a family friend, was pregnant with her fifth child, Nell asked if she was taking precautions. When she said she was, Lady Rank observed, 'Well, they must be old stock!'

Nell was known for her occasional chidings of her husband, of which there were two kinds: the more gentle one would begin, 'Oh Arthur... '; but if it was serious she would say, 'Arthur, I will talk to you in the morning.' He would react by getting up, putting his arm round her and saying 'Now Nell dear, you can't do that,' and she would reply, 'Well, you can't get away with what you just said [or did].'

Rank probably enjoyed the limelight more than he let on and only in deference to his wife did he say 'no' to a number of things. He listened to her. If she thought he was going over the top, she would say so. 'Now, Arpie, you shouldn't say that,' was her response. When they got older she would just take him off and say, 'It's time for bed.'

She accepted that his business and his intense motivation meant interminable hours of meetings and functions. If she had had her way, she would rather have been alone with Arthur doing those things in which they were both interested. Her patience was truly amazing as, night after night, she would sit, saying little and usually knitting, while Arthur dealt with some difficult business associates. She had a bad leg which would have been easily cured today but it meant a lot of sitting, so she occupied herself with tapestry and knitting.

When they got home later there would be an inquest on the evening's activities. She would show great discernment as she assessed the characters involved and she would shrewdly evaluate the conversation. What she said and wanted was often the deciding factor with her Arpie.

For example, Rank once had his eye on a moor on the Isle of Arran and struck the deal, but in the morning he cancelled it because Nell had discovered that there was thirty miles of water to get across to it and she didn't like being on the sea. Another time, at dinner one evening, he was offered part-time fishing rights on a river in Norway. Rank was keen to go in on the deal, but unfortunately while he was playing bridge after the meal ('trying to earn an honest penny', as he put it—though he never staked more than a few pence), the guest who had offered the opportunity was talking to Nell. He described how beautiful the river was and how marvellous the mosquitoes were. By the morning Rank had decided against the river because Nell couldn't stand mosquitoes—'If there was one within a mile it would attack her.'

Most of the guests at their social functions were men, and often the most popular guests were bachelors, who played bridge and were good shots. Douglas Hutchinson, Rank's nephew, was one of them:

> The reason for this was that Nell Rank didn't like
> having women around. She thought they were a
> nuisance. She was more than half way to being a
> recluse and she didn't like having to look after them.
> She was very sweet and simply devoted to him, too
> much so, he could do no wrong.
>
> She was all there and half-way back again and no
> one would pull the wool over her eyes. If she had been
> a stronger character and stood up to him, it would
> have been no bad thing. She was very nice, cosy and
> antisocial. She wasn't very interesting and was rather
> shy. Life for her revolved around Arthur.

At dinner parties the men she liked were assigned to sit next to her. Two of these were Maurice Goodbody and Wilson Impey, both friends of Rank from the milling industry. She liked Impey, even though she made him more nervous than

Arthur did. During one dinner he revealed to her that he was a Quaker, and he learnt from her that the original Rank money was Quaker money and not Methodist. Joseph Rank's real mother was a Quaker and she had left him some money which he used to buy his first mill. The morning after this revealing conversation, Nell handed Impey a cheque for £10,000 to be donated to the Quaker Education Fund.

Nell was known to be a good judge of character. She was even described by one newspaper as 'a shrewd businesswoman'. However, she hated the social side to Arthur's life. She was most uncomfortable at premières and big dinners and was quite choosy as to who came to stay at Sutton Manor. She didn't like having film producers in her house and she really didn't like being left with their wives for small talk and social chatter. She was all right at dinners for Rank's shooting parties but, as she said to her daughter Shelagh, 'I'd go and live on a desert island with your father quite happily.' She hated the thought of outsiders intruding in her world.

When Rank had to be in London for the week, she would go with him to stay in the Dorchester, in the suite of rooms he often took, where he would entertain his City contacts. They had a sitting-room and a bedroom, and Nell often ate a sandwich alone in the bedroom while a waiter served the men lunch.

On less business-oriented occasions, when Rank's researcher Edgar Youdell came on his monthly visit, she would stay and talk, and although she showed no interest in Arthur's business affairs, she was interested in his religious films and was often quite critical of them.

Ellen Rank remained a very private person throughout her life. Arthur asked for privacy and respect in his and his wife's personal life. When his fame had grown, his home was often besieged by the press, and there were exaggerated reports of the size and number of rooms in their mansion, as well as greatly enhanced numbers of the dogs that he owned. Ellen must have hated such gossip and intrusion. She loved her home life and wanted things to remain settled. However, the husband whom she loved above all had taken her into a life-style that invited publicity and put pressure on her. She was terribly upset when Arthur decided to leave their first house in Reigate and move to Hampshire, but she was so loyal and devoted that she didn't stand in his way. She did what was necessary to help him even if she didn't like it.

For all Rank's fame, I found only one occasion when the Ranks found themselves in a gossip column, albeit for the most innocent reason. Under the headline 'Romantic Echo', the *Star* of 6 November 1948 remarks that, at a big film dinner given by Paramount:

> Mr J. Arthur Rank does not have much time for dancing. But he danced with his wife last night at the Savoy ballroom. Afterwards he told me, 'I said to my wife, we must just have one dance. You see, it was in this room thirty-five years ago that I first met her.

It is remarkable that there was little gossip about the Ranks. Obviously, they didn't court publicity for their private lives, but the truth is that their honest living was devoid of any scandal. Devoted, faithful married life doesn't titillate the tabloids.

Her daughter Shelagh recalled, 'Mother was totally different. She had a quiet faith, she wasn't the extrovert Father was, but she was full of good works.'

In later years their butler, Michael Harnett, was a beneficiary of some of these good works. When his children were born Nell would come down every day to visit his wife and check on her well-being. And when the children eventually went to school she paid for all their uniforms, and when his son went to St Mary's Roman Catholic school they paid all his fees. Lady Rank's generosity could be rather embarrassing. Dinah Sheridan, who was married to John Davis, remembers that at Christmas time 'Auntie Nell' would tell her to go and buy Christmas presents for her children and then send her the bill—'A deed I hated doing!'

Rank's nephew, Douglas Hutchinson, commented:

I think Arthur loved his wife, they seemed so close and happy. They used to go down to a hotel in Cornwall in March, the Carlyon Bay Hotel, and again in November. They looked after them well. It was quiet and had a good golf course and they would play a bit and he used to read to her, novels like Geoffrey Farnell. They were both fond of flowers and they would often walk together round the garden. When he had time he used to read to her in the loggia.

Alan Wood describes how Arthur's wife was overheard in a Reigate bookshop wishing she could get her husband more interested in reading. He read so little that of one book which he did manage to get through, *The Letters of Erasmus*, he commented, it 'took me a long time'.[1]

Their grandson, Fred Packard, remembers:

Granny was very saintly, full of the milk of human kindness. She was a good judge of human character. But really they were chalk and cheese. Grandpa's life should never be seen in isolation. My parents said, if Grandpa hadn't been married to Granny, he might have gone off the rails.

While Rank would read nothing more taxing than horse-racing novels, Nell was a member of the *Times* Book Club and she read a very great deal. She enjoyed reading in bed so much so that Rank had to tie a scarf round his eyes so that he could go to sleep. (Rank's literary ignorance was surprising. Once he even admitted that he'd never heard of Thomas Hardy.)[2]

As the tributes were flowing at Rank's eightieth birthday party, held by the Rank Organisation at the Dorchester, Mrs Rank was included in the praise. When John Davis mentioned that Arthur had been lucky to have had such a wonderful wife, there was a chorus of 'hear, hear,' and bangs on the table.

Michael, their butler, remembers how terrible it was for Rank when she died.

He rang me at 7.00 and I went up and she was laying in the bathroom [in the same position that Rank was to be found when he was dying] and we got her into bed. Lord Rank sent for the doctor and from then on she got worse.

Despite the attentions of a private nurse Nell died about a fortnight afterwards on 18 August 1971.

He wasn't the same afterwards. He became quiet, and before that he was full of life. He said to me, 'Michael, it's for the best, she was really ill and she would only have gone on suffering.' But in his heart, I knew that he was now a lonely man.

One day, after her death, there were some dog trials—a hobby Rank followed for many years with some intensity—and Rank, as usual, won several prizes. But when he came home he was sad; he told Michael how depressing it was that there was no one to share his joy now that his wife was dead. They were so devoted that he had a big picture of her in his dressing-room with a light shining on her and Michael would often find him staring at it.

Fred Packard remembers his grieving as the only time he had ever seen his grandfather miserable:

I went to visit him in August '71. We had lunch, just the two of us, and he talked about the last twenty-four hours with her. It was like he had both arms cut off. She would drive him mad, she would lose things and she lost her memory and it did get on his nerves, but their marriage was a wonder to behold. I only saw him sad that once. I also went to say good-bye—it was just before I went to Brazil—and he was sitting behind his huge desk in his study and he was so alone and so strange without Granny. I think he knew he would never see me again and there were tears in his eyes.

Mrs Joan Powell, sister of Rank's son-in-law Robin Cowen, had known Rank since she was six:

> When she died he was heartbroken. He made a little sort of fortress round the fire, with his desk and chair forming a little square where he sat, and he didn't want to go out or do anything.

Sir Francis Pemberton, CBE DL, who was a friend from Rank's involvement with the Royal Agricultural Society, recalls giving lunch to Rank ten days after Lady Rank had died. They spent some three hours talking together, during which time Rank spoke as if his wife was in the room with him. Sir Francis described this as one of the most marvellous experiences of his life.

The Rev. Dr Kingsley Lloyd, former president of the Methodist conference, wrote a letter of sympathy to Rank. In his reply, dated 14 September 1971, Rank said:

> I am so glad she is glad today, living in the fullness of God's love. This sudden change has brought me nearer to God. In great thankfulness that I had fifty-five years of joy with my dear one. Yours, Arthur Rank.

8 HOME AND FAMILY LIFE

Happy the home where man and wife together
Are of one mind believing in your love.
KARL SPITTA

I spoke to a very large number of the Rank family who were all very fond of 'the old man'. He obviously inspired great affection in those close to him and their reminiscences help to build up a portrait of him as a family man. I started writing this book the day after the death of his eldest and closest daughter, Ursula Newton, and during my research she had always been too unwell for me to visit. The closest relative I spoke to was his younger daughter (by four years), Shelagh, and her second husband Major Robin Cowen. Robin's parents had been very good friends with Arthur and Nell and he became practically a surrogate son to Rank. Rank had asked Robin to be Assistant Agent on the estate when he was just fifteen-and-a-half, and when Robin was seventeen he left Marlborough and took up the post. He was to manage the Reigate estate before the war and after the estate in Sutton Scotney.

One can only conjecture as to the disappointment Rank and his wife felt at not having a son and heir. There was a baby son but he died at birth. This must have been the biggest tragedy in Rank's life although I have been unable to find much information on the subject. It was reported in *The Leysian*, the Leys School magazine. The entry was brief, simply stating that J. Arthur Rank and his wife had a son, 'who did not survive his birth'. Shelagh was the last child to be born; Nell had been so ill with the birth that there could be no more. Maybe these tragedies gave Rank an extra drive to achieve even more; it is clear that they did not blight his life. Because he was able to apply his religion to every aspect of his life, he was able to be happy even when things were going wrong.

The house in Heathfield, Reigate Heath, to which Nell and Arthur moved after the First World War, was a proper family home and a happy place. At that time Rank was not the busy man he became in later life, and he spent plenty of time with his wife and daughters and enjoying the farm. He kept some horses, and took a keen interest in the management of the land, and in farming techniques. Later he was to start his kennels, which became very important to him.

Rank had the happy knack of being able to shut his business out of his mind on Friday nights. On Saturdays he liked to go golfing in Reigate or shooting in Sutton Scotney, but nothing would prevent him from returning to the Sunday school to take his class. It was no problem to switch from the jollity of the golf course to the serious business of teaching. Stories are told of him playing bridge in the evenings at Reigate. Suddenly his father would ring him on business. He would immediately answer the phone and become totally involved in business matters, and then return without a hitch to the game and resume playing. But although Rank certainly enjoyed his playtimes, he could only do so after work was complete; 'Play is always more enjoyable after work,' he would say.

Although there was some land at Heathfield, there was not enough for someone who was as keen on shooting as Rank. He began looking around for new land to shoot on and in 1929 he began to rent Tichborne Park in Hampshire which introduced him to the delights of the Hampshire countryside while keeping the Reigate home.

Robin Cowen remembers going to Reigate for the weekend as a teenager before the Second World War:

> We used to play penny accumulator golf matches on a special putting green with two holes, one at each end.

We'd play nine holes and we always had a bet. But he'd have this uncanny habit of always sinking the last long put and scooping the pool—but it was great fun; he loved his golf.

Shelagh, too, remembers those days:

Every minute was full of action. We used to go and stay by the sea and Daddy liked to take a bag of golf balls onto the cliff top. He was late for lunch one day and Mother was just saying grace and a golf ball came straight through the window, sending splinters all over the cold ham.

His family all observed that his faith was the guiding principle in his life, but none of them took it on board for themselves. His daughter Shelagh blames this on his over-enthusiasm and for his being a bit heavy-handed when they were young. Now, however, the family have nothing but respect for the 'old man's' faith and remember with great affection how he would pray every morning and never do anything without consulting the Almighty. It must have been a terrible disappointment to him, though, that neither of his daughters were interested in the Christian faith. They went along with it for as long as they had to, but there was no commitment after that. The girls were not sent to his Sunday school class in Reigate. He would go off on his own and during the war he would cycle back in time for lunch. Shelagh continues:

Around tea-time we would have family prayers. Father would read to us and give a tiny sermonette, sometimes talking for two or three minutes on the sins of the week. Mother would play the piano and we would sing a hymn, and then in the evening we would go out to his service at the church in Reigate. It was all terribly jolly, with coffee afterwards, but then it would get embarrassing with extemporary praying.

On Sundays Rank didn't immerse himself in his papers in the same way as on other days. He might do a little reading. In later years he would always have a long chat on the phone with Ursula (his other daughter) on Sunday morning. She rarely went to Sutton Manor. Arthur was particularly fond of Ursula and he used to like her being around. Because of his slight deafness and being somewhat short-sighted he valued not only her company but also her practical help and encouragement.

According to some of Rank's former Sunday school pupils, the girls were fortunate not to have to attend his classes. Rank was Superintendent of the entire school for many years and then in 1947 became leader of the Senior Department at Reigate Methodist church. This was for children aged eleven to fifteen. Rank had actually stepped down from Superintendent to become leader of the senior group, but he never resented this. As Alan Wood comments, this sort of 'demotion' would have been unimaginable in his business life.[1]

Rank's ability as a Sunday school teacher was surprisingly lacking. There were thirty or so children and, despite his attempts to be strict, he had trouble keeping control. They weren't intimidated by him, as you might have imagined, but there was much fondness, love and respect for their extraordinary teacher. He would take autograph books to the studios and would come back with such treasures as 'with love from Margaret Lockwood'. Occasionally he would bring some of his VIP guests into the Sunday school so that they could see what was going on. But the main problem was that he was rather boring. On one occasion the pianist, Mr Laker, who accompanied the singing, had fallen asleep by the time Rank came to the closing hymn. Rank announced it twice and then had to go and wake him up.

One old scholar remembers with shame that they were not very appreciative of Rank's efforts. He would try to come down to their level but they would make fun of him. Even his regular importation of the latest electrical gadgets, record players and slide shows would fail to impress. It can't have helped the atmosphere when there were often reporters at the back, wondering why such a powerful businessman taught in Sunday school when he clearly had so little talent for it.

Alan Wood visited Rank's Sunday school class and, maybe because his biographer was present, it seemed to go quite well.

> Inside we will find him going round giving out the hymn books and Bibles himself. Then he stands, not in the pulpit or behind the communion rail, but in the aisle before the children, girls on the right and boys on the left; he will smile at one or other among them as they catch his eye, and he speaks with a simple ease and fluency which would astonish his business associates. He is, in fact, a completely different man from the Rank of films or the Rank of flour; even in his clothes. His brown suit almost has a baggy look about it; and the collar of his blue shirt is crumpled.[2]

Sunday school and the teaching he did there was an integral part of Rank's life and his character was built upon it. It would be difficult for the normal member of the public who knew Arthur as the film and flour magnate to even remotely imagine how he spent his weekends. But Rank was terribly committed to young people and the Sunday school meant a great deal to him. His pupils loved him as a dear uncle, and his real nieces would refer to him as 'happy Arthur', partly in jest, since he was perceived as being very stern, while they all had a great sense of humour and irrepressible giggling fits.

Sundays in Reigate also included a walk round the farm which was still viable and working. This went on until both Shelagh and Ursula were sent to boarding school. To this day, Shelagh still thinks he is watching over her and she still refrains from things if she thinks he would disapprove. As a father he didn't believe in corporal punishment—he preferred to reason with the children, and point out the ethical and religious reasons why they shouldn't have done what they did.

In the Reigate days Rank would catch the 8.15a.m. from Redhill, be in London for 9.00a.m. and come home every evening. But as the film business increased his workload, he took rooms at the Dorchester Hotel. His daughters became aware very slowly that their father was becoming a household name and was perceived to be 'the man with the gong' (as in the famous logo at the start of his films). Although he didn't change in character, the main difference was that he was no longer around. By the time the adult Shelagh got back from the States she had to make an appointment to see him.

Away from the business world, Rank had many interests in addition to his Sunday school teaching. Some of his activities might now seem to be at variance with his strongly-held beliefs—the paradox of Rank is intriguing. He smoked cigarettes for a large part of his life. He was certainly still smoking twenty a day at the age of sixty. He used to give up every February, possibly as a token gesture to the Lenten season, but also because it was the shortest month. He would insist that his clients gave up with him so that he didn't suffer alone.

His somewhat 'easy' views of gambling, described elsewhere, indicate a rebellious streak. As well as being a Freemason, which some would find inconsistent with the Christian faith, and which is now disapproved of by the Methodist Church, he used to enjoy reading Mr Lindo in *The People* newspaper. Mr Lindo would prophesy, along the lines of an astrologer, about what was going to happen that week. Apparently, Rank rather enjoyed this and identified himself with the writer, since he too was an optimist. If it was raining on the day of a shoot Rank used to say, 'Oh, it's just a clearing-up shower.' During the Second World War he kept saying, 'It will all be over by Christmas.' He was endlessly optimistic. Other than *The People*, Rank read the *Daily Express* and the *Sunday Express* as well as *The Times*.

He was fond of driving. This became a family joke, since he was so bad at it. His nephew, Douglas Hutchinson, remembers one driving story:

> A friend of his, Vincent Routledge, who was an
> exceedingly good shot, was being driven hell-for-
> leather by Arthur on the way to London and Arthur

147

outrageously overtook a car which then overtook them and hurled abuse. 'What did he say, Vincent?' 'He says, Arthur, that he thinks you're a f—ing bastard.'

Rank drove Lancias and, at one time, a German Stutz, before falling to the inevitable Rolls Royce. After fifty years of accident-free driving he was made a Knight of the Road amid much family hilarity. He had been an aggressive driver from the early days of his business career. A former secretary of his, Miss D.N. Nyst, who worked with him for many years, remembers him giving her a lift to work during the General Strike. 'He was a fast driver and his pet phrase was 'Mind your back, woman, your stomach won't save you," if anyone dashed across the road in front of the car. Luckily, we never hit anyone!' His bad driving and his refusal to admit defeat nearly had disastrous results while on holiday in Scotland, as Colin Rank, Arthur's great-nephew, remembers:

> Maurice Goodbody told me that Arthur, Nell and Wilson Impey had gone off to church in the Landrover one Sunday morning. They were late and Arthur was driving too fast to make up time, since he was a stickler for punctuality, and it went out of control. The wheels went off on to the rough where there were periodic ditches and everyone was thrown all over the place, and after the tenth ditch, still out of control, Nell said calmly, 'Arpie, I think you've made your point!' When he got back he parked the Land Rover next to the wall so that the chauffeur couldn't see the damage.

Although Rank was devoted to his wife and family, and would come home as much as he could, the ten years during the height of his movie successes was very short on family get-togethers. But one time they were all together was for a period during the war. His daughter Shelagh has one particular memory which indicates Rank's involvement in high places.

She was home on leave when, the day before D-Day, her father stood all evening, looking out of the window. She and Nell couldn't understand what he was doing. They asked him what was wrong, but he said he was only thinking. When morning came they heard on the wireless that the D-Day invasion had begun and Rank was able to say why he had been so anxious.

Apparently Eisenhower had been down to see him in secret. He had taken Rank out into a field where no one could hear, and had explained his mission. He told Rank of the plans for the top secret D-Day operation. Adverse weather conditions had been indicated which might delay the troops' landing by another three weeks. What Eisenhower wanted was, in the event of bad weather, to borrow all Rank's cinemas on the south coast in order to entertain the troops, and keep them hidden and well-briefed for the invasion. Rank had agreed to the proposal but was sworn to secrecy, even from telling his family. So his relief when he heard that the invasion had gone ahead on schedule was understandable. There is no doubt that this plan would have been financially damaging for him, but Rank's patriotism was such that I doubt such a thought crossed his mind.

During the war Rank also visited America on behalf of the Government to see about food supplies. He claims to have gone deaf on the flight and from then on, as is recorded elsewhere, he used his deafness to his own advantage in business situations, choosing to be deaf when it suited him. For example, if Rank was completely stumped by a shareholder's question he would either reply with a Yorkshire anecdote—which would go down well—or he would use his defence of periodic deafness to great effect. On one occasion there was a particularly unpleasant shareholder who stood up and shouted at Rank for about five minutes, after which Rank stood up and said, 'Can't you speak up a bit, we can't hear you up here!'

This deafness meant that he answered what he wanted to and said what he wanted to say. Amazingly, he got away with it. John Davis joked about this 'little difficulty' at Rank's eightieth birthday dinner:

Arthur has suffered from a little deafness from ever
since I can remember [much laughter]. There were
those times when he didn't want to hear, there were
those occasions when he heard and took no notice, and
the occasion when a side remark was made which he
was not intended to hear and which he heard very
clearly.

But he could become deaf with his family too. Shelagh
remembers his technique:

I said there was something I had to talk to him about
so he asked me up to London and there he was,
surrounded by papers piled up all around him. Then
he looked up at me and said, 'Sit down and tell me all
about it.' And then he took both hearing aids out.

Deaf or not, he wasn't always the easiest man to talk to since
he would sit at his desk riffling through papers. But apparently
he was always listening. A story is told about when he was
president of a golf club near Winchester. At one meeting he was
told that an awkward issue was going to be raised. So he
switched off both hearing aids and made the man repeat the
question three times because he said he couldn't hear what the
trouble-maker was saying. In the end the matter was dropped,
out of frustration.

Rank's life as a landowner and countryman was mainly to do with
shooting and dogs. In 1934, despite Rank's willingness to spend a
lot of money at Tichborne Park in Hampshire, the 21-year-old heir
to the estate decided he wanted it for himself so Rank was forced
to look elsewhere in Hampshire for a country retreat. He found
Sutton Manor, in Sutton Scotney, and bought the house and the
first 2,000 acres of the adjoining land from the Courage family,
paying about £20,000. By 1939 this had grown to a 9,000 acre
estate and after the war a further 5,000 acres were added.

By 1953 he considered it unnecessary to have two big houses
so he decided to sell the Reigate home—which was heartbreaking

for Nell. At Sutton Manor there were many staff—eight or nine in the house, eleven gardeners and thirteen gamekeepers. About 3,000 acres were in hand and farmed. In those days shooting was merely considered a rich man's hobby, and Rank obviously had no moral qualms about building up a wonderful shoot on his estate. He was actually considered one of the best game shots in the country before the Second World War.

In Reigate he had built up an impressive pack of gun dogs, of which he was extremely fond: 'I named all the dogs after generals and the bitches after movie stars.' Indeed his dogs were fond of him. When he was at death's door with a burst appendix in 1934 his favourite dog sat and cried by his bedside for hours at a time.

Rank founded his Reigate kennels in 1936. They moved to Sutton Scotney in 1953. At its peak he had forty-six dogs (twenty-four Labradors and twenty-two pointers) and three kennel-men to look after them. (He kept his greyhounds at other kennels.) He had no interest in Crufts—rather, he focused his competitive nature on working trials. He would open his land for these trials, but since he usually won he was only too pleased to be generous.

When there wasn't a shoot on, Rank would spend as much time as he could walking his favourite dogs and setting them challenges to find hidden dummies. Even his dogs had to work hard! And he would often challenge other top dog owners to see if their dogs could beat his to the prize. 'He was very competitive, was his Lordship,' observed Manners, who looked after Rank's much-loved pointers and labradors with great skill. Lady Rank would go up to the kennels on Sundays and talk to the dogs. She would bring Scrap, the house labrador, who would hold her hand in his mouth.

The record of the Scotney kennels is very impressive and the Scotney prefix was a household word in both retriever and bird-dog circles. According to *The Shooting Times*, 'few, if any men have done more for field trials than Lord Rank. Well may he be proud of his achievements.' Jingle was probably his most successful dog (Manners described him as 'the dog of a lifetime'). He was field champion in 1959, 1960 and 1961. But Rank's favourite, which was also his personal shooting-dog, was called Kate. One of his most famous dogs was Scotney Doodle. Of five puppies she produced in one litter, all became champions—an all-time record. Scotney Doodle was the product of a mating between a British bitch and an American sire, acquired from a friend in the US motion picture industry which, no doubt, made Rank especially satisfied. There was also the labrador Dusty and two pointers, Regent and Jack who, on one occasion, were loaned to the Queen.

Paintings of Rank's favourite dogs adorned the walls of his house. He was President of the Southern and Western Counties Field Trial Society and also of the International Gun Dog League. His love of animals also led him to be President of the Animal Health Trust. His dogs were enormously important to him and were a great source of comfort when his business enterprises were not going so well. John Davis remembers a period of financial crisis at the Rank Organisation and how Arthur would arrive at work and, rather than address the problems at the start of the day, would first tell him all about how his dogs had got on that weekend.[3]

Another popular employee was Ted Critchley, who arrived at the Sutton Scotney estate as Farm Manager in 1959 and ended up Farm Director, with 4,000 acres to look after. As well as confessing to knowing nothing about films, Rank also admitted that he knew nothing about farming. However, Critchley recalls that Lord Rank came up with lots of innovative ideas. One was a machine which lifted five or six inches of soil, sterilized it, fertilized it and then put it back. The advantage would have been that it cut out ploughing, drilling and hoeing. He also had several strange ideas about farming techniques that he was keen to experiment with. He had heard that one farmer was trying to farm without fertilizer, so Robin Cowen was instructed to try this out on one plot of land. It was 'reasonably disastrous'.

Rank did have an occasional temper, and he could get cross if things weren't going so well. In such a situation he would never blame himself—it was always someone else's fault.

Although this seems slightly at variance with the general picture of his character, nonetheless it must be added to the portrait. In the same vein, Rank had an odd way of dealing with confrontation; if a shoot had gone wrong, he wouldn't tell his keeper directly, he would tell one of his friends in front of the keeper.

Rank's farm was actually losing money when Ted Critchley arrived and he asked Ted, 'How long before you can make some money?' By 1961 the farm had started producing. Ted also remembers Rank's keen eye for detail:

> He would rub his nose or stroke his chin while talking and once he said, 'Tell me, Ted, why haven't you got as many grains as last year on this barley? Last year it was twenty-seven, twenty-eight. This year you're one or two grains lighter.' It was a fantastic observation for me as a farmer.

Rank also had a very positive attitude to the weather:

> We were out shooting and there was a gale and it was raining. After it was over I said, 'What an awful day!', but the governor says, 'It was glorious, all the rain and the wind, you should feel happy!' And I thought, 'Yes, you're probably right.'

Critchley describes Rank as a good landlord who treated all the tenants and farmers on his estate as friends. Once a year he would hold a big party for everyone in the village hall. Everyone, smokers or not, found a packet of twenty cigarettes by their place setting and, despite Rank's own teetotalism, there was plenty of drink for all. Rank would also provide top entertainment including Jimmy Edwards, Nicholas Parsons, Dick Emery, Arthur Askey and Russ Conway.

Rank's role amongst his estate employees was the benign squire. It was a little community with no worries. Robin Cowen comments:

> He was a benevolent feudalist. Essentially he was a great family man, and regarded his workers and tenants as part of the family.

Rank's memory, so helpful to him in business, was also an aid to his caring nature both as boss and landlord. He probably remembered little things because he would pray about everything every day. Douglas Hutchinson recalls:

> He did have a very good memory and if you'd say to him, 'Look, Arthur, will you do something?' he'd say, 'I'll think about that,' and then months later he'd say 'You asked me about that and yes, it's OK.' Often I'd forgotten what I'd asked about! He used his memory all the time so he retained it and it was built in, so to speak.

His attention to detail in terms of his gratitude is often referred to. One weekend in December 1966 he went down to Wilson Impey's shoot in Essex. After a good day's shoot Rank had to leave quickly. He had his car brought down to the final drive so that he could make a quick exit. In the rush Rank omitted to tip Jarvis the game-keeper, but the next day his secretary, the indispensable Gookey, was on the phone to find Jarvis' address. By Tuesday morning there was a five-pound note in Jarvis' hand and he bounded around the pubs showing off his hand-written thank-you letter from Lord Rank. Rank also wrote a hand-written letter to every mill manager at Christmas.

For all his shrewdness in business, he was not always a good judge of character in his personal life. Among his estate staff were examples of his ability to believe the best about everybody. One in particular took to the bottle but Rank remained loyal to him, even though he sometimes spent the afternoon sleeping off his over-indulgence. Maybe it was just naivety. The family was also irritated a great deal by one of Rank's long-serving members of staff, whom they considered difficult and very lazy. Robin Cowen remarked:

> It was infuriating that there were people living off him that weren't friends. I'm sure he knew, but he wasn't going to do anything about it.

It seems surprising that Rank sometimes ended up employing difficult characters since he had a very definite employment principle. Above all, his staff must have integrity. In the employment of staff on his estate, integrity came before knowledge of farming, although Rank would insist that they came from an estate that was profitable.

The most important of Rank's domestic employees was his butler, Michael, who was to be with him from March 1954 to Rank's death in 1972. He was to have a unique insight into the life of the Ranks. Michael had been a steward in the Merchant Navy when he answered an advert in *The Times* for an assistant butler. At the subsequent interview with Lord Rank Michael mentioned that he was from Limerick and used to pass Rank's mills there in Sexton Street on his way to school. When Michael arrived he was betrothed to his future wife. After four months in Rank's employ, Rank asked when he was to get married. When Michael told him it was to be in July, Rank said: 'I'll buy you a house if you stay.'

In fact, Rank provided a house for all his employees who worked on the estate—some twenty or so houses—rent-free for the rest of their lives. Rank looked after his own.

In 1957 the incumbent butler, Thomas Smart, died and Michael took over. As assistant butler, Michael had laid the tables and polished the silver, as well as looking after Lord Rank's wardrobe, including his considerable collection of suits. Rank also had a large number of silk dressing-gowns and handkerchiefs. His idea of relaxing was to wear one of his dressing-gowns with a cravat.

When Michael became butler he took over the running of a well established routine. By this stage Rank was already well into his sixties. Once or twice a week Rank would go up to London, but when he stayed at Sutton Manor, this was a typical day. The Ranks would wake at 7.00a.m. and Lord Rank would turn off the alarm so that Michael could get in. After bathing, their breakfast was taken upstairs—bacon and eggs, and sometimes sausages, toast and marmalade. Rank liked his tea very weak. At 8.30a.m. this was cleared away, Rank would come down to his office and meet Mr Dalton (his secretary), and they would work through the post until 11.00a.m. when he would take tea and biscuits. Lunch was at 1p.m.. Rank loved steak and kidney pie with vegetables from the farm, followed by fruit, also from the farm. After lunch he would sit with his wife in the living room and, if time allowed, they had a walk and he would read to her out loud. He would continue to work then until 4.00p.m. At tea-time, his favourite cake, 'Old Faithful', which came from the Rank bakeries, was enjoyed. Dinner was taken at 8.00p.m.— lamb chops were a favourite. Arthur loved his rice pudding, while Nell liked her cheese and biscuits.

Rank's blind spot about some employees was mirrored in his devotion to certain articles of clothing. Michael recalls that he had one sports jacket that he had worn on his first shoot and he always liked to wear it on the first day of any shoot. It got terribly old and decrepit. One day he asked Michael to take it to Winchester to get it repaired, but such was its condition that no one would mend it. Still not satisfied, Rank gave it to Mrs Goulding, his wife's maid, to mend. She did, which made him very happy.

Rank was very fond of Michael and pleased that he was a practising Catholic. He made sure Michael had time to get to Mass in Winchester. Once Michael needed £400 for a new car and asked Lord Rank if he could borrow it. Rank asked him what collateral he had, Michael replied: 'The only collateral I have is that I work for you until you or I die.' Michael recalls Rank's response: 'He said that was good enough for him, and after that I got a new car every two years.' This kind of generosity was in addition to cash presents at summer and Christmas.

Michael remembers seeing Rank angry on one occasion. He was holding a tea-party for all his keepers on the estate in the loggia at Sutton Manor. Caterers were supplying all the food, and the bread for the party came from a Rank bakery in Eastleigh. It can't have been fun serving bread to Rank at any time but on this occasion he felt the bread and discovered it wasn't fresh out of the oven. He hurled it against a wall saying, 'I expect the bread to be first-class.'

He once had a row in a hotel with a waiter who had dared to contradict him when Rank said the bread wasn't fresh. 'Yes, it is!' the waiter insisted. Rank called the manager who went and checked, and returned grovelling, 'I'm terribly sorry, my Lord, but we haven't got any fresh bread.' Rank just knew these things. He had a real aversion to brown bread which he used to describe as sweepings from the floor and bad for you. White was the only bread to have because it was pure.

Rank was a very private person. He hated publicity, and when he and Nell went away on holiday he insisted on a private dining- and sitting-room. The villagers in Sutton Scotney would not have seen him often, unless they went to his special Sunday Film Services which he organized in the village hall. But he liked having his hand-picked parties around him. It seemed that as long as he was top dog and in control of the hierarchy, he was happy. A less charitable view proffered by a good friend of the family was that he liked to be surrounded by 'yes' men. He was a very charismatic figure. When he came into a room you noticed him. When his house-party guests were all assembled at breakfast he would ask them what they would like to do. Then he would proceed to put forward his own idea to do something else, the thing he had wanted to do in the first place. He was also very competitive and always had to win. While he was playing tennis with younger opponents and out of breath, he would never admit to it, but would bend down to re-do his shoelaces in order to have a breather.

While he was a good sportsman in some fields, Rank's artistic ignorance and plebeian tendencies remained firmly intact. He was totally uninterested in music and especially hated opera. He was himself tone-deaf, a great sorrow to him as he couldn't sing in tune—not that this stopped him from singing in church with great gusto. He wasn't fond of the organ and it was to be a great sadness to Methodist organ-lovers that the Joseph Rank Benevolent Trust never gave any money to build organs. He was so unmusical that it is hard to imagine Rank being able to choose eight favourite pieces of music if Radio 4 had asked him onto the programme 'Desert Island Discs'. He would certainly have taken 'Onward Christian Soldiers', his favourite hymn, but the only other song I heard mentioned in association with him is the slightly more controversial ditty:

Does your mother ride a bike
in the middle of the night
with nothing but her garters on?

One has to remember that he was not always as straightforward as he might seem.

Nell played the piano and painted water-colours, but neither had any informed interest in art. The pictures they had at Sutton Manor were described as hilarious by one regular visitor. The Ranks never went out and bought anything, so there were no interesting *objets d'art* anywhere, except for some rather extraordinary art deco bronzes of half-naked girls which are now in the possession of his grandson Fred. Rank mainly liked to have pictures of his gun dogs and pheasants on the walls.

It is not surprising to report that their unexotic tastes ruled in the food department as well: they both liked their roast beef and Yorkshire pudding followed by the sponge pudding Spotted Dick—the very meal Rank chose for his seventieth birthday party. When partaking in the high life of big business (which Rank did only when essential), he always ate the food placed in front of him, but he had a warning to potential hosts on a smaller scale: 'Don't give me mucked up food and desserts in flower vases!'

The original house in Sutton Scotney was quite unexceptionable, but as his weekend shooting parties developed, Rank wanted more bedrooms to house his 'guns' for the night, so an extension was built. This was purely functional in design, and spoiled the look of the place. Douglas Hutchinson commented:

It was a simply hideous house. It wasn't very large and not attractive and he built a wing of bedrooms for shooting guests. I stayed in the wing very often and J.V.'s wife [Rank's sister-in-law] said, 'Oh God, it looks like a public lavatory.'

His leisure pursuits were a challenge and channel for his boundless energy. Shooting was one of his great loves, especially partridges. For a controlling personality like Rank it was a constant challenge. While he could manipulate people into doing his will, try as he might, he could never get game birds to perform to his expectations. That was probably why he remained so keen on shooting.[4]

Apart from becoming one of the best all-round shots in the country, Rank created one of the finest sporting estates in the south of England, where he loved to entertain friends. By the time of his death in 1972 the Sutton Manor estate was described as one of the finest landholdings in Southern England and his creation of it over thirty-eight years as 'an outstanding rural estate achievement'. Worth about £3.5 million, it was the largest single asset that he left, the biggest estate in Hampshire with fifteen let farms, 3,637 acres of home farm and an estate staff of more than a hundred. He carried on developing it right to the end of his life. Overall he spent some £2 million on farm buildings and modernizing 250 cottages.

Shooting was a good focus for Rank's single-minded attention to detail. There would be the same ritual at the start of every day's sport. The time for leaving was 9.30a.m. prompt but the 'guns' would arrive earlier, at 9.15a.m. M.J. Thompson, a regular member of the party, recalls: 'God help you if you weren't there on time. I'd appear with one minute to go and he would look at his watch.' Rank would appear and Michael, his butler, would be behind him with some apples. Rank would go to each gun in turn and shake their hand and they would be expected to take an apple. Then at 9.30a.m. everyone would leave. They were expected to go home after shooting on Saturday. Rank liked to enjoy a peaceful Sunday as a special day when he would go to church.

In addition to the shoots at Sutton Scotney, Rank rented a Scottish moor from Lord Cawdor. The estate near Nairn included Drynachan Lodge on the Findhorn river. Every year for sixteen years, all through the sixties, he used to go up for three weeks in May, and then from the end of July to the end of

September. Michael the butler would drive up the day before with the clothes; the chauffeur took the guns and the dogs in a lorry; and the family came up by train. Michael remembers how much Rank enjoyed it: 'He couldn't wait to go to Scotland. When he got up there he was whistling and full of life—like a schoolboy really. Such a break from big business.'

Rank spent a lot of money on the estate. He built seventy miles of roads and bridges, and he gave the roads names, such as Santa Fe Junction and Union Pacific Highway. It was a big lodge with twelve bedrooms, and there were turf fires. But of course Rank was not on holiday the whole time: he would also do considerable amounts of business. He took a secretary and spent many hours, as he did in Hampshire, surrounded by papers. His secretary's wife also had to muck in and cook for the party.

Rank's guests had to help themselves to alcohol, which put some of them, including John Davis, under considerable pressure, so much so that he did not visit often. Dinah Sheridan (Davis' former wife) remembers: 'We stayed only once at his house, mainly because J.D. did not enjoy a weekend there. He was embarrassed by the teetotal atmosphere. There were a few bottles placed on the sideboard but a drink was never mentioned and it would have been conspicuous to stand up and help yourself.' It was the same at the Dorchester. Edgar Youdell, his researcher, was a teetotaller himself and was impressed with Rank's insistence on it. He remembers that Rank would deliberately make guests feel awkward and they had to ask the waiter themselves for what they wanted.

This was not the experience of Ealing Studio boss Michael Balcon, quoted in *The People*, March 1968:

> Lord Rank is the most tolerant of men. He is a
> teetotaller himself, but when entertaining he will drink
> ginger ale and lime because it looks like a real drink
> and guests don't find it uncomfortable.

Golf did not come so easily to Rank as shooting. He was never in the first class (although at one stage he played off a two handicap), but this was another area where he would always be experimenting. He would insist that his house-party guests try out his new theories on grip and techniques on putting, with a bent knee or a left foot cocked. He was very hard to beat because of his amazing powers of concentration and a keen desire to win. This also characterized him at bridge. Douglas Hutchinson (to whom Rank was known as 'Daddy-long-legs') remembers:

> He played very shrewdly, with match-winning determination. He also developed a highly personal and effective technique in gamesmanship, so that, even if you did take a few points off him (the stakes were always 3d a hundred) he almost invariably got it back at some dreadful game with appallingly one-sided house rules. He didn't often lose—partly because he was always partnered by Lance Newton (his son-in-law, who would sometimes come down for shooting parties without his wife) and they both understood these goulash hands. Meanwhile I would have to play with someone who I wasn't used to, and in the unlikely event of me being in front he would say 'let's play *chemin de fer* through the pack' and you'd play until he won.

One Hollywood film producer who stayed for a weekend reported that his millionaire host played bridge for a sixpence a hundred stake, sipping lime juice between deals, and how he chortled with a schoolboyish delight when the close of the evening's play showed him to be the winner of three shillings.

On one occasion the chairman of the bank used by the Rank Organisation was shooting with Rank for the weekend. Rank knew that his guest was a very sound bridge player and, as he was his bank manager, Rank didn't want to appear too speculative in his bidding. He reported to John Davis after the weekend that he had played a different game of bridge, one without too many risks. The result was that they both won, but the chairman expressed surprise that Arthur had played with such caution.

In work or play Rank was a great tease, and some of his greatest friends were those who enjoyed submitting to his particular type of wit and sense of fun. He expected people to retaliate, and the more they did the more he teased. It wasn't cruel, and he would not expose shrinking violets but, if you fancied your chances, he would use you quite mercilessly. He chided and remonstrated, and it could be quite wearing to be the butt of his humour; it required a strong constitution. Rank, of course, enjoyed it all immensely. All this, like everything in his life, was done in a kindly way and completely without malice. It has been suggested that, just as kings of old had court jesters, so Rank needed someone in the group to be the target of his jokes and the source of fun. But I have seen the occasional wince at the memory of it.

One of Rank's main victims was Fred Packard, his grandson. He remembers Rank teasing him until he went wild. It was a sort of constant bantering criticism. One of the few people who could usually stand up to Rank was a family friend, Lewis Powell, who chastized Rank, pointing out that it was ridiculous to tease a boy of four. Then Fred remembers that the teasing fizzled out. Maybe Rank was giving Fred special attention for other reasons. Douglas Hutchinson remembers:

> Arthur was rather concerned about how Fred would turn out, bearing in mind his father. He didn't have a high opinion of Fred's father [Shelagh's first husband]. He was worried Fred would take more after his father than his mother.

But, despite the ragging, Fred can't speak too highly of his grandpa:

> He was the greatest influence in my life. If I think of doing something dodgy, I think of Grandpa looking down from heaven and I refrain. He represented total integrity and taught me never to break my word. Of course, it sounds very basic, but when you hear that from someone you love and admire as much as I did Grandpa then it has an enormous effect. He led by example.

Fred also recalls a very formative experience and a story which he has re-told again and again at significant moments during his life.

> I was about twelve years old. We were on holiday in Scotland at Drynachan. I was sitting on the toilet and I had a sheath knife and I took it out of the scabbard and carved my initials and the date on the wall which had been newly decorated. My mother summoned me and said that Grandpa was furious. The house was owned by the Cawdors and Grandpa wanted to see me. I thought 'Hell!' There was this long thin corridor and at the end was the drawing room where he was waiting to see me in his multi-coloured dressing-gown. I thought he would ban me from shooting or something, then he said, 'Don't carve your name in dark and gloomy places—carve your name with pride for all the world to see.'

When this story was repeated at Fred's twenty-first birthday party Rank had tears in his eyes.

But Rank's teasing did sometimes verge on the edge of acceptability. Valentine Powell (Lewis' son) recalls his father being teased unmercifully by Rank. When Valentine was a little boy, his father was playing golf with Rank. He missed a crucial putt, and Rank called him yellow and a coward and then insisted that young Valentine call his father the same thing.

In the world of religious films, Colonel Hake was always regarded by Rank as being good for a laugh. If something went wrong during a shoot 'old Hakey' would be blamed and be the butt of a number of Rank's jokes. Everyone would roar with laughter and then move on.

There were some wonderful times on the Drynachan estate. Regular house guests included Maurice Goodbody, Wilson Impey, Lord Blakenham and Lord Cobham. Colin Rank, Arthur's great-nephew, remembers an incident involving Joe Nickerson (later knighted) who had built his business on some credit given to him by Rank. Joe was very intense and after a day's shooting Rank went to his butt and found only seven cartridges there. Apparently on Joe's instructions his loader had picked up all but seven of the empties to save Joe's blushes because he had shot so many and was missing so badly that day. At dinner Rank asked him, 'How many birds did you get at the third drive?' 'Nine,' Jo Nickerson lied. Rank left it a while, then commented, 'Very clever, with only seven cartridges.'

Another of Rank's favourite guests was M.J.M. Thompson who was Rank's land agent. He was both a good shot and a good bridge player—in Rank's mind, this was the perfect combination. Thompson describes Rank as 'the most outstanding man I ever met'. He says:

> We all knew he was the boss, it was purely natural for him; he was the most revered and he was the oldest there.

Rank was free and easy at distributing the ragging but, as it turned out, he wasn't too good at taking a joke aimed at himself. As Thompson remembers:

> I prepared a box with two wooden kitchen spoons and I made a very small third one. These ancient golden insignia were presented to Joseph Arthur Baron Rank, JP, on the occasion of his election by unanimous acclamation as President of the World Association of Pudding Stirrers. They were presented at the end of dinner. He looked at it and got up and went out. The butler, Michael, who was playing the game, said they had been left for him. Lord Rank grilled him so much afterwards that his wife had to intervene, 'Oh Arthur, stop making Michael tell lies.' Eventually he put them in the office safe. About five or seven years later I was having tea, chatting before I went, then the doctor came and the doctor went on and on and on about all the terrible things in the world. Rank then said, 'He sounds like he's a candidate for the President of the World Association of Pudding Stirrers. I think we should elect him.'

Rank did not bear a grudge against Thompson for his humour and, indeed, continued to do business with him right to the end. In January 1972 Thompson was looking after the sale of one of Rank's properties in Leicestershire. Rank rang him to arrange some shooting dates and also asked if the property would fetch a good price at that moment. Thompson said it would and Rank, with his money-nose twitching, said 'Right, John, collect the spondulicks!'

Rank hated lavatorial jokes as well as jokes against himself. He wasn't prudish; he just didn't like them. He would be horrified by some of the humour today. He enjoyed his own practical jokes, however, and once, during a summer holiday in Scotland, when it was dark outside, he dressed as a ghost and then started tapping on the window. It was interesting that his public persona did not include his humorous side. *The Observer* profiled him on 13 November 1949:

> Mr Rank is no joker. He is a large, tall man now aged
> 61; kindly to meet but not oncoming. A man who finds
> it hard to talk and harder still to laugh; a man you feel
> of a simple intensity.

Fred Packard remembers there being a lot of talk about religion in the house at Sutton, and particularly about the success and failure of Rank's religious films and the effect they had on people. Rank would sermonize and there would be heated arguments. Shelagh remembers a long debate about missionaries—whom Rank, of course, was defending. Fred felt able to be more courageous with his grandfather than some people were, and thought that he liked people to stand up to him. Also, unlike others, Fred did what he wanted, even if Rank disapproved. He recalls Rank's response to his decision to go to Brazil:

> I was eighteen and Grandpa was very negative about
> going to Brazil. He said, 'I won't help you. You could
> go anywhere else. I will open any door, but not in
> South America. I was legged over with some wheat
> deal in Argentina. The South Americans are very

unethical in business and I don't want you to be tainted at such an early age. I'm not going to help you, you're not going with my total blessing.' Later, however, he did relent and he gave me £100.

Out-and-out rows were rare but Fred recalls one such which is quite revealing about Rank's attitudes to child education and his inability to lose:

The biggest row, between my parents and grandpa, was when I was sixteen and we were at Drynachan in Scotland. Grandpa said, 'I will give you £1,000 if you refrain from drinking, smoking and having sex before you are twenty-one.' My parents said it was bribery and that it was far better to learn to drink and smoke in moderation. They had a tremendous argument and the whole house party joined in. Grandpa, who never wanted to be trumped, sent the chauffeur to buy a dictionary and he looked up the word 'bribe', and he read it out and proved to his own satisfaction that he wasn't bribing me. He just had to prove that he was right. Eventually the subject dissipated.

In fact, the reason he had made this offer to Fred was because his father had done the same to him. And Rank only started smoking at twenty-one, having successfully resisted to that age and having received the promised £250 from his father.

Rank had a Churchillian gift of being able to sleep at will. When shooting in Scotland he used to like to have a nap on the moor in the afternoon. Before he got too old he would simply wrap himself up in his old trench coat (a relic from the First World War) and roll into the heather, saying, 'Wake me up in twenty minutes.' Later, his Land Rover called 'Dog's Delight' would come out with a big, purpose-built, portable couch for him to sleep on. He would wake up instantly like a child and be ready to shoot again. Like his couch, few of his treasured possessions were standard; they all seemed to be converted or built specially for the job. He used to take the 'guns' round in a converted Bedford army truck, which was very uncomfortable. He would never take no for an answer. If he was going shooting and he couldn't walk up the hill he would buy, invent or commission something that would help. He was a very tall man and as he grew older he found walking difficult. He therefore commissioned an amazing caterpillar machine, a sort of Land Rover on huge wheels, to get him around the hills. He also had his Rolls Royce altered so that he could stretch his legs out as on a bed.

Rank liked fishing but not as much as his other outdoor pursuits. To him fishing was a means to an end and the means were not all that exciting. He would go out with Michael the butler, after all the others had gone out. He would fish for an hour and, with Michael's considerable help, he would return with a fish. That, for him, was what it was all about—there was no point in spending hours at it.

While on holiday in Scotland he used to have the cricket scores sent up so he could follow the fortunes of his beloved Yorkshire. He would have a 2s 6d bet with certain house guests that Yorkshire would beat Surrey—in those days, a fairly likely occurrence. Michael the butler would take down the scores from the radio and announce them to his Lordship. Rank was not very interested in football although he would ask how Leeds United got on.

At Sutton Scotney he had an enormous array of white roses and he would show them to Ogden Mills, a Lancastrian and a former Managing Director of Ranks Hovis McDougall: 'This is Yorkshire here. You're out of place—but I'm letting you stay.' And in a jocular way, although he probably believed it, he would say: 'A good Yorkshireman will always beat a good Lancastrian.' It is perhaps notable that such a committed Yorkshireman never went back to live in the county, nor indeed did he ever holiday there, preferring to dwell in Hampshire and relax in Cornwall or Scotland. When there was talk of a peerage the local papers in Hull were excitedly speculating that he would become the first Lord Hull. Again, Rank chose to ignore his roots and plumped for the very Southern-sounding 'Baron Rank of Sutton Scotney'.

9 FLOUR

Bread of heaven
Feed me now and evermore.
WILLIAM WILLIAMS

Rank was at heart a miller. He had been born and bred for flour. He was strongly motivated by the belief that he was chosen by God to provide the people of Britain with the best-quality flour and bread, 'the stuff of life', as he called it. In a letter written in December 1955 he declared:

> Our constant aim is always to move with the times; to give our customers goods of the highest quality in the variety they require at an economic price and with the service they rightly expect of such an organization, which is, in fact, the justification for the company's existence.
>
> Eighty years ago, my father first set up in business and gathered round him men of integrity, energy and ability. Today, we also have a team of like-minded men directing the affairs of the company. We shall strive to continue to build on the foundations he laid down and to follow the ideals he pursued so that the company may go from strength to strength in the coming years.[1]

As a young man, Arthur had worked his way up in his father's mill with very little privilege shown to him. He always remembered how to operate the machinery. In later life, when he visited a mill, he would put his apron on and make adjustments to the machines and end up leaving white finger-marks all over his bowler hat. Flour was probably the only thing he really did understand, but because he was not the eldest son he was not under so much pressure to go into the family business. Indeed, even if he had wanted to, it would have been difficult for him with his brother Jimmy in charge. They were both big personalities and the company was probably not big enough for both of them. His nephew Douglas Hutchinson[2] believes that this was very significant:

> He would never have got into the movies if he hadn't had an elder brother. He liked running his own show and he was in a subordinate position in the family business and it didn't provide the outlet for his energies.

The milling trade was very cut-throat before the First World War and was even worse in the 1920s. During this time Joseph Rank was the guiding light. Then there was the birth of the Millers Mutual. Every miller could be a member and everybody had a yearly amount of flour they could trade in. All members paid a subscription; if they sold or delivered less than the specified amount they received a top-up payment and if they went over the limit they had to pay a little extra subscription. This gave the milling industry some sort of structure and backbone that worked successfully until 1939, when it was taken over by the Ministry of Food.

Arthur's first important contribution to the expansion of Joseph Rank Ltd was in the 1930s. At the time he was living in Reigate. He helped the company acquire and merge some small London-based mills whose flour milling by-products were animal feed. This brought his father's business into the production and sale of branded animal feeds, which was to be an important part of the company's future. When Joseph Rank's middle son Rowland died in 1939 the Rank family took over Associated London Flour Mills and Rowland's company was brought into Joseph Rank Ltd. Arthur described his brother Rowland as having 'more brains than anyone else in our family but he was so damned lazy that he didn't use them'. (Rowland's legacy, though, was a son, Joseph McArthur Rank, the last of the Rank millers. He took over the flour business when J. Arthur Rank died, and retired in 1989.)

Rank and his brother Jimmy turned their attention to the organization of the Irish flour market, which was supplied solely by the Ranks-owned Ocean Mills at Birkenhead. The Irish trade from England entailed imported wheat being brought past Ireland to Liverpool, and then shipped back after milling. J. Arthur Rank joined W.H. Raylor and spent some time living in cottages around the Irish countryside in order to find out exactly the right types of flour needed by the people living in the locality. Joseph Rank came himself to inspect possible sites for a new mill in Ulster and also to look at potential business in Southern Ireland. Early in 1930 the Ranks acquired the mills controlled by the Goodbody family. Subsequently the Irish government prohibited the import of flour into Southern Ireland..[3]

Joseph Rank died during the Second World War, but not before he had witnessed the destruction of his beloved Clarence Mills in an air-raid in Hull. The mills had been so successful that they alone were producing animal feedstuffs for a vast area—extending from the Eastern Counties north to the Scottish border, and encompassing Yorkshire and the counties of Nottingham, Derby and Leicester. Joseph's eldest son, Jimmy, took over the business. Jimmy Rank was different from Arthur—a shrewd and tough businessman, he was perhaps a bit more flexible than his younger brother. Jimmy's main passion in life was horse-racing. Knowing this was useful information to the various mill managers around the country, who could predict that James Rank would be coming to see them whenever there was a race meeting in the area. There was a mutual respect between the two brothers, but they were never best friends.

By that time, the Ranks probably ground about a third of the nation's flour. In the 1930s the Ministry of Food started stockpiling reserves of basic foods and Jimmy Rank was very involved with this. As soon as war became a possibility he bought up enormous supplies of wheat. He acquired it from all over the world, but so clever was his buying strategy that the markets were unaffected and no one became suspicious. The outcome was that Britain had enough bread in strategic reserves to survive the war.

When the milling industry was taken over by the Ministry of Food one new milling company was formed. Jimmy Rank became Chairman of the new Millers Mutual Pool Ltd. He and Spillers negotiated the way in which the milling industry traded with the Ministry of Food. They received all the money from the Government, and distributed it to the millers through the Millers Mutual Pool. This was a complex financial procedure which had to be unravelled after the war.

When Jimmy was seconded to the Ministry of Food as a bulk-buyer during the war, the milling industry saw a different side to Arthur, his younger brother. Although always polite and often appearing silent and meek, there were times when Arthur was roused to speak his mind in public. All flour millers had been summoned to hear the Minister of Food, Lord Woolton, who wanted to discuss with them 'a plan for changing the wheat extraction rate'. The implications of Lord Woolton's proposal caused the chief chemist of Joseph Rank Ltd to write an article condemning it. He wrote this in his own name as a scientist, rather than as part of the Rank flour mill. Apparently, Lord Woolton read the article and came to the meeting in a bad mood. But when he started to criticize Jimmy Rank who, being employed by the Ministry of Food, was therefore not able to argue with the Minister, Arthur took it upon himself to stand up for the chemist. He pointed out that the chemist had acted on his own behalf, not writing on Joseph Rank notepaper, and asked why someone who felt strongly about something shouldn't express it publicly. The assembled meeting was absolutely flabbergasted that Arthur had it in him to speak out so strongly.

During the Second World War, Arthur was actively involved in the family firm—at the same time as financing both his religious films and the box-office hits. Many of the Rank employees were called up and only essential personnel were retained, so the bulk of the administration staff were transferred to J. Arthur Rank's house at Sutton Scotney in Hampshire. Rooms were found in the village, and those who couldn't fit into Arthur's house slept in barns and outbuildings with beds being hastily improvized with wood and wire netting.

A country mansion, the Priory, at Reigate was also obtained for the milling business. Offices, a restaurant and living quarters were found there. As Rank did not have a son he offered work to his nephew, Douglas Hutchinson, when he came down from Cambridge in June 1939.

In 1943 Arthur and his brother Jimmy were in charge of one of the largest flour-milling concerns in England. Rank was quoted as saying, 'Most of the day is given to flour. In the evenings I turn to films.' In 1949 *The Observer* newspaper reported him as saying he worked 'at flour all day in the City and at films all night'. Arthur's capacity for hard work was boundless.

When Jimmy died in 1952 he left an even bigger business than he had inherited from Joseph Rank. He had bought a new mill at Victoria Dock in London, and others in Newcastle, Edinburgh, Belfast and Southampton. The newly rebuilt Clarence Mills were also in production from this time.

Apparently a number of people thought it unlikely that J. Arthur Rank would become Chairman. When Jimmy Rank had been in charge a man called Askew—who had married Rank's eldest sister, was a Director and was conscientious, thoughtful and diligent—seemed the more likely successor, while Arthur seemed too involved in building up his cinema company. Maybe the whiff of flour was too irresistible for Arthur and he exercised his *droit de seigneur* and leapt in to take up the reins. It certainly came as no surprise to Sir Charles Norman, a retired Director of Joseph Rank Ltd:

> I always said—and I was proved right—that if anything
> happened to Mr James, Mr Arthur would be sitting in
> the Chairman's seat the following morning at
> 9 o'clock—which was the case.

So in 1952 J. Arthur Rank returned to run the family business, but he didn't stop running the Rank Organisation just yet. Initially he merely doubled his already colossal work load. Before taking over as chairman of the flour business he was already on the board of sixty-five companies, including the Gaumont-British Picture Corporation, Odeon Properties, Odeon Cinema Holdings and

Manorfield Investments. He was also chairman of twenty-three of them. He worked an eighteen-hour day. His right-hand man at the time, known as Micky Norman (later Sir Charles Norman) said that Rank 'did the flour' in the early morning till lunch-time, played a round of golf and went into the Rank Organisation at 4.00p.m., worked till 4.00a.m. and then took three hours sleep. Such a punishing schedule would not have been performed with a heavy heart, though, because Rank was back where he wanted to be. His grandson Fred Packard sums it up:

> The Rank Organisation did not interest him that much—he was far more interested in flour. The milling and the bread side was in his veins and the people in the film industry were not his sort. He wasn't happy with the people he rubbed shoulders with. He remembers the film tycoons, they couldn't possibly understand him. He'd be asked 'Do you want a blonde or a brunette?' It was a sleazy world.

Rank's main problem was the decontrolling of the milling industry after the war-time structure run by the Ministry of Food. This meant that for all practical purposes any rewards for lost profits voluntarily absorbed to help the government during the war were limited on a pre-war basis. At his first AGM as Chairman he said: 'We are looking forward to freedom from control as soon as the government feels that this can be done, and meanwhile I can assure you that the millers, as represented by their association, are pressing the government to review the remuneration arrangements... to bring them more into line with current circumstances.' He was also keen to continue to develop the milling business and explore new possibilities in animal feeds. Every flour mill made bran and wheatings but the animal feeds company, Blue Cross, was pioneering new ideas and together with Ranks they developed animal feeding nuts.

Arthur's style was very different from Jimmy's and, indeed, different from what life would have been under Askew. Rank was described as swashbuckling in comparison. Jimmy had always thought that Arthur was too flashy by half and that his

cars were too fast. But, despite these traits, the new management style he introduced was welcome. He trusted his
subordinates much more and encouraged less confident staff to
stand on their own feet. At his first AGM he stated his belief in
the importance of a contented staff. 'I should like to say how
pleased I am in the happy relationship which exists between the
various sections of the Organisation, for it is by co-operation
between the milling side, the selling side and the administrative
side that the company prospers.'

From the very beginning of his career, Rank had been much
loved by his staff. A former secretary of his, Miss D.N. Nyst, who
worked with him for many years, said in 1924, 'He very rarely lost
his temper, [he was] quick to notice any mistake but was forgiving
with "don't let it happen again," which, of course put one on one's
honour and was usually effective,' and he kept this office
management style throughout his business life.

In those days, before the National Health Service, Rank, in
line with his father's principles, always insisted that employees'
health care should be at the firm's expense. He also brought
with him some useful experience from the film world—an in-
depth knowledge of company law and the ability to read a
balance sheet like a trained accountant. His fascination with
new techniques and technologies was not limited to projectors
and cameras, but was transferred into new projects and
research into the milling industry. But, most of all, he brought
his enormous personality, which was the greatest inspiration to
the family business.

From the day Rank took over, the policy of the firm seemed
to change. One of his first jobs was to sort out the mess after the
Monopolies Act. Rank discovered there had been a lot of
broken promises and underhand dealing in the milling
industry, and this annoyed him greatly. He launched into a
tirade one day against the inability of so many milling
companies to keep their word. Before the war they could have
been checked by fines, imposed by the Millers Mutual, but now
Arthur decided to set up his own milling industry watch-dog
under a retired Governor of Aden, Sir Tom Higginbottom. This

organization worked well, refereeing various disputes over price or trading conditions.

However, it came as a surprise to Arthur to realize how useful it could be. One morning he was breakfasting with Wilson Impey, who had introduced Rank to Sir Tom. There was a problem in the company which was causing Rank some grief. Impey suggested that he should call in his own special committee. He looked at Impey and said, 'What committee?' He was reminded of the watch-dog. 'Do you think I'm going to ask them to sort out *my* difficulties? Humph!' It wasn't that he thought it was a bad idea, it was just that he hadn't thought of it himself.

In 1953 there was considerable chaos in the milling industry. The profits and the hassles were growing hand in hand. Wilson Impey looks back:

> Rank was a man of tremendous energy. He didn't mind how much effort he put in to sort out the problems. He had been through two wars and knew about the difficulties of the twenties, and it's understandable why it was that he wanted to try and prevent a repetition of what happened then. In any industry there are always plenty of greedy boys. In the Millers Mutual they could be kept in check but now if they wanted to go berserk they could do so.

In the early 1950s Rank started a series of face-to-face meetings with millers from all round the country at his suite in the Dorchester. Every Wednesday at 7.30 he would host a dinner for six guests and try to build up trust and understanding and set up a sort of gentleman's agreement to replace the old Millers Mutual. He carried on with this until he had seen a hundred or so executives. Rank kept peace in the industry in those heady days of deregulation by dint of his personality; this was his major contribution to the flour industry.

Around this time, too, Rank took over the Irish flour-milling business and the Chairman, Maurice Goodbody, came in to deal with Rank. Goodbody was looking for some interesting hobby that Rank could relate to, and suggested that Rank should take over his brother's horses. Rank wasn't keen on horses so Maurice suggested greyhounds. Rank thought this a good idea and wanted to start off by buying the best grey-hound—the winner of the Waterloo Cup, an Irish greyhound. Goodbody was dispatched to buy this animal which, at the time was owned by a country priest. A meeting was arranged, and Goodbody and the priest began to negotiate the price in a hotel bedroom. One of the beds in the room was covered in pound notes and the priest waited until there was no bed showing before he signed the deal.

Joseph McArthur Rank (Rowland's son) who was later Chairman of Ranks Hovis McDougall remembers him:

> To him business was fun, life was fun. He was a great
> one for practical jokes. He would pretend to fall over at
> tense moments in discussions, or pretend he was going
> to drop something. Once he got irritated with Mr
> Askew, who used to put the microphone of his hearing
> aid on the table, so Rank rustled his papers right in
> front of it.

The younger Joseph was grateful for the things Rank had taught him—to see business as fun, to get rid of pomposity and to reduce problems to simple terms. He also took over his uncle's specially thoughtful style of management, never failing to send hand-written notes of condolence or appreciation after a special contribution had been made.

The milling industry had left government control in 1951 and Arthur had worked harder than anyone, in very difficult circumstances, to get a sensible price for flour. Garfield Weston was to become a key player in the flour world. He was a Canadian miller successfully making Burton's biscuits. But what he wanted was an outlet for his Canadian flour, which was no good for his biscuits, but was good for bread. In 1954 he decided to buy two or three bakeries of his own. Rank realized that Weston's move was a serious threat so he started buying bakeries; so also did Spillers. Spillers created 'Wonderloaf', Ranks formed 'Mother's Pride' and Weston's formed 'Sunblest'.

Despite all this Rank and Weston remained friends.

As a result of Rank's 'if you can't beat them, join them' attitude, Ranks became the biggest bakers in the country. After this turn-around Ranks started to buy agricultural merchant businesses and at one time they had the finest agricultural merchanting business in the country.

J. Arthur Rank was respected as a boss. One of his former British Bakery area directors is Sid Kenrick:

> People were mesmerized by his involvement in so
> many things and astounded by his multiplicity of
> interests. If anything, the general opinion was that the
> firm was a bit old fashioned but he made some good
> decisions, particularly when he saw the Garfield
> Weston threat so early. He was a good boss, he didn't
> dispose of people. Rank was loyal, not like Weston. We
> felt safe; we felt we had the best in the business. We
> were as good as Sunblest at baking bread but we were
> better than them because they were ruthless. Ranks
> were not ruthless, although there were closures later.

Ranks was remarkable in the loyalty it instilled in most of its workforce. It was not only a family company, but it also employed people who stayed on and on—some of them working fifty or sixty years of their lives. It was company policy always to look for new ideas and never 'rest on its laurels'. But staff morale was important to management as well. All employees were given pension schemes and, so the company claimed, widows and children of employees who died were well looked after. The philosophy behind the way the Rank employees were treated was deliberate; the management always felt that a spirit of well-being and comradeship among the employees resulted in increased efficiency and interest in their work. 'For an organization that neglects the human side will soon find that the human side will neglect them'.[4]

Rank was impressive in his shrewdness and the planning he would do before negotiations. Ogden Mills was Managing Director of Ranks Hovis McDougall:

You were unaware of the strategy of the conversations but it was amazing how he introduced 'punchlines' and 'hammer blows' after preliminary gentle and apparently inconsequential talk. He would very occasionally back down from a desire and he was big about it when he did, but if he was having difficulty about persuasion he would have recourse to his favourite theme—that accountants and economists had no idea whatsoever about running business and they were a complete menace. He did, in fact, use accountants to the full— economists were his pet aversion.

Rank was to say towards the end of his life:

I've got no use for these economists. The economists [Britain's had] in the last few years have got us into queer street; they've got other countries into queer street as well. And I don't know an economist who's ever made money. I wouldn't put an economist into a fried fish shop.

Economists were there to stop you making mistakes but all they did, according to Rank, was make you make more mistakes. Rank was generally unenthusiastic about anything that lacked originality and independence of spirit. Not only economists, but any kind of bureaucracy, got him down, especially when it stood in the way of new initiatives or restricted the speed of advancement.

Most of Rank's immediate colleagues in the flour business found working with him an exhilarating experience. He had considerable presence and he was a great leader. Nothing ever stood still and he was always looking for the next project. His insatiable drive and enthusiasm are often quoted. Once he had decided that he wanted to do something, it would inevitably happen because everyone got swept up in his vision. In all his dealings he was always a straight talker and dealer, which meant that he was rarely misunderstood.

It is said that when Ranks Ltd joined with Hovis McDougall in the early sixties it was a marriage. In fact it was a take-over, masterminded by Joe McArthur Rank with the then Hovis-McDougall chairman, Kenneth Moore. Hovis McDougall wanted to be taken over by Ranks Ltd, mainly because Moore was terrified of being taken over by Garfield Weston. There was also some hard feeling between Moore and Spillers' Chairman, Sir Wilfred Vernon (they were actually better friends than Moore and Rank). But some of the Hovis McDougall board must have lived to rue this decision. Out of the twelve board members that were taken into Ranks, all but three were sacked. Wilson Impey was one of the lucky ones: 'They had nothing to do, they were all dead wood.'

The plans for the take-over were announced in December 1961 when it was estimated that the new flour milling group would be worth £100 million. It consolidated Ranks' leading position in the British flour milling industry and made a strong force to meet the keen competition within the industry which had been reducing profit margins. Ranks and Hovis-McDougall were largely complementary and covered a wide field. Flour milling and bakeries made up the largest part of Ranks, but there were also important interests in animal foods and manufacture. Hovis-McDougall, through the Hovis subsidiary, produced the well-known Hovis flour and, through other subsidiaries, made self-raising and plain flour for home cooking. The company also had important interests in groceries and importing, blending and packaging butter and cheese. Both sides were happy with the terms and 'wholeheartedly' recommended the proposals.

Rank certainly used his money. He was an enormous spender. Just as in the movie industry things seemed not to have a real price so, it seems, Rank viewed the flour business. In Ranks Hovis McDougall (RHM), for instance, he would pay over the odds to buy a bakery he had set his mind on, to make sure he secured it. This, over a time, built up problems for RHM which had very considerable financial difficulties aggravated by these take-overs of bakeries and agricultural businesses.

Like his father, Arthur was a strong employer who would not take any nonsense. In later years he was very cross with the Pakistani contingent among his bakery workforce who were causing him some industrial problems. There was talk of a racial war. 'I don't know anything about a racial war, you do your job or else get out! That's what I'd say. And they don't like it.' Rank was convinced that Britain had the best potential workforce in the world, but he firmly believed that they had to be treated fairly and with integrity to get the best from them. 'If you give them a square deal and an incentive—we'll never get out of the mess until we do that.'

He was sometimes ill-advised. His head of research Arnold Spicer, Research Director at Hovis McDougall when Ranks took them over, persuaded Rank to spend money on certain research projects which came to nothing. Douglas Hutchinson says:

> Arthur thought he was marvellous. He was very articulate, full of enthusiasm and bright ideas. The problem with Arnold Spicer was that all his geese were swans; he was a super-optimist and so was Arthur— that's why he liked him.

Rank remained very proud of his milling business. It produced a large range of brands of flour but he was always looking for more.

> What new brands nature and science may combine to provide is for the future to decide. But it is no idle boast to say that if finer flours can be produced and better bread baked than has been possible in the past, an undertaking, with roots planted well over a century ago and which through five generations has made milling its business, is well qualified to achieve that object.[5]

Arthur described his milling business as being less spectacular than the Rank Organisation but said that it had wonderful opportunities. A year or so before he died, he said that RHM:

... is going to do wonderful things for the human race and make a great deal of money for the shareholders. I've given them a new job... I'm interested in research and you might say that I don't know what I'm talking about, but I'm perfectly sure that if you want to you can, and I've told my researcher, Arnold Spicer, that I want to be able to put into bread something that is going to regenerate the brain cells when a man gets to sixty. I don't say that I'm going to lengthen his life, but I don't want him to get senile—in five years' time.

His commitment to research had led to the establishment of the Lord Rank Research centre at High Wycombe, which was designed to cover a wide range of scientific and technological investigations, from plant genetics to baking technology.[6]

By the time Rank retired he had seen twenty years of unprecedented growth, diversification and expansion. Ranks Ltd had developed from a milling business to a multi-faceted food processing concern opening up opportunities at home and abroad. In its final integrated form the company's interests had extended beyond flour and animal feeds into farm products, grain trading and cereals. Adding Hovis McDougall and Cerebos Ltd also introduced the well-known grocery division behind many popular products like McVities:

First, the Ranks grew the corn, then they ground the grain, now they bake the bread. The cycle is complete and logical. Fine flour badly baked is no advertisement.[7]

J. Arthur Rank was made Life President of Ranks Hovis McDougall Ltd in 1969, having retired in that year as Chairman. RHM had since been taken over by Tomkins plc.

10 A MISSION TO COMMUNICATE

My talents, gifts, and graces, Lord,
Into Thy blessed hands receive;
And let me live to preach thy word,
And let me to Thy glory live;
My every sacred moment spend
In publishing the sinner's Friend.

CHARLES WESLEY

While the 'golden years' of the British film industry made Rank famous with such classics as *Henry V*, *Blithe Spirit* and *Brief Encounter*, his work with the Religious Film Society continued. Rank was continually looking for ways of communicating the Christian faith.

During the war, George VI had called for a national day of prayer, and Rank had been asked by the Archbishop of Canterbury, William Temple, if a local vicar could go into his cinemas and conduct prayers on that day. Rank thought this over; instead of local clergymen being called on two or three times during the course of an evening to slot in on the continuous programme, why not have the Archbishop himself, on film, and make it available to all the cinemas?

The Archbishop was on holiday at the time, but a request was sent to him and he replied by telegram saying, 'Returning to London, will make film.' It was August and therefore difficult to secure choirboys for the filming because they were on holiday. But enough were found and the filming took place one

Saturday morning in the church just outside Lambeth Palace. Dr Temple was very grand, but he made it easy for everyone, 'Don't be afraid to tell me if I go wrong, I'll do it again,' he said. He was a popular archbishop and Rank's idea was a great success.

With all the disruption of war it took until 1945 to fully amalgamate the Religious Film Society (RFS) with the Christian Cinema Council (CCC). The Archbishop of Canterbury was to be President of the new society, which was set up as a non-trading organization. That meant that the work of the RFS in film-making and distribution must now be done by Religious Films Ltd (RF), which in 1945 became the parent company, commissioning the films.

It was decided that the first project under the amalgamated CCC and RFS should be the film series *Two Thousand Years Ago* (1946), which had taken three years to prepare. There are five twenty-minute films in the series: *The Day's Work*, *The Home*, *The School*, *The Synagogue and Passover* and *The Travellers*. Described as 'instructional films', and showing a reconstruction of everyday life in Palestine at the time of Christ, they were to be shown through Children's Cinema Clubs of which Rank had become President. When he asked what the effect of the usual films they showed the children on Saturday mornings was, the reply was, 'They don't do the children any harm.' Rank replied: 'Hm, why not show some films that would do them good?'

When Rank heard about the new project he asked, 'Who's going to pay?' Dr Gregory, who had worked with him right from the beginning, replied, 'You are, Arthur.' Rank said, 'Well, that's the first I've heard of it!' This was a time when he turned to a rather unlikely source of funding. Having earlier expressed horror that his youngest son was going into the movie business, just before he died, Joseph Rank told his son: 'If I was twenty years younger, I would be going in for this too.' According to Alan Wood,[1] Arthur replied that he ought to give him some money for an experiment. This his father did, just before he died, and with the £20,000 Rank was able to fund this new project.

The film series went into production at the Gainsborough Studios in Islington and was directed by Mary Field, a pioneer of educational films. She had been working on children's films

183

for the Saturday morning clubs (Rank's daughter Shelagh was on her staff). After Rank had financed the production, he donated the negatives to the Methodist Church so that they could profit from the rental fees and from the sale of film strips which also were made from the film. Eventually hundreds were sold to schools, both in Britain and abroad.

After the war the Methodist Church Home Mission Department, no doubt with Rank's encouragement and financing, organized ecumenical 'commando' raids on various towns. A 'hit squad' of ministers would go into the chosen town and tell people about their faith in pubs, works canteens, clubs and dance halls. Religious films were to be a part of this campaign. The indefatigable Walter Knights served on eighteen missions. There were two big campaigns in London: one night there were fifty open-air speakers in Hyde Park with thousands of people in attendance.

Although Rank was not expecting a financial return from these endeavours, he was expecting a profit in people turning to God. It was happening. In Derby, films were shown one evening to five hundred soldiers and an appeal was made to see if anyone would accept the challenge of a changed life. To everyone's surprise the Major of the regiment went forward, and afterwards he agreed to start a club in which forty or fifty soldiers supported each other as Christians.

After his release from the army Noel Evans, formerly secretary of the Christian Cinema Council, brought the operation of Religious Films Ltd back from Dunstable to London, to offices in Eaton Gate. Film production at this time was entirely in the hands of Norman Walker. He directed the majority of Rank's religious films, giving them their style. 'Captain', as he was known on the set, was popular and created a relaxed atmosphere. His Christian faith influenced those he worked with: there was no swearing when he was in charge; he didn't shout when things went wrong; and many of the non-religious crew and actors were impressed with him.

To save money, production staff, cameramen, set builders and technical staff were hired on a freelance basis, and studios only booked when filming was ready to start. However, when the Gate Studios in Elstree became available, Rank bought it and let RF use it. This gave a new impetus to production. It was a very efficient studio and produced a number of very good films.

It is worth emphasizing the colossal financial load Rank's passion was putting on him: the income from sales, hiring and the only occasional success in the box office was totally insufficient to match the expenditure involved. This inevitably slowed down production and things got worse—after the war, production costs went up and up. Some of the Shakespeare films, for example, took five years to recover their production costs, let alone make a profit. One of the reasons was the post-war need to take back workers into the industry who had returned from the Services. In addition, the unions doubled the number of technicians working on the set. It was no longer possible to use an outfit or studio for odd days: the whole unit had to be taken for a week as a minimum. This no doubt helped employment, but it became very costly unless enough films could be made to cover the costs of using an expensive unit for a week.

As a result of all this Religious Films activity, notice was being taken overseas, most notably in Canada, Australia and the States. In the mid-1930s the Religious Film Society was the only body engaging in the production of religious films. However, in 1938 the Rev. Brian Hession, Vicar of Holy Trinity Church, Aylesbury, formed the Dawn Trust company in order to produce and distribute his own religious films. He began by acquiring and reissuing an early silent feature film, *From the Manger to the Cross*, to which he added his own narration and a musical soundtrack. Around the same time in the States the Rev. James Friedrichs formed his Cathedral Films Company which produced both biblical and contemporary stories in both black and white and colour, with the benefit of studio facilities in Hollywood. Later other US companies, such as Billy Graham Productions and Fact and Faith Films, set up distribution centres in London. Some of their films were outstanding. Much improved equipment— projectors and other visual aids—was also available from the States.

Many schools were able to get their first audio-visual facilities, including overhead projectors. There was also an improvement in screen material, and special box screens were developed for daylight showings. Churches, however, still found the idea of projectors and film screens somewhat distasteful and blacking them out was always a problem because of their large windows.

Walter Knights recalls:

> There was general opposition to the use of a projector in an actual church. Many times I have met committees who were dead against this. My approach was to say, 'Let me show you the film first and then we'll discuss it.' On one occasion the discussion was going well when a lady inquired, 'Are the actors and actresses in your films Christians?' After a few seconds' hesitation I replied, 'I will answer that question by asking you one. You have a beautiful church, well appointed, and I presume you must have had a good architect, a good builder and workmen. And did you ask them if they were Christians? I doubt if you did. What you wanted was the best you could get with the money you have available. We do the same in Religious Films.' The result was that I was allowed to show a film in that beautiful church and it was accepted, gracefully.

Just as Rank was busy funding commercial films illustrating the British way of life, so he was not averse to using his religious films to promote the Methodist Church in general and the Home Mission Department in particular. Walter Knights produced *Young Strong and Free* (1950) about the Methodist Association of Youth Clubs London Weekend. The film was full of young people (all looking in their forties) and was healthy, wholesome fun. It went badly over budget but Rank picked up the balance. This was the beginning of a number of such films publicizing the vibrancy of the Methodist Church. *See His Banners Go* (1950) followed, showing the post-war activities of the Home Mission department all round the country and in Germany.

One film that did particularly well was *The Promise* (1952), which told the story of a newly appointed social worker who found it hard to meet the standards set by his predecessor. He discovers that his predecessor was working with the guidance of God's Holy Spirit, and eventually discovers the Holy Spirit for himself through the medium of some religious paintings. *The Promise* won a Golden Globe Award in the States as well as the US National Evangelical Film Award and an award from the World Council of Christian Churches. Rank showed it to the Methodist Church's annual conference in Preston, where it played to large crowds. (It failed, however, to teach Rank's Yorkshire character to show any grace to Lancashire. The former Mayor of Blackpool invited Rank to dinner during the conference to show Rank the famous seaside resort for the first time. His host asked him what he thought. 'I shan't want to go again!' was Rank's gruff reply.)

Rank's critics often enjoyed quoting that his business genius had triumphed over his Methodist principles. They used, among other things, a commercial film, *The Wicked Lady*, to make their point. It was released in 1945, with James Mason, Margaret Lockwood and Pat Roc, was a phenomenal success in the box office. It was held in great contempt by the critics for its racy content, and caused a storm of protest in *The Methodist Recorder*. It told the story of a highwaywoman who was also a prostitute. Queen Mary asked if she might be invited to the première. This caused slight consternation: apparently there was someone in the projection box throughout the showing, ready to turn down the sound so that any potentially offensive words would become inaudible to royal ears. However, at the end of the film, Queen Mary said to Arthur: 'A very good film, Mr. Rank, and a fine moral.'[2]

Rank was delighted with such royal approval.

Queen Mary is the only person to see in the film what I see myself. I only agreed to it because there's a moral in it. You have two pretty girls, Margaret Lockwood and Pat Roc. One of them falls to temptation, and gets

shot in the end; the other lives happily. That's the
moral. Both girls are pretty, you see; it wouldn't have
meant anything if one of them had been plain. Oh yes,
I didn't like some of the dialogue... I didn't know about
that... [3]

The object in Rank's mind, although his theology was
completely satisfied by such a film, was to get people talking
about it.

In 1949 Edgar Youdell, a Congregational minister, was interviewed
by Rank who wanted a researcher into the effect of visual aids in
religion. Youdell was offered the job and went on to work for Rank
until 1957. His second research project was on the use of film in
religion generally and especially in Christian worship. During the
eight years it took him to write up his research, Youdell moved
outside the terms of his contract and became at Rank's beck and
call. About once a month during this time they would travel round
the country together, talking to various meetings. Youdell would
write many of the speeches Rank made on the subject of religious
films. On one occasion they had a disagreement, probably based on
Youdell's fear of Rank's often proclaimed intellectual weaknesses.
Youdell remembers:

He was invited to speak to the Cambridge Students'
Union about the use of film in religion. I was to go
with him and he asked me to do an outline for his talk
as he had done many times before. But for this I wrote
out the whole thing because I was worried that he
wouldn't do it well. It was the first disagreement with
him. I had spent hours into the night writing it and he
put the script on the table in front of him and then he
didn't look at it.

Youdell wanted Rank to talk about the theory of using
audio-visuals—and he had the right background knowledge to
help him do this. Rank, however, preferred to talk about one of
his films and then use it to start an argument.

The object of these meetings, which Youdell organized on behalf of Rank, was to promote films from the RFS and also from the Dawn Trust[4] which distributed US religious films. Rank did not want to join with the Dawn Trust, but he couldn't ignore the portfolio of imported product. Eventually, during a visit to the States, he set up a department of Religious Films in New York, which did very well. In 1951 Rank accepted an invitation from the US World Council of Churches to go to Green Lake, Wisconsin to a big Baptist Assembly. Two weeks before he was due to go he had to pull out and Youdell was sent instead. The following year Youdell was invited to be Chaplain for the whole event and Rank paid for him to go by plane, since the ship took too long.

Another of Youdell's responsibilities was to organize religious film conferences at Mansfield College, Oxford. There were five in all. People were invited from abroad and Rank used the opportunity to introduce a brand-new religious film at each of the conferences. It was a publicity idea as much as anything and Rank was always pleased to discover that they had made the front page of the *Oxford Mail*.

The relationship between Youdell and Rank extended to Rank paying occasional visits to the Youdell household.

Once we were going to Luton to visit the Rev. Bill Gowland at the Luton Industrial College (which Rank had supported financially). Rank asked me over the phone if we could have a cup of tea before we go. I asked him if he'd come and pick me up and suggested we'd have tea at my place. We lived in a terraced house and the sort of area where a big Daimler outside causes a bit of a commotion, and a crowd of twenty or so folk gathered. Inside, he showed gentleness to my family and spoke to my wife about the wonderful work I was doing. Rank always wore a waistcoat with a gold watch and chain, and my son Andrew went up to Rank and asked him if he could see his watch. Rank took it off the chain and gave it to Andrew to look at. I told

Andrew to be careful, and a few moments later he came back with his Mickey Mouse watch and said, 'Swap you!' Rank thought that was hilarious.

Youdell was prepared to work incredibly hard for Rank. And Rank didn't leave his special workers without reward. Every Christmas, the Youdell household would receive a huge hamper from Fortnum and Masons, and Rank took care of other needs as well:

I had my own car when I started the job and on one visit I went out to Colchester. On the way back the car broke down and eventually someone gave me a tow. I had to go home and leave the car, but the expense was quite heavy and I rang Rank to tell him what had happened, and he asked me to go down and see him. He asked me if I had a garage I was pleased with and I told him about one in Berkhamsted. He asked for the particulars of my car, and I told him it was a Vauxhall, that I had been very happy with it and I thought no more about it. (In those days you had to wait six to nine months to get a new car.) I think it was about a fortnight later when the manager of the garage rang and said, 'I've got a new Vauxhall here for you.' I rang Rank's secretary and she told me that he had written to the garage in Luton and she said, 'You must make an arrangement to go and collect the car, it's going to be his gift to you.' He even let me keep the car when I left.

Eventually Youdell had to leave Rank's employment because of pressure from his family. He had simply been working too hard. He remembers verbatim the conversation they had when he took his notice to Rank:

'I thought you were happy working for me.'
'I'm happy, but it's not good for family relationships.'

'Well, if you're in an important job you've got to be prepared to go anywhere at any time.'

'Look, Mr Rank, I know you work terribly hard [his secretary told me that he was always in his office in South Street] but you're an older man than I am and I'm only just starting my family.'

'This is not a matter for me, but for the committee.'

I could feel that underneath he was controlling himself. He didn't make it easy for me. But after he had talked to Mrs Rank about it, he rang me the next day and said he was very sorry and he and his wife had talked about the many happy occasions that we had had together.

It was not the first or last time Mrs Rank was to calm her husband down.

Although Rank did expect a massive amount from those working for him he never neglected the personal touch and he had a deeply Christian attitude to his employees. When Youdell's father died while Youdell was in Rank's employment, Rank took the time and trouble to write a sympathetic letter in his own hand and said there was no need to hurry back to work.

Noel Evans was another employee who was intensely loyal to Rank and understood what his faith meant to him. Evans was very secretive and protective of Rank; he had great power at Religious Films and practically ran the organization. He read hundreds and hundreds of scripts, looking for new stories, which were surprisingly hard to find. He was largely responsible for the script of *The Shield of Faith* (1955), the scenario of which he worked on with Rank[5]. Later Evans gave up being Secretary of the CCC and RFS and succeeded Dr Gregory as Secretary of Religious Films Ltd. This brought him into greater contact with Rank and after Dr Gregory's death he did more and more for him.

Rank was clearly proud of Evans. Once when Bob Hope came over Rank was really anxious for the two to meet. Hope was being driven by Youdell back to the Dorchester from Clubland in the Elephant and Castle when he asked, 'Do you know Noel Evans? The first thing Rank said to me this time was "Have you seen Noel Evans yet?" I'm going to see him in the morning—is he important to Rank?'

While he was happy to leave the big commercial films well alone, Rank interfered enormously in the script writing and the editing of his religious films, particularly towards the end of his life. It is perhaps cruel but true to say that this may be why some were not as good as they might have been. Rank would be shown the script and make comments and modifications, then he would see a rough cut and make editing suggestions, which were often impractical from a technical point of view.

Perhaps the difference was that the aim of these films was not commercial: he was trying to convey what he felt. He wasn't very good at expressing his faith, but he desperately wanted to. In his later years, his inability to communicate his faith became more marked. Colin Rank, his great-nephew and like Rank a committed Christian, remembers him trying to explain the potential of the Holy Spirit, but people wouldn't pick up on it. While Rank knew what he wanted to say, he found it difficult to share it with others.

Rank was absolutely convinced that if he could make the right religious films he could spread the Christian message to the entire world. He was so enthusiastic about his religious films, he wanted everyone to see them—his long-suffering family included. His grandson, Fred Packard remembers:

> We used to be dragged to see them in the blasted
> village hall and they were so bad. Grandpa had
> selective judgement; he was not great at being self-
> critical if it didn't suit him. He wasn't driven by money,
> he was driven by faith.

When Rank was at Sutton Scotney he organized monthly film services on Sundays at 2.30p.m. during the autumn and winter. The services were put on in the village hall for the local community.

The family and the estate would go too. A free bus was provided to get people there from the surrounding countryside and Mr and Mrs Rank would greet everyone at the door. Valentine Powell, a family friend who lived on the estate, has grim memories of them:

> They were rather bent... they didn't overtake you with a burning faith. They were horribly dated, ponderous and slow, if you compared it with Zeffirelli. They weren't controversial and they didn't test your belief by asking you questions, they just gave the syrupy bit. He was convinced that the films were exposing people to the word of God, and he hoped people would react.

Rank admitted later that some of his early films were not good. This is now a generally held belief. But in those days they proved very popular among the churches, who had to book a long way ahead to get one. Rank's failures only spurred him on to greater efforts. Robin Cowen remembers the first time a religious film service was held in a cathedral. Chichester had agreed to host the event. It was freezing cold, the projector broke down and the sound didn't work, but Rank refused to be despondent.

Andrew Youdell (Edgar Youdell's son) from the British Film Institute, an expert on Rank's films, describes Rank's later religious films as awful, singling out *The Challenge* (1970) in particular. This told the story of an idyllic Christian community in the north of England which was about to be shattered by the building of a huge power station. In their various ways and with the help of God they all come to terms with it. Youdell describes it as 'completely out-of-date and lacking in any audience involvement'.

Rank's last religious film was called *Remember Me* (1972). It was about the Last Supper and turned out to be a theological minefield. Rank's idea was for it to be distributed through the Rank Home Film Fellowship (see below) and used while people shared Holy Communion in their homes. Unfortunately, due to his death the scheme did not work out as he had planned.

Rank was always looking for more ways to communicate to the masses. Eventually Religious Films Ltd was to find another home and another outlet into the fast-growing world of television. In the late fifties commercial television had become a major force and each evening a short slot was devoted to the Epilogue, much mocked by some. This simple programme involved a clergyman, often in an armchair, delivering a 'thought' to the camera. Many clergymen were used and, since virtually none had experience of working in front of a camera, Rank thought it important that they should receive training in the skill. He therefore established the Churches' Television Centre (CTVC), which began life in Tooting Central Hall. It was set up so that ministers could be trained in the art of mass communication.

The first director, heading a staff of six, was the Rev. Cyril Thomas. In 1962 the centre moved, with more staff and better equipment, to some former BBC studios opposite Madame Tussaud's on the Marylebone Road. Rank was the first person to realize that ministers needed this kind of training. Hundreds of them went through the process, and so even better facilities were needed. In 1965 a site was found at 'Hillside', a large country house in Bushey near Watford, and CTVC began to be even more professional. When Rank was interviewed by a local paper about the Centre, he said:

> The churches have been asleep and we have to find a
> way of getting through to the masses... We haven't yet
> found a way of putting over the gospel story in a way
> which is entertaining, but I have a team working on it
> at the centre, where we train ministers, even bishops—
> everybody—in the methods of television presentation.
> We believe, because we believe in the teaching of Jesus
> Christ, that the Holy Spirit will guide us and I am sure
> that we are going to break through.

In 1970 the Rev. Leslie Timmins became the second director. Under him, on 1 January 1973, thanks to Rank's enthusiasm for new technology, CTVC went over to colour pictures and thereby became one of the most up-to-date closed television studios in the world. There was also further expansion of production facilities, including a second television studio and two sound studios.

Rank was keen for religious television programmes to be as well produced as all other programmes, and CTVC was encouraged to pursue excellence in all fields of production. The early product was sold largely to ITV companies, although *The Weekenders*, about the Methodist Association of Youth Clubs, was shown by the BBC. These days the studios make as many programmes as they can, but they have to rely on the four terrestrial channels to buy them for broadcast. Quite a lot of the work is done in co-production and some fourteen projects for network transmission were completed in 1994. They have considerable resources available, both financial and technical, and a staff of seventy to run them. With the vision of Lord Rank behind them and his portrait hanging on the wall to remind them of it, they are always hoping for greater exposure. When there are not enough religious programmes being made, the studios are let out for secular work.

The early, overtly evangelical broadcasts found air-time probably because they were sold cheaply to the commissioning editors rather than because they were first-rate television. Every network takes on some responsibility for showing religious programmes and this would have been a way of fulfilling the brief without seriously denting the budget.

Another branch of Rank's involvement in religious films was the founding of the Rank Home Film Fellowship. This came about indirectly through his Presidency of the Royal Agricultural Society in 1969 and the founding of the Arthur Rank Centre at the National Agricultural Centre in Warwickshire.

Rank's great interest in farming, which he had pursued from his early days in Reigate, combined with his position as one of the most important businessmen in the country, made it inevitable that he would one day be President of the Royal Agricultural Society. He was to bring to this not only his enthusiasm for agriculture, but also his faith. The Royal Show, held in early July every year, had been permanently based at the National Agricultural Centre at Stoneleigh near Kenilworth since 1963.

The British churches hosted a pavilion at the Show for four years, but were unable to fund it after that. They were given an old fertilizer stand on the main concourse but it was not very big and was unimpressive. It was also only there for the four days of the Show and was not a regular presence on the permanent site.

While President of the Society, Rank decided that a fertilizer stand was not good enough for the churches' pavilion. His thoughts coincided with the thinking of the churches' team at the Show. At the time the emphasis in churches was all for 'industrial' chaplains; the future seemed to say that parish boundaries would disappear and the rural church would be largely forgotten. So the then Archdeacon of Warwick (who was Chaplain to the Royal Show), the Vicar of Stoneleigh, Canon Parks and the Rev. Peter Buckler (who was part of the churches' team) thought they should do something to redress the balance. In the late sixties they had a conference and decided that they needed a permanent centre for the rural church. When Rank said a new building was needed, it all came together. Peter Buckler takes up the story:

> I was charged to go and see Lord Rank at the
> Dorchester. Major Evans was there to stop Rank from
> spending money, so I went with one or two plans for a
> modest building. Lord Rank listened very attentively,
> but he told me he had gone cold on putting money
> into buildings, because he had invested £60,000 in a
> new church building, and he went to visit it. He didn't
> have the red carpet put out and he turned up without
> warning for the evening service and there were only
> forty there. 'This won't do. If the people won't come to
> the church, the church must go to the people.'

Rank then took the opportunity of exploiting the presence of a young man eager to please, by talking of the exciting new developments in mass communication coming from the United States. He predicted the advent of videotape. But this was still in the future so, in the meantime, he wanted to launch the Rank Home Film Fellowship, a development of Religious Films Ltd. It would work like a book club. Rank had got projectors with screens, and the idea was to have a projector for use in the home or in small groups. A film would be issued once a month and sent round the churches. Rank was very excited about the idea and was really pushing it. So instead of a new building Canon Buckler came away with £3,500 of projectors and films, and the promise of more films to come. He commented:

> I thought the films were awful and entirely unsuitable
> but I went round promoting the scheme. Rank was the
> sort of man who would inspire you to get on and do
> something.

Buckler believed, like many others, that Rank had not been well advised as to the content of his religious films. However, many churches became enthusiastic about the Rank Home Film Fellowship. The films were naive, but they did serve as useful promoters of religious discussion. There was no limit on getting projectors and no limit on films, and the project was successful. Then, according to Canon Buckler, the organization became more bureaucratic. Full-time staff were appointed and better organization took over, but the whole thing was too expensive and folded up. If it had only bridged the time to the arrival of the video, the idea could still have had a future. The concept was good, even visionary but, as was sometimes the case with Rank, before its time.[6]

Rank's constant quest for new ways of communicating his precious faith continued right into his final years, and his ideas were often far in advance of anyone else. Just before Walter Knights retired, Rank had the idea of using a church in a smallish town and running wires to houses nearby so that the film could be relayed by close circuit TV to the houses where groups of people would gather together. In effect, this would have been the first cable TV. The idea was prepared, but the Post Office would not agree to the wiring and he had to drop it.

Rank told Colin Rank in the last year of his life that he was still involved in various exciting new adventures. He was becoming enthusiastic about the idea of 'talking pages'. Rank frequently had imaginative ideas well ahead of his time. He envisaged using a television screen to call up a picture which would give you options of how to proceed. Rank saw potential here as a learning device. He was intrigued by the idea that you could sit in front of a screen and teach yourself almost anything you wanted. This would, in effect, be an interactive computer programme. Unfortunately technology was not up to it and his death intervened before he could pursue it further.

11 HIS FAITH

Crowns and thrones may perish,
Kingdoms rise and wane,
But the church of Jesus
Constant will remain;
Gates of hell can never
'Gainst that church prevail
We have Christ's own promise
and that cannot fail.

SABINE BARING-GOULD

Rank was brought up in a strictly Methodist home, and his faith was very much a part of his daily life from childhood. As a child he was infused with Sabbath observance, chapel and hymns from his birth. He was sent to a Methodist boarding school, The Leys in Cambridge, but despite this powerful indoctrination it was still his own free choice to become a Christian at a rally when he was thirteen years old. Apart from a short period as a young man in Hull, there is no indication that he ever rebelled and his faith grew strong. Later on, it was to go through some testing times and some dramatic changes but it remained the single most striking thing about him. For Rank was not just a lifelong member of the Methodist Church; he was also an evangelical Christian. Even his severest critics acknowledge that he was totally true to his Lord and Saviour.

Rank's nonconformist background was absolutely crucial to the shaping of his life. Had he not possessed the convictions given to him by his father he would never have ventured into films. It gave him the 'God-given' confidence and evangelical zeal to tread where no Sunday school teacher had trod before: his faith gave him a moral right to stand in the strange world of films. His daughter Shelagh, among others, describes his faith as 'marvellously simple'. One or two less close to him might have described it as marvellously simplistic, but it meant everything to Rank. He would say it was the hardest thing in the world to live up to.

Every day began with prayer and he would not do anything in his business or private life unless he believed he had God's blessing. He was never too busy to talk to God before breakfast. This would usually be alone, but at night he and his wife would pray together. When the weather was fine, and especially in Scotland, he would say his prayers outside, walking with the dogs or sitting by the river. He was never pushy about his faith in social situations but he would always make it very clear where he stood on things. For instance, Rank was very fond of his weekend shooting parties but there was never any sport on Sundays. In fact, very few guests ever stayed on to the Sunday—they were all sent packing on Saturday, to leave the Sabbath free. Rank also made Sunday a day of rest for all his staff, except during harvest and other busy times, when estate work had to be done on Sundays, when it always stopped at 5.00p.m. to allow people to get to an evening service. Despite having very firm principles himself, Rank was remarkably non-judgmental of family or friend who had got themselves into trouble. He said on more than one occasion: 'If you read the Bible, sins of the spirit are worse than sins of the flesh.'

Rank was an interesting mixture of a 'strict and particular' Methodist (Sabbath observance, teetotal tendencies) and a very broad-minded man of the world. Maybe it was Jesus' teachings on forgiveness and the challenge to 'take the plank out of your own eye' that made him so understanding. He would be judgmental about the sin, but show great compassion to the sinner. This part of his nature was very important at the time of his daughter Shelagh's marriage breakdown. She had married an American called Packard and gone to live in the United States. But the relationship went wrong and Shelagh came home. He was very understanding about it and showed great compassion. His spirits no doubt lifted when she re-married, as Robin Cowen was a close friend of the family. Robin was also divorced and he remembers Rank's compassionate attitude to his situation: 'When I went to tell him about the break-up of my first marriage he said, "My poor boy, I'm so desperately sorry for you and for your poor wife." '

Rank also had to come to terms with the fact that his other daughter, Ursula, also married a divorcee. This was certainly contrary to his view of marriage and its importance in the teachings of Christ, but again he made himself understand and was wonderfully supportive. He explained later that he had got through these times so well because he had been in constant contact with his Maker.

He had a firm faith in the power of the Holy Spirit, who—he believed—had intervened in his life and guided him in many of his decisions. One such was his commitment to total abstinence from alcohol, to which Rank held firmly throughout his life. This stood him in good stead when a burst appendix threatened his life; his doctor kept him alive for two weeks by giving him sips of brandy. Arthur's father-in-law, Lord Marshall, was about to send for the best liqueur brandy but was told by the doctor that the local stuff in the pub would be best as it would have more bite to it and thereby the stimulation would be greater. It is said that having been a teetotaller probably saved Arthur's life, because the effect of the brandy would not have been as useful had he been a seasoned drinker. But if the brandy saved his life, it didn't convert him to alcohol. 'I lived on brandy for a fortnight and I liked it even less at the end than the beginning. They say it's an acquired taste; I didn't acquire it,' he commented. Rank preferred to give his gratitude to God. At the start of his recovery he said to his wife, 'I am one step further away from the brink, thanks to God.'

The Rev. Dr Kingsley Lloyd, former President of the Methodist Conference, was fond of Rank and has this to say about his faith:

> His religion was genuine but he had some
> extraordinary ideas. He thought he had a special line
> to God, some divine imprimatur. His ideas of

orthodoxy were very vague. He had some rather eccentric views about the church and religion. He had a great belief about the guidance he received from God, which he called the Holy Spirit, and had a strong belief that his schemes were working towards a religious goal and that all the things he was involved in were part of God's purpose. Revival for the church, he believed, would come through technology. At the time of *Honest to God* [a controversial book of popular theology], I said 'You're as bad as the Bishop of Woolwich. You want to change everything.'

The Rev. George Sails, former Secretary of the Home Mission division of the Methodist Church, wrote in *The Methodist Recorder* after Rank's death:

His faith was simple in the extreme but none of us who knew him would ever dare to question its depth or validity. He was a good man, and full of the Holy Ghost and of faith.

Rank's faith was also well-practised. A member of staff at Methodist Publications Ltd, working under Walter Knights, was found stealing payments made for advertisements. Knights couldn't sack him but he had the man suspended and informed Rank. Then it was also discovered that the man had other debts and was threatened with proceedings. Rank's response was, 'This fellow has fallen in the gutter, hasn't he? If Christ came along and saw a man in the gutter what would he do?' Knights replied, 'Pick him up and give him another chance,' so Rank said, 'That is what you and I must do with this man. Find out how much he owes and I will send him a cheque.' Rank helped him to get another job with the Eat More Bread campaign.

The man then stole again and ended up at Bow Street Magistrates Court. While in the dock he claimed that Rank was a friend and Rank was summoned. In court, Rank admitted to having helped the man. When the man was sentenced to eight months in prison, Rank got Knights to find out where he was and arranged to visit him. The man had a wife and three sons and Rank paid for the children to be looked after while their father was inside so that the mother could work to earn money to keep them all more comfortably when her husband was released. That way the family stayed together.

There is some firm and respected criticism of Rank's theology, and particularly of his contribution to the Methodist Church. For example, for all his involvement in the church, Rank did not lend his support to the Methodist anti-apartheid stance. It was well-known that if you wanted to set up some evangelical organization and you used the right terminology, you could get his support, but an issue regarding ethical investment in South Africa was of no interest to him.

Joseph Rank's commitment to building huge Central Halls was continued by his son. This emphasis has found disfavour in some quarters. Former President of Conference, the Rev. Dr Colin Morris, explains:

> Once you start a building, you make it static, and they went in a big way for walls and a roof. So, far from showing the flexibility of the Holy Spirit, it lumbers people down with the structures.

The well-known Methodist preacher and life-peer Lord Soper was another leading Methodist who had little respect for Rank, his money or his methods:

> I was appointed to the opening of the Islington Central Hall, bringing together two Methodist churches. Our financial problems were acute but the name of 'Rank' meant you could face financial difficulties. My first contact with his emissaries was to get sums of money and there was, even at that stage, a collision of our attitudes. He seemed, through his emissaries, to treat me with a certain amount of suspicion. I don't think he thought my social gospel was the kind of thing that he thought I should proclaim in Islington.

Soper, famous for his open-air 'soap-box' delivery, had been challenged many times on London's Tower Hill about the behaviour of capitalists, and Rank had been a frequent focus of the discussion. So Soper decided to get to the facts. He wrote to Lord Rank, requesting an interview to ask him about his methods and his business practice. Rank's response was to fob Soper off with a representative:

> He was very suspicious of my form of Christian advocacy... I would have been a better evangelist, in his opinion, with a simpler message.

Soper genuinely believed that Rank was a sincere Christian man with a strong sense of responsibility for his wealth, but who had, at the same time, a very narrow funnel through which he believed it was possible to distribute that wealth.

> It seemed to me then that he epitomized a particular form of Christian advocacy that I thought was far too narrow and unrelated to the Kingdom of God, and channelled it into quite personal terms, like laying off the booze and no serious gambling. The evangelism was focused upon, and very largely circumscribed by, the processes of personal conversion and individual responsibility, rather than the realization that we have to translate that commitment into the language of a society, completely different to the one Jesus Christ was talking to.

Soper did feel uneasy about criticizing a sincere Christian man, but it was hard for him not to, since Rank's simplistic capitalism was in Soper's opinion fundamentally incorrect.

> It's one thing to speak to God, it's another to listen to the reply. He had a simplistic faith and he took the precaution of not asking too many questions about it. I've no doubt he was wholehearted. I don't think anyone thought of him as a cynical exploiter of religion for his own aggrandisement. His motives were limited but honest.

A family friend admitted that Soper was probably right—Rank did take the precaution of not asking himself awkward questions. In fact, he may have concocted his religion slightly to suit himself.

While Soper was critical of Rank's world-view, Rank thought that Soper wasn't a man of the world and that he was unrealistic. Soper imagined that everyone would be happy with the barest minimum requirements, but Rank thought he knew people better than that. He maintained that Soper did not understand communication. He would talk despairingly of Soper's opposition to him. More might have been made of their mutual disdain in the press had it not been for the fact that most people thought that Soper, who had married a wealthy lady, was married to Rank's daughter (not true) and that explained why Soper was apparently well-off; and that he was only masquerading as a Methodist minister.

When I questioned the Rev. Dr Kingsley Lloyd, he said he would not go along with Soper, because it was too easy a judgment to make. He proffered an explanation:

> He was his father's son. He was a tycoon—a great house, a suite at the Dorchester, offices on South Street—he had all the trappings and he genuinely believed that God gave him these things. I found it hard to reconcile the image of a man of great faith with some of the things he promoted like his movies, bingo, etc. but that didn't seem to worry him. Why not... ? He went into pictures really with an idea of promoting religious faith. And the other things were making money so that he could promote good causes.

Rank's own understanding and interpretation of the Christian faith left him a staunch Tory. After the *ad valorem* tax debacle after the Second World War, when the Labour government, and Harold Wilson in particular, let him down so badly, he was left with very little faith in the socialists; they simply did not keep their word. Rank would have been a great fan of the Thatcher years and would have echoed her quotation from John Wesley (as his father had done), 'Earn all you can, give all you can, save all you can.' He would have said that we were all born equal, but balance that truth with Jesus' parable of the talents: it is up to each individual to make the most of life's opportunities. Of those who are given much, much will be expected.

One extraordinary insight into Rank's private spiritual life was provided by Michael, his butler. He told me that Lord Rank used to keep a crucifix in his dressing-room and would kiss it as part of his daily prayer routine—hardly nonconformist orthodoxy. He would often talk to his Catholic butler about the Roman Catholic faith and the Pope, and was impressed by Michael's complete commitment to attending Mass every week.

Like the founder of Methodism, John Wesley, who spent an awful lot of time being a 'Christian without' before his heart was 'strangely warmed', Rank too went through the majority of his life without the strongest spiritual experience of all. Like Wesley, who used to follow the adage 'preach faith until you have it,' so Rank replied, when a friend asked, 'How do you get to believe so strongly?', 'You've got to pretend at first and then it will come.'

Although Rank was keen on the new medium of film for Sunday schools, in all other ways he was a traditionalist, liking the old hymns and prayers, saying that even if they were not immediately understood by the children, eventually the meaning would sink in. When the *Methodist Sunday School Hymn Book* was published in 1950 and Rank discovered that it did not contain some of the older Victorian hymns, such as 'What a friend we have in Jesus', he protested. When the minister at Reigate argued that this hymn would not mean much to the average boy scout, Rank argued back that it was just the sort of thing the average boy scout needed.

J. Arthur Rank believed very strongly in the power of prayer. Once he was at lunch with the Powell family. It was towards the end of his life. Mrs Powell was four months pregnant with her fourth child and he asked whether she wanted a boy or a girl. When she said 'a girl', Rank put his hand on her stomach and prayed that it would be a girl baby. As it turned out, the baby was a girl. What this says about Rank's understanding of human biology is questionable, but it does give an interesting insight into his beliefs about prayer.

The Holy Spirit was to play a large part in Rank's final years, and he had always been very aware of his presence. When Wood finished his biography in 1945, Rank was freely expressing the Holy Spirit's guidance even then. Wood records that while they were having lunch and discussing a religious film Rank was making, he suddenly said:

> I can never understand how anyone can take on
> responsibility in planning any big show without guidance
> from God. No man can rely on himself. But, of course, it's
> a damned dangerous thing to ask for guidance of the
> Holy Spirit. It may tell you to do things you don't want to
> do. You never know where it may lead you. I am in films
> because of the Holy Spirit.[1]

The more powerful his faith, the more private he became about it, which explains why so few people knew about the following event. Rank's faith was always strong but four years before the end of his life he was to have an experience that was to confirm his trust in God. Colin Rank, Rank's great-nephew, became a convinced Christian in the last year of his uncle's life, and he was to hear the story first-hand:

> Four years before he died he met Donald Coggan, then
> Archbishop of York, and they were talking and praying
> together when the Archbishop leant and touched the
> side of his head and told him that he was going to
> experience a wonderful gift in the near future.[2]
> Later that year he was out walking in Scotland. He
> would go out with half a dozen of his dogs every
> morning before breakfast and walk with them up to the
> pony bridge and back. By now he had forgotten all
> about what Lord Coggan had said, but as he looked up
> he saw what he described as a kind of revelation in his
> mind's eye, of the glory and splendour of God, and he

became powerfully aware of the presence of God. Thus in a new and revitalising way, from then on, he experienced the presence of God in his life.

This event completely changed Rank's understanding of God. He had been a Christian since the age of thirteen, but this changed everything. Now it seemed to him that up to this time he had been trying to achieve success purely by means of his own strength, without relying on God. His wife did not seem to be particularly affected by his change of emphasis, but for Rank this was a massive moment in his life, and he set about tirelessly to reform everything he was doing. His renewed enthusiasm for his faith caused much consternation among some of his companions who could not understand what was going on. He was very keen to find out who was preaching 'in the power of the Spirit' as he called it, and giving the Holy Spirit proper emphasis. This raised eyebrows in some church circles from those who thought that Rank should stay out of theology.

After this, Rank visited Cliff College, one of Methodism's more evangelical centres and asked if they were teaching the doctrine of the Holy Spirit. They told him that they were, and that they appreciated his financial support. Rank, his new energy not satisfied with that as an answer, went off and asked for details of all the students that had been through the college. He followed them up and found that the ones who preached the Holy Spirit saw their congregations growing. So he went back and set out the facts to Cliff College: this person, who had been preaching the Holy Spirit, had had growth; this person, who hadn't, had not had growth. Membership figures are well kept in Methodism and Rank would not have had a problem in proving his case. The authorities at the college understandably took deep exception to his interfering. But Rank with his new zeal remained adamant; if they didn't teach the Holy Spirit he wasn't going to give them any money.

In the course of his duties as President of the Royal Agricultural Society (RAS) in 1969, Rank visited the Royal Show and met the people involved with putting it on. Canon Peter Buckler, who was part of the churches' team, remembers him approaching the churches' pavilion:

> He was big in every way and he came with one of the senior stewards of RAS Christopher York, who was even taller. As they came across they were met by the Archdeacon of Warwick, Archdeacon Proctor, who was the Chaplain of the Royal Show and the vicar of Stoneleigh, Canon Parks, who was a nice man. Both Parks and Proctor were not tall, so from a great height Rank said, 'And what is your teaching on the Holy Spirit?' Proctor got in a tizzy and said, 'Well, we do say the grace!'

Rank, instead of talking about agriculture or films or flour, apparently spent twenty minutes preaching to the assembled clergy about the activity of the Holy Spirit. He told them of his belief that the Holy Spirit was involved with every aspect of one's life, whether it was a decision on flour or church life. It does seem extraordinary; this great important man on an official duty suddenly starts revealing his simple faith to the first clergymen he sees. But it left a lasting impression. Canon Buckler was in no doubt of Rank's Christian conviction:

> He was in constant contact with God. He had a very simple faith and, where some of us have difficulty knowing what God wants, he felt clearly that he was God-directed. He couldn't understand why it wasn't everyone else's experience.

As with many other stories about Rank's involvement with projects, his role was inspirational as well as financial. As Canon Buckler says:

> You couldn't meet him without going away having gained something. It was more than the money you got when he backed your idea—you became convinced it was right as well, and part of God's plan. The money was secondary.

Rank was very influenced by the US evangelist Oral Roberts, famous for his prayer tower. This small-time evangelist had gone to Madison Avenue in New York (the centre of the advertising industry) and said, 'God's told me no longer to be a tent evangelist; I want to set up a university in Tulsa, Oklahoma.'

The advertisers believed him and gave him a new image. Oral Roberts became a well-known television evangelist and faith-healer. In the 1960s he came over to a big rally at White City in London, and Rank, who was becoming interested in faith-healing, organized a meeting with him. Rank read a lot about faith-healing and the laying on of hands, and this interest became wound up with his obsession with the work of the Holy Spirit. The second time Oral Roberts came over, Rank paid all his expenses to encourage Roberts in order to set up a healing centre at the Westminster Central Hall. Once again, Rank was behaving in a way which was baffling to his family; they were all under the impression that Roberts was some sort of con-man. The whole family was dragged off, largely against their wills, to hear Roberts preach at Central Hall. It was something of a disaster from all accounts. Roberts was too American in his style—he had them all holding hands and it didn't go down at all well. Rank, however, was completely convinced and talked a lot about the 'healing hands'. Towards the end of the second stay Oral Roberts came down to Sutton Scotney for a game of golf.

Later, when Fred Packard, Rank's grandson, was going to the United States, Rank asked him to go and stay at The Oral Roberts University—something which Fred was none too pleased about.

It was the summer of 1970 when I went to Oklahoma. I had a summer job in Brazil and was going to come back through the States. Grandfather told me that if I was going to be in America he wanted me to see Oral Roberts because he said, 'I think he's been blessed with the ability to communicate about Jesus Christ.' I felt uncomfortable about smoking at the university and I thought the guy was a complete charlatan and he gave me the creeps... However, it was fascinating, it was real mid-town Oklahoma. There was a slightly ingenuous, naive streak in Grandpa when it came to some people. Other people connected with his spiritual life fooled him as well. His relationship with Oral Roberts in no way led to anything disastrous. I reported back that I found it fascinating, but that he's not my cup of tea.

This strange fascination with Oral Roberts may be explained by, as Fred says, Rank's naivety, but it also shows another characteristic: an interest in unconventional people, people who were saying something new. Rank was always ready to listen to a fresh approach to a subject. Towards the end of his life he read a number of books on the charismatic movement and also became interested in the Jesus People.

The Joseph Rank 1942 Trust was only small compared with the Joseph Rank Benevolent Trust and the Rank Foundation, but it gave a lot of money towards the Oral Roberts University. The committee comprised only Colin Rank, Douglas Hutchinson and Rank himself. After he died they were left with a commitment to Oral Roberts of which no one else had totally approved. But Rank was completely absorbed by Mr Roberts' ministry and even circulated his daily blessing.

Oddly, Rank was less fond of the more conventional evangelical figures. He once said: 'I've heard Billy Graham once on television and I don't want to hear him again!' Apparently, he was not fond of the blatantly evangelical approach, even though during one of Billy Graham's crusades at Easter time, Rank had arranged with the Dominion, the Odeon, Leicester Square and the Empire, Leicester Square, for Graham to go on stage for four minutes in each one. Rank no longer thought that religious films with someone just preaching to camera were good communication, although he did not dismiss it. He preferred the message to be hidden in a story.

Rank was fond of circulating written material associated with his latest theological thinking. One such hand-out was a small card with 'The Christian's Prayer'. He circulated bundles of these things to all those he thought might benefit. It went as follows:

Dear Heavenly Father:

You always love me. I ask in Jesus' name for a strong, active and continuous faith so that I may always be conscious that the Holy Spirit lives within me and that he will teach me to love Jesus, keep His words, walk in His ways and learn no longer to rely on myself, but with certainty place all my hopes and cares in Your loving hands, dear Father.

I believe—Father, Son and Holy Spirit, help Thou my unbelief.

Rank was not known for his own theological writings but he was asked by one publisher to lend his wisdom to the back of Andrew Murray's book *The Spirit of Christ* (published by Marshall, Morgan & Scott in 1963). In that he confesses, 'As I am not a theologian, I often find it difficult to follow the highly technical approach of some writers who deal with the Person of the Holy Spirit. But Andrew Murray writes with clarity and simplicity, yet profoundly, so that my own understanding has been deepened and my spiritual life blessed and enriched.'

He liked to get his own way all the time, and he would often bring in the Almighty in one form or another to add backing to his arguments. He was known to have banged the table at a board meeting and say, 'But we have the Holy Spirit on our side.' He definitely felt that when the Holy Spirit came, he dwelt within you and everything that you were involved with he was involved with. Therefore, as Chairman of the Rank Organisation, it went without saying that the Holy Spirit was with him there as well. He had no doubt that God was as much with him in his business dealings as he was with his religious films. His faith was always there. Once, after the signing of a contract for a big film deal, he turned to one of his secretaries and said: 'It's curious, isn't it, to think that Jesus Christ is in the room with us now?'

Rank was always enthusiastic about new developments and new ways of communicating. In the late sixties, on a cold February day during the power cuts, and after a full day's business and a 5.00p.m. meeting at the Home Mission Department, he took himself off to see the new West End show *Godspell*, to find out how God was speaking through young people today.

Colin Rank remembers that they had lots of discussions about faith, apart from how he received the Holy Spirit: 'We had a private joke about "the ministry of damp water" in the church. He was always complaining about those people who were cynical about his ideas.'

At home, the Sabbath was always strictly observed and Rank would attend the little chapel in Sutton Scotney every Sunday morning. He liked the simple hymns and the simple Sunday service. He sometimes led in prayer and enjoyed communion at the Lord's table. A fellow worshipper at the church, Rita Braybrooke-Tucker, remembers Rank arriving every Sunday, one minute before the service was about to begin. 'He would walk tall and upright up the aisle, with his Bible and hymn book in his hand, to the front pew. As soon as he was seated, the service would start.' He would put £5 in the collection and sing wholeheartedly if out of tune. He would usually have a word with the preacher, but everyone was rather in awe of him and he could seem a little austere. She also remembers a six-week mission in the area when she looked after two young Methodist ministers. Twice a week Mr Rank's dairyman would deliver two pounds of 'beautiful golden butter and a jar of thick yellow cream'. He would also hold all the Methodist garden parties in the grounds of Sutton Manor. And although he spent vast sums of money on a national scale refurbishing Methodist properties he didn't forget his own chapel and paid for new furnishing and decorating as well as rich velvet curtains with 'God Loves You' written on them. The words typified his gospel.

I have found an example of what a Rank sermon might have been like. It is not strictly a sermon, because it was part of an appeal he made for more money for the Methodist Home Mission Department in 1971, and it was distributed on a 45rpm disc. It demonstrates some of his theology and gives an insight into his optimistic faith:

> New opportunities are confronting us and we are ready. For this purpose God has given us the gift of the Holy Spirit to enable us to mission in the areas of life and need to which we are truly sent... The church of the first century was deeply aware of the movement and guidance of the Holy Spirit and they were triumphant. We believe... that the power of the Holy Spirit is ours for the asking. It is He and He alone who can and will renew the life of our church today... The Holy Spirit is using the work of the Home Mission Department mightily. We pray that you will play your part in His work... You cannot do this effectively unless you first realize that the Holy Spirit is within you. Then you will be able to meet with love and generosity the challenge that I put before you.

Rank kept up with his Sunday school teaching all through his life, and regularly attended his local 'class meeting' in which Methodists traditionally found teaching and friendship. Alan Wood writes: 'It was religion that gave Arthur Rank the driving force to work and the energy to play, so that he returned refreshed to work anew. The secret of what Rank did during the week in Wardour Street was always to be found in what he did in his Sunday school at Reigate, and during weekends at Sutton Scotney.'[3]

12 RANK AND THE METHODIST CHURCH

Let us take up the cross,
Till we the crown obtain;
And gladly reckon all things loss,
So we may Jesus gain.'
CHARLES WESLEY

The *Methodist Recorder*'s obituary published on 6 April 1972 described Lord Rank as 'an unresisting evangelist... one of Methodism's outstanding laymen and among the connection's most generous benefactors.'

Officially he had held two posts, Treasurer of the Methodist Home Mission Department (1933-72) and General Treasurer of Westminster Central Hall. But his actual relationship with Methodism was far more complex and interesting than those titles may suggest.

It is almost impossible to be a Methodist and not know that J. Arthur Rank was one, too. His name is on so many churches, and whether you agreed with his theology or politics or not, everyone was at least a little proud that Methodists could call Lord Rank their own. He lost some of this respect over the issue of his Bingo Halls, of which more later, but it is impossible to calculate just how much money and time Rank gave to the Methodist Church. He argued with it, very nearly fell out with it, but the church would now be a much smaller place materially if it hadn't been for his massive financial input. An Osbert Lancaster cartoon summed up his financial significance: a bishop and a minister are crossing Westminster Bridge and the

Bishop says, 'We've got the Church Commissioners but you've got J. Arthur Rank.'

Rank was a faithful church-goer, and sang very loudly and badly. By the time he lived in Reigate he was instantly recognizable because so few church members swept up in a Rolls Royce. He was not over-friendly to his fellow worshippers when in Reigate and some considered that he 'flashed his money around'. He was described as being aloof and cold in the church situation, but he was more open and generous when he moved to Sutton Scotney. His commitment to Sunday school teaching was wholehearted and constant, but it is interesting to note that some have considered that he did it in order to make the world at large think well of him.

The Rank/Methodist relationship began with his father Joseph and the Joseph Rank Benevolent Trust, which gave an enormous amount to the Methodist Church and was responsible for the legacy of all the Central Halls around the country. Joseph Rank's vision, backed with his money, affected the development of Methodism. If you didn't do it his way, there was no financial help. The Rev. Dr Kingsley Lloyd, former President of the Methodist Conference, remembers:

> In 1939 I was minister in north London and involved
> in a new church in Grange Park near Enfield, and we
> went to some trouble to get an architect. We appealed
> to the Joseph Rank Benevolent Trust and they refused
> it because my plans were too ecclesiastical. We went
> ahead anyway, as it turned out, but that was typical of
> Joseph Rank's attitude. He wanted preaching halls all
> centred around a popular preacher. J. Arthur Rank got
> away from that mentality. He showed sympathy with
> the aims of the ministers who wanted to emphasize
> worship rather than just preaching, so gave money at a
> later stage to some of these Central Halls to create
> worship areas within the halls. The decline set in after
> the war and many of these huge places were only half
> full, even the famous Kingsway.'

Arthur was a somewhat less tyrannical figure than his father for the Methodist Church to deal with and altogether less imposing. Even so, as Kingsley Lloyd remarked, 'His suits always looked as though they would stand up on their own if he took them off'. Arthur was much more jolly than his father. But he shared his father's view that an empty church was nothing but abject failure. Even though there might be many factors contributing to the decline, he still saw it as unacceptable that the great preaching halls of his father's vision were not packed as they used to be. The Rev. Dr John Tudor, who has recently retired as minister of the Central Hall in Westminster, remembers having an argument with Rank on the subject:

> I was a junior minister at East Ham mission and the Superintendent invited Lord Rank to come and chair the evening service. I was the junior minister and when he arrived he said, 'Take me to the gallery, young Tudor. Tell me, how many people do you get here on a Sunday night?' This was the time in the fifties when people were beginning to drift away. 'About three, four hundred, perhaps five.' He pointed out that it seated two thousand. 'When this place was built and my father gave money for it, it was packed.' I said, 'Yes, and there were no cinemas, no films on a Sunday, all the things there are that take people away from church today.' Then he turned on me and really took me to task, and for two minutes we argued and then he put his arm round me and hugged me saying, 'You'll do, you'll do.' He really was the kind of man that if you challenged him, he loved you.

J. Arthur Rank was genuinely concerned to promote his brand of Christianity and to bring people to faith. Although he had some slightly eccentric views, he was genuinely religious and believed that his great wealth should be used to promote Christian aims. Fortunately for the Methodist Church, he chose to spend a vast amount of it on them.

Rank had a deep conviction that the Methodist Church should keep a firm hold on its evangelical tradition and this made him a great supporter of the Home Mission Department as well as acting as their treasurer. Rank gave a lot of money to Home Mission. He was a regular visitor to their offices and was well known for sticking his head round the door and asking: 'Is everything well? And is there evidence of the Holy Spirit in all the work?'

George Sails, a former Secretary of the Home Mission Department, paid tribute to Rank's contribution in the *Methodist Recorder* on 13 April 1972:

> He combined outstanding business ability with deep
> Christian conviction and a personal commitment to
> Jesus Christ as Lord and Saviour, always exercising a
> true Christian stewardship of expenditure.

And of course his religious films were a big part in his contribution to the work of the Department. Through it he pioneered the Family Film Services and, by the time of his death, 340 circuits out of 800 were operating the scheme. In 1967 there were no less than 9,000 such services being held in the country. He also financed many building and modernization schemes, seizing opportunities for mission in the new towns.

Rank used his business expertise and contacts to good use, introducing the knowledgeable and highly respected merchant bankers Lazard Brothers into the work of the Department. They became advisors to Home Mission. His main concern, based on his father's principle of 'never spend your capital', was to build up enough capital reserves for the Department so that they could cover their administration costs. Once they were catered for, all the money that was given by Methodists in the churches could go straight to the good causes the Department wanted to support.

The Home Mission Department was involved in many projects, but some of the ones introduced during Rank's time had his hallmark. He was very concerned to help film evangelism, especially in rural areas, and he funded the cinema van project. This was effectively a mobile cinema using back projection, with somewhat disappointing viewing quality. Despite this, Rank was keen on the idea. The first cinema van was owned by the *Methodist Times* and was taken round the country by a man from Doncaster. The idea was picked up by the Home Mission Department, which bought a few of these vehicles. One even went out to France at the beginning of the war and got caught up in the Dunkirk evacuation—only the driver, however, made it onto the boat, the van was left to burn. The Methodist Church also provided caravans for deaconesses to use and these were equipped with audio-visual aids. Over the years Rank provided money for cassettes, cassette recorders and projectors, and was also responsible for providing cars for ministers in country circuits, as well as scooters and car loans for other ministers. The Overseas Mission field was not forgotten about either, and the Rank Foundation funded a third of the cost of providing film-strips and projectors to carry the work of the Religious Film Society all over the world.

Where Rank was not able to help in person, he was very good at ensuring a suitable stand-in. Kingsley Lloyd remembers one such occasion:

> I was in a strange financial job in Westminster Central Hall, to do with connexional funds. We had to allocate the general assessment to the districts, a pension fund, a school fund and so on. It was the 1950s and I thought the set up was all very Victorian—we had no conception of financial management. We applied to Parliament for a bill to set up the Central Finance Board of the Methodist Church which gave us enormous freedom of investment—a totally tax-free fund. We were opposed by the Charity Commission but we got it through because the Church of England had a very similar set-up. I thought it would be good for Rank to accept the Chairmanship of this board and at first he didn't say no, but then he came back and said no, he wouldn't

accept, but he would ask Lord Mackintosh and he was our first Chairman. Rank was very helpful to me and we would never have got Lord Mackintosh without his help.

As late as the 1950s, Methodist ministers were still expected to buy their retirement houses out of their own resources. But in 1952 the Methodists set up the Ministers' Housing Society, which was backed by the Rank Trust. At this time, when some ministers died in active work, their widows were stranded. Once again, Rank was approached and as a result the Methodist Church was the only church at the time to guarantee that ministers' widows could live in a house of their choice.

Rank took the responsibility of giving out his money very seriously and always preferred to do business face-to-face. He also insisted that the cause needing the money should be prepared to put up half the cost. These 'pound for pound' deals were popular and successful. One such was at Kingswood School, a Methodist boarding school in Bath, founded by John Wesley. In 1967, the school needed £150,000 to build a new sixth-form study complex. Kingsley Lloyd was Chairman of the governors at the time and he wrote to Rank asking for the £75,000 on the pound for pound deal. Rank insisted on coming to see Kingsley Lloyd.

He said, 'This is your show, isn't it?' He then gave me three cheques, each for £25,000 from the Rank Trusts; the Rank Foundation; and him and his wife.

There is a recording of Rank making a pound for pound appeal for the Methodist Church Home Mission Department. It was made in 1971, a year before he died, and when membership was falling steeply:

How do we get more money from fewer members? First by refusing to accept defeat, by believing that God is with us, and as we enter more deeply into the life of the Spirit, our whole attitude to life will change, and a new surge of generosity will flow from our grateful hearts. I am therefore led to make the greatest challenge offer I have ever made to the people of

Methodism through the Department. The church has responded magnificently to previous challenges; now I offer pound for pound, up to £40,000, for new income. This money will help to maintain our man and woman power in circuits under pressure. It will enable us to advance in the new towns, to experiment in the rural areas and to remould our work in the central areas of the old towns and cities of our land. This challenge expects much, but it is made in the strong conviction that the Methodist people, conscious of the Holy Spirit within them, will meet the challenge.

Rank thought that theology was a lot of gobbledy-gook: the important thing was to communicate the faith through technological developments, and that would bring about a new age. He had a frustrating feeling that the Methodist Church was not getting anywhere. He was enormously successful—why was the church hanging around? The great thing, as far as he was concerned, was to fill the churches. But of course, it was not as straightforward as all that. Rank was a man who was used to making things happen. He only had to say the word. But, despite his frustrations, he did not complain much and kept on signing the cheques.

As with all his decisions in the last years of his life, Rank needed to know that the Holy Spirit was behind each venture that was put before him. It was difficult for some; if the ideas were Rank's he took the approval of the Holy Spirit for granted but other people had to demonstrate, in the way they presented their case for money, that the Holy Spirit had been involved in their vision and preparation, and it was quite a difficult thing to persuade Rank what was Holy-Spirit based. He was simply convinced that nothing could work unless the Holy Spirit was at the root of the idea. This became a bit of a joke among Methodists and one presumes that a few less scrupulous, money-hungry applicants invented a certain amount of divine activity in their presentation to Rank. The Rev. Dr Kingsley Lloyd had some sympathy for Rank in these situations:

I liked the old boy. People with that much money find people are always after something and this was very hard for Rank.

Colin Morris is far less light-hearted about this business of using certain code-words to get money from Rank:

One of the most demeaning aspects of the Rank Trust was the way one had to cast one's applications. You called geese swans and had to use the right code-words to get the money, even if that was untrue to the cause. There was not a chance of Rank's name being a light under a bushel—his name's on all the buildings. No one had to work for the money, they were just dispensing largesse, throwing fish to seals.

Rank was totally consumed by the subject of the Holy Spirit. While he was working as treasurer for Westminster Central Hall, Tony Reddall remembers Rank grilling Maurice Barnett, the then minister of the church, on what he was going to be preaching about on the Sunday morning and whether it would be about the Holy Spirit. He really could not be led away from the subject. It was, as many said, almost an obsession.

A successor of Dr Barnett's at the Central Hall, believes that without Rank's money the Methodist Church would not have survived:

You can take that two ways. You can say 'Thank God it was there,' and we would be in very poor straits if it weren't, but if it hadn't have been there it might have made the Methodist people give a darn sight more money than they were giving.

Rank was a great supporter of the Methodist stance on teetotalism and defended it when there was a move to make the rules slightly more liberal. But another point of Methodist orthodoxy was to be a real problem, and it almost brought Rank and the Methodists to a parting of the ways.

The Methodist Church has long been a vociferous opponent of gambling in all its forms and when it was known that Rank was proposing to have bingo in some of his Odeon cinemas, there was an outcry. Some very heated debate ensued; horror was expressed at the thought of such a prominent Methodist showing favour to such an abhorrent activity. The Methodist Conference of July 1962 had to come to a decision as to whether Lord Rank should be allowed to continue as a member of the Methodist Church, having consented to this outrage.

Rank had a defender in the Rev. E. Rogers, Secretary of the Christian Citizenship Department, who wrote in their report to Conference:

> It has been a real concern to us, and to many Methodists who have written to us, that Lord Rank has been so prominently associated with the development of Bingo clubs. We have conveyed this concern to the Home Mission Department and to Lord Rank. The Department is fully convinced of Lord Rank's integrity, and that his opinion that bingo is a harmless amusement is a sincere conviction. The Department, moreover, agrees that the guidance given on such questions is a matter for personal decision, and must not be regarded in any way as a condition of membership of the Church. Mainly because of the eminence of the person concerned, the particular question has caused us real anxiety, but we should be prepared to defend the right of any individual to act according to his conscientious conviction. At the same time we claim the right to express our own conscientious conviction that Lord Rank is mistaken in his judgment.

Rogers said at Conference—the Methodists' highest decision-making body—that Rank was obviously a man of the deepest faith and there was no hypocrisy. Rank himself held that bingo was a rather dreary game that did no real harm and, as a matter of personal conviction, he counted himself to have acted rightly. It was left to Lord Soper to say what many members of Conference were feeling: 'I hope we shall not involve ourselves in an acceptance of the theology that lies behind what I believe to be the delinquency of Lord Rank.'

But Rank's business sense and commitment to money was on occasion stronger than his commitment to the rules of Methodism and, unperturbed by the hullabaloo, he went ahead with the uneasy acquiescence of Conference. It was the fifties; all the glory days of the picture palaces had faded as television had begun to take over, and now Rank saw a future for bingo in his old cinemas. He really couldn't see anything wrong with it; after all, bingo was really just an excuse for a social club, and the stakes were so small that no one could come to any harm. Rank thought it was a little titillating to have your palm tickled and he imagined that most folk didn't have much joy in their lives. He genuinely thought that bingo was doing a service to the community. As with every decision he ever made, he took this to the Lord in prayer and apparently, after some thought, he felt that the Lord gave his project the go-ahead. For Rank this was a straight business proposition and he thought that the Conference's opposition was narrow-minded. Because he had prayed about it, his conscience was clear and, despite some cutting criticism, he didn't change his plans. Interestingly, there must have been a slight question mark over gambling as an activity becoming to a good Christian in Rank's mind, since he would never play any of his hobbies for money on a Sunday.

Despite some of Rank's critics, such as Soper, standing firm, there was a marked resistance in the Methodist Church against going too far in shouting the great man down. It was sensed that it was not a good idea to offend Rank too much—the need for his money was perhaps greater for some parties than the upholding of principle. This incident, however, did not do Rank's public relations with the average Methodist any good. Many really felt betrayed by him; someone whom they had been proud of had now gone too far. In fact, Rank had always been unorthodox in his attitude to gambling and he had also enjoyed upsetting the strait-laced Methodist clergy. When in 1925 he bought the *Methodist Times*, he used to go to all the editorial meetings and took a delight in 'baiting the parsons present'¹ by purposely mentioning that he had just placed a bet on a horse. This would inevitably result in a heated discussion about the rights and wrongs of gambling.

The Rev. Dr Kenneth Greet remembers another occasion when Rank's attitudes were rather surprising:

> When I was secretary of the Christian Citizenship Department, we invited Lord Rank to one of our standing committees to discuss the cinema. When he was about to leave he remarked casually, 'I don't know if your department deals with Football Pools, but I think they are rather a good idea.' This caused a few raised eyebrows and perhaps indicated a not very clear understanding of the finer points of the Christian social witness.

At one time Rank's name came up for Vice-President of Conference, always a lay appointment. But interestingly he turned it down saying that 'it wasn't really his scene'. Maybe he didn't want to be too closely associated with the establishment because then he would have to toe the party line.

Less controversially, Rank was a great supporter of Anglican and Methodist union, and was very disappointed when this failed to come about. He was very ecumenical himself, shown in his approach to his family film services, and I would imagine he was far less bothered about denomination than the Spirit-filled nature of the preaching. On this subject he said in 1967:

> I think the churches need to be completely woken up. They realize now that they are not doing their job and that they have got to get together. I am sure they will get together in the next ten years. As Charles Wesley wrote and sang, 'Faith, mighty Faith, the promise sees and looks to that alone, laughs at impossibilities and cries, it shall be done!'

Undoubtedly Rank's biggest contribution to the Methodist Church was his money. This came in various forms: sometimes from his own private funds, but an enormous amount came through the Joseph Rank Benevolent Trust (JRBT) of which he was Chairman. Douglas Hutchinson says:

I don't think the Methodist Church would be the same thing at all without the Joseph Rank Benevolent Trust. Roughly speaking, we raised one-third of the funds required to be raised by local congregations. If £100,000 is required for a job and £40,000 is raised from sales of property etc., £60,000 from the congregation, JRBT would offer £20,000. The effect on Methodism is more than very considerable. We are amazed how local people are able to raise so much money and sometimes we wonder whether we are justified in maintaining local churches with small congregations, but they worked so hard. Sometimes we have a separate category and we support in principle, but they don't come forward for a contribution until they are well down the road.

Interestingly, some requests for money would be dismissed for being too small. One church in the sixties wanted £250 to improve their facilities and it was rejected.

Rank probably spent more than £1 million on Central Hall, Westminster. In 1967, during the early days of Maurice Barnett's time as minister (1964–80) he asked Rank if he would be Treasurer. Rank was pleased to be asked, despite all his manifold commitments. He said, 'I really do appreciate the fact that someone has asked me to do something without asking for my money.' Apparently, it was the first time the Methodist Church had done so. He acknowledged that money would obviously be involved and said he would see to that, as long as they did the work.

The hall was in a very run-down state, the seating was poor and the lifts were still on ropes. After a few meetings, Rank decided that the place should be refurbished and he asked Maurice to sort out a list of priorities. Tony Reddall, who was a member at the Central Hall and an employee with Bowmaker the Financiers, was the other treasurer:

The meetings were very interesting. We would get into Maurice's room and Arthur would insist that the first half hour was a class meeting! But instead of a normal class meeting he would lecture us on the Holy Spirit. After the class meeting he would appear to completely withdraw from us and apparently sleep [he suffered from angina]. All of a sudden he would wake up and say, 'Right, we're going to do a tour of the building.' He would never use the lifts and we would stomp up the stairs, walking everywhere. Then, having looked, we would say what needed doing.

One such tour ended in the auditorium itself, and resulted in the transfer of an entire set of seating from an Odeon which was closing down to the Central Hall. Those very cinema seats are still in place today. After returning to Dr Barnett's office, Rank would ask how much today's viewing decisions would cost.

We weren't experts, but we'd give some idea. Then he'd go to sleep again, or appear to, then he'd say, 'That's too high. Get some better quotes and the cheque will be in the post tomorrow.'

An appeal for £2 million misfired, so the Joseph Rank Benevolent Trust decided to make a £250,000 contribution, which repaired the roof. The Central Hall had also carried a debt of some £60,000 since 1912. There was not much hope of raising that kind of money. Rank went to talk to a few of his influential friends, but at the end of the day most of it was cleared by him.

At one stage of Rank's involvement with the great building he was all for knocking it down and building a multi-storey block of offices to incorporate everything the church needed. So keen was he, and so opposed was everyone else, that Rank took the matter as far as the Prime Minister, who would not or could not help him. The City of London, and probably Methodism, should be grateful that it never happened. 'Practical' was Rank's watchword; elegance and beauty were largely wasted on him.

When Rank heard that the Central Hall had never had a manse for its incumbent minister he decided to pay for one. It cost around £10,000 in 1970. He said it was his gift to the mission.

I asked Lord Soper, himself much respected by Methodists, to assess Rank's contribution to Methodism:

> In the first place I would say that his contribution to Methodism was, at heart, a valid one. He believed and expressed it financially in getting to the masses—epitomized by the Central Halls. The sacramental side of Christianity was almost totally absent from his understanding of church. Reverence, contemplation and sacramental worship did not play a part in his Christianity. Rank was the executor of the wilful attitude of his father Joseph. The Central Halls were in fact a disaster.

Paying the piper and calling the tune was always going to be a suspect activity, for there was no 'control mechanism' on Rank, except what he believed God was telling him to do. And since there was no judgment on that except his own, mistakes were going to be made.

Kingsley Lloyd, former President of the Methodist Conference, reflected:

> Rank had no malign influence unless you take the view that any capitalist money is corrupting. Short of that the things he promoted were largely philanthropic, like support for ministers' pensions, housing etc. They didn't influence the character of the Church, nor did he have any influence on the counsel of the Church. His money was no more tainted than anyone else's. I could say with hand on heart that he had very little influence. He didn't attend Conference or speak on any topics or complain about Soper's socialism. It is easier to criticize Joseph. He was much more about suppressing the workers. Arthur was well aware that the general view of

the Methodist Church was rather left of centre; he may not have agreed with that, but he didn't curtail his support of the church. The church was perhaps too dependent on these charities which was perhaps not too healthy. There used to be a general feeling '... the Rank money will see us through... ' The 'pound for pound' helped against senseless benefacting.

The Rev. Dr Colin Morris, another former President of Conference, disagrees:

The Rank Trust helped to distort the theology of the church, and the problem is that there is no doubt that whoever waves the cheque book will determine which way the church will move. It also restricted the activity of the church to the evangelical charismatic sector, to the neglect of other very important work which would have benefited: multi-faith projects and organizations and pressure groups, racism, apartheid, feminism, social responsibility...

If it is a law of nature to fill empty spaces, Rank, perhaps unfortunately for the Methodist Church, filled a lot of empty spaces that might just have been filled with more creative and theologically sound activity. Lord Soper again:

Benevolence with what you've got is not a justification for getting it. The Rank era was a menace—it filled up the pit of opportunity with the wrong ingredients. The whole ethos as represented by Rank is a terminus *ad quem*... an end and not a gateway. Giving money away was the easiest way to ease his conscience...

What should he have done?

... recognized that the greatest danger is the possession of wealth. It is there in the teaching of Jesus—the hardest thing was for a rich man to enter the kingdom. The process of how you get wealth should be tempered with the Christian gospel in the first place. You need a clear vision that the only justification of accumulating wealth is to share it. You should not possess wealth; you should administer it. Unfortunately Rank was from a group of human beings with a capacity to manipulate and no creativity.

I asked Kingsley Lloyd whether he felt that the Methodist Church needed another Rank:

No, I don't think it's healthy for Methodism to be so supported by one individual... But we've moved on a bit since then... it's far healthier for the church to be independent.

Colin Morris believes:

Rank was theologically naive, and the way he gave his money away reflects that. But whether he was simple or naive, he was perfectly entitled to do what he liked with it and you can't really blame him for doing what he did. A cool analysis would show that you've ended up with churches where they shouldn't have been. It definitely put a bias on the strategy of the church, but... if any good at all was done by it then it's been a good thing. Why should his money go to things he didn't like?

For a man whose philanthropy was every bit as important to him as his flour, faith and films, it would be impossible not to mention his charitable foundations and the staggering quantity of money that Rank gave away to what he thought were just causes. Several have already been mentioned and it would be boring and inappropriate to give endless lists of the good works his money has supported. But there are many.

It is estimated that Rank gave away £100 million during his lifetime. He had a very strong sense that one day he would be held accountable for all the good fortune he had received in his life and the massive wealth he had created for himself. When it came to the point that the Rank Organisation had become one of the biggest companies in the country and was therefore attracting attention from across the Atlantic, Rank became fearful that the Americans would stage a take-over. He turned all his shares, around £65 million, over to the J. Arthur Rank Group Charity which later became the Rank Foundation. This not only saved his company from a US buy-out, the thought of which horrified him, but also created what is still today one of the six biggest charities in Britain. The trustees have now divested the Foundation of nearly all the shares in the Rank Organisation, and its beneficiaries are no longer tied to the fortunes of any one company. Its market value is £160 million and it has an income in the region of £6 million per annum. As a charity the Rank Foundation states three aims:

● The promotion, by means of the exhibition of religious films, of the Christian religion, Christian principles, Christian religious education and the study of the history of the Christian faith. Also, the promotion of the Christian religion by any other lawful means.

● The promotion of education.

● The promotion of any other objects or purposes which are exclusively charitable according to the laws of England in force from time to time.

This gives a broad canvas on which the charity can operate. It supports all the work of the Churches' Television Centre, education and youth work in the community, the YMCA, youth and disabled sailing projects, care for the elderly, the National Youth Orchestra and sporting activities, to name but a handful.

The Joseph Rank Benevolent Trust represents the amalgamation of the three trusts established between the wars by Joseph Rank and continued by Arthur. It is about half the size of the Rank Foundation and is more specific on where its money goes. Arthur's nephew, Douglas Hutchinson, is Chairman of the Joseph Rank Benevolent Trust (JRBT). It was originally concerned mainly with building or restoring Methodist Church property. As a result of the Second World War there was a tremendous backlog of work that mopped up all the income. After J. Arthur Rank's death, Douglas Hutchinson suggested that a limit of 70 per cent was put on the funds for bricks and mortar. The Trust also supports Christian social work including the Mission Alongside the Poor work with both elderly and young people. 30 per cent of its giving is exclusively for Methodist concerns, but the rest is focused on more general Christian social work This also now includes the money from the 1942 Trust. The Trust helps maintain Methodist property, as well as building and adapting existing structures.

Paul Bartlett Lang, another of Rank's nephews, joined the JRBT in 1954, mainly working for his own father, the Rev. F. Bartlett Lang, who had married Rank's sister Hilda. Paul had reason to be grateful to his uncle:

> When I first came into the trust I did not have a title but in 1961 I was brought into a sub-committee to get to know the plans we were considering. At the time I felt my father was holding me back but Arthur thought I should be doing more. He gave me my head and said that he wanted me to get out and about and see the work at first hand... I held him in very high regard because he treated me as an adult person.

Paul Bartlet Lang later became secretary of the trust and recalls how Rank's ecumenical leanings guided their grants:

> Rank believed very strongly in the churches working together. People had to tell us at the JRBT that they were prepared to work in relation to other churches in their area and, if it seemed appropriate, to become united. He was a man ahead of his time.

All Central Halls were heavily supported by the JRBT. They fitted the style of the man—big and simple. J. Arthur Rank caused a bit of embarrassment at the JRBT by committing money without asking the trustees; he was the most important voice on the board after his father died, but he was still only one voice.

The Joseph Rank Benevolent Trust and the Rank Foundation still both bear the hallmark of their respective founders who were, for many years, remembered in prayer at the start of each meeting.

As well as these big charity set-ups, Rank considered almost every Christian claim on his money and had pet projects far too numerous to mention. One, perhaps, showed a forgiving side of his nature: Rank helped to pay for the Langley Houses project, the vision of John Dodd, a Methodist local preacher on the Isle of Wight. He was a prisoner of war in Japan, and afterwards became interested in the plight of prisoners in British gaols. After a time visiting various gaols he set up, with the backing of Rank and the Home Mission Department, the Langley House Trust to help rehabilitate discharged prisoners. Rank was proud of this work and especially of Wing Grange in Rutland, which he described as 'seeking to do something for men who have spent most of their lives in prison'. Rank also gave time and money to the work of Jimmy Butterworth and his Clublands project in the Elephant and Castle district of London. This was a charity which Rank was to introduce to actor and comedian Bob Hope, who visited the centre on a number of occasions. Mr Hope gave all the money he earned in England to Clubland and showed an interest in Religious Films.

Wealth and the Christian faith have never been easy bedfellows. Rank was an extraordinary phenomenon whom the Methodist Church found both exhilarating and uncomfortable. Of course, funds to back various charities and building projects are always needed, but just as money can't buy you happiness, they say, it cannot build a successful, growing church.

The Rev. Dr Kenneth Greet reflects:

> His generosity to Methodism is well known, and he primed the pump for building schemes and all sorts of good causes. I believe that he took seriously the Christian requirement of good stewardship of our possessions. Perhaps Methodism demanded too much from him, but then we are a bit short of millionaires.

13 THE END

O may thy Spirit seal
Our souls unto that day,
With all thy fullness fill,
And then transport away:
Away to our eternal rest,
Away to our Redeemer's breast.

CHARLES WESLEY

J. Arthur Rank died First Baron Rank of Sutton Scotney (created 1957) on 29 March 1972, aged eighty-three, on the day of the Rank Organisation's Annual General Meeting. With his death the barony became extinct. Rank left an estate of only £6-7 million. His home, Sutton Manor was valued at £3.5 million.

Rank was always reluctant to admit to his age. His father had lived to be eighty-nine and Rank assumed he would do the same, if not live longer. He was ever hopeful and ever full of new ideas and changes. At the dinner given by the Rank Organisation to honour his eightieth birthday, three days before the day, he had said, 'You'll be pleased to know that I've only got three more days to be an awkward cuss, because when I enter the eighties I'm going to be a reformed character.'

Rank spent the last two weeks of his life in St Austell, staying at the Carlyon Bay Hotel. Michael, his butler, remembers that on the way home Rank said he didn't feel too well:

So the chauffeur stopped the car and then carried on when his Lordship said he felt a little better. At home that night he came down at 8.00p.m. and again he said he felt a little better. He said to put his clothes out because he was going to London tomorrow morning. So in the morning (I always got there by 7.00a.m.), I rang him from the pantry so he could turn off the burglar alarms, and when I came up shortly afterwards with his pills I found him lying in his bathroom on the floor, in exactly the same position that his wife had fallen, and he said, 'Michael, I don't know what happened.' He asked for a drop of brandy. I got the doctor and I rang Major Cowen. Then I gave him the brandy and we got him into bed with some difficulty because he was a big man. Major Cowen got a consultant from Winchester and they took him into hospital round about 12.00. Mrs Cowen rang around 3.00 p.m. to say he had passed on.

The funeral took place in Sutton Scotney, surrounded by masses of daffodils.

The Rev. Dr Maurice Barnet, writing in the *Methodist Recorder* on 6 April 1972, quoted from a letter that Rank had written to him the day before he died:

We must manufacture a spiritual bomb that will wake up the churches. We may look down on the Jesus People and the Children of God, but they are getting excited about what the Holy Spirit is doing for them. It might be good to let them loose among the theologians.

In the same issue the Rev. Kenneth Greet wrote:

Lord Rank was man of simple and uncomplicated faith, with a passionate devotion to our Lord and to the cause of evangelism... We all prize the memory of a loyal Methodist who, even at the apex of worldly success, never deviated from his simple testimony to the power of the Lord he loved.

John Davis remembers:

On the night before he died he phoned me. We had an
awkward cuss who always came to the AGM and made
a fuss. Rank said, 'I'm looking forward to hearing you
deal with this fellow tomorrow because you always win.'
Robin Cowen rang the next morning and said he'd got
bad news for me. The doctors said he wouldn't live out
the day and he didn't.

That year John Davis wrote in the *Rank Organisation Annual
Report*:

Whilst our Annual Meeting last year was taking place, I
knew that Lord Rank, President, friend and colleague
of us all, was slowly passing to a happier place... It was
my good fortune to know Arthur Rank, both as a
business colleague and as a friend, spanning nearly
forty years; my relationship with him was both an
inspiration and a source of great personal privilege.
    His deep and abiding faith, his unshakeable integrity
and principles coloured all his life, whatever the
circumstances. He was a great family man; he was a
wise businessman. He loved the country and country
life; he had a lively sense of humour and an
enthusiastic sense of fun. Above all, he loved his fellow-
man, not patronisingly or pompously, but as a man
whose sensitive approach to life made him conscious of
his own good fortune and anxious to help others. We
have lost the wisdom, friendship and advice of a great
and unusual man.

One may imagine Rank giving the Almighty a really hard
time when he arrived in heaven because there was still so much
for him to do and achieve. At the time he died, he had several
projects on the go and several new ideas to be developed,
including a new charity emphasizing the work of the Holy
Spirit. On the afternoon before he died, after he had returned
from Cornwall, Robin Cowen went to see him and they spent

two or three hours talking about the new trust. He had set aside £1 million specifically to fund the new charity. However, it became impossible after his death to implement this, and his vision was never realized.

From his obituary in *The Times* of 30 March 1972:

His strength lay in his business acumen, his Yorkshire solidarity, in an entertainment world prone to emotional instability and excesses of alternating optimism and pessimism, and his ability to choose shrewd and reliable lieutenants to implement his policies.

His grandson, Fred Packard:

He had this brown leather coat which he'd had since the First World War. It was tatty but Grandpa adored it and wouldn't let anyone throw it away. When he died, we were clearing out Sutton Manor and we came to the coat. There was a bonfire going in the courtyard and we decided to burn it. It was a moving moment, my mother, the loyal butler and I, watching the coat burn.

Rank didn't want a memorial service but the demand was so great that the family agreed to it. It was a wonderful service and there was a huge turnout. The service was taken by the Rev. Maurice Barnet on 24 April at Westminster Central Hall. It reflected Rank's simple Christian faith that shone through every facet of his life, a life that the world called 'successful'.

In his address the Rev. Dr Maurice Barnett said:

Arthur Rank's remarkable life can never be interpreted without understanding the deep concept of his religious convictions. For him commitment of the Christian way was basic. It was the power of God that gave direction to his undertakings. He had a brand of religion that was practical and earthy in which there was no separation between the secular and the sacred.

Among those present were the Speaker of the House of Commons, Mr Selwyn Lloyd, and men and women from City boardrooms, the film industry, members of staff from his various enterprises, heads of the various Methodist Departments, Chairmen of Districts—the Methodist equivalent of bishops—and ordinary people who wanted to show their respect.

The Bible reading was from Paul's first letter to the Corinthians, chapter 13—'the greatest of these is love'—and they sang his favourite hymn, 'Onward Christian Soldiers'. Barnett went on to say:

> We were touched by his magnetic presence. We discovered that this was a man whose word was his bond: who did things because they were right, not because they were convenient or profitable, a lover of families and of home, and a profound Christian with a burning practical faith.

The *Methodist Recorder* of 6 April 1972 devoted an editorial to paying tribute to Rank:

> ... A man of strong faith, whose shrewd energy and driving will were never allowed to submerge his warm humanity. He believed in giving back to God what God had given him. His compassion ran deep. This was a man who knew how to hold on to eternal things but was as modern as tomorrow.

The Rev. Dr John Tudor:

> Everyone that knew him admired him tremendously; he was a man of conviction. He moved among the great of the land and kept a very humble spirit really and felt that he wanted to live to the glory of God through the medium of whatever he was doing.

Alan Wood writes:

> If we want to sum up Arthur Rank, we can only say that he is good and he is bad, he is wise and he is foolish, he is shrewd and he is gullible; old fashioned and up-to-date; reactionary and progressive; a failure

and a success; a capitalist and a Christian; a devout man and a joker; a man of immense simplicity and therefore a man of surprising complexity... [1]

Douglas Hutchinson said:

He displayed in everything he undertook his unique energy, enthusiasm and single-minded determination. 'I work hard and I play hard.' During his last holiday in Cornwall, replying to a letter to me, he said, 'I have started my golf again. My putting's alright but the rest is awful. However I'm getting my swing back!' Ever an immense optimist. Always planning for the future.

BIBLIOGRAPHY

All Our Yesterdays: Ninety Years of British Cinema, Barr, Charles (ed.), BFI, 1986.

The Cinema for Christ, Burnett, R.G., 1934.

Crying with Laughter, Monkhouse, Bob, Century, 1993.

The Devil's Camera: Menace of a Film-Ridden World, Burnett, R.G. and Martell, E.D.

The Future of British Films, Bond, Ralph.

The Golden Gong, Falk, Quentin, Columbus Books, 1987.

Harold Wilson, Pimlott, Ben, HarperCollins, 1992.

The History of Broadcasting, Briggs, Asa, OUP, 1995.

Hymns and Psalms, Methodist Pubiishing House, 1983.

J. Arthur Rank and the British Film Industry, Macnab, Geoffrey, Routledge, 1993.

The Master Millers, issued by Joseph Rank Ltd, published by Harley Publishing Co. Ltd.

Mr Rank: A Study of J. Arthur Rank and British Films, Wood, Alan, Hodder and Stoughton, 1952.

Policy and Politics in British Methodism, Thompson-Brake, Esdall, 1984.

The Story of the House of Rank, The Northern Publishing Co. Ltd, 1922.

Talking of Films, Minney, R.J., Home and Van Thal, 1947.

Through the Mill: The Life of Joseph Rank, Burnett, R.G., Epworth Press, 1945.

FOOTNOTES

Chapter 1

1 Wood, *Mr Rank*.
2 R.G. Burnett, *The Master Millers*, p. 9.
3 John Rank, J. Arthur's great grandfather, was born in Hollyn. It was only the fact that John Rank's father emigrated to the United States that resulted in John being brought up by his grandparents which, in turn, meant that he did not feel the need to automatically take over the farm from his father. His father never returned to Britain.
4 This mill on Holderness Road can still be seen today and, as a beautiful irony, the mill and the cottages next door where Joseph (the great man of temperance) was born have only been kept standing by a brewery firm which has turned them into a rather attractive pub.
5 *The Master Millers*, reprinted from *Milling*, 2 September 1922.
6 ibid.
7 ibid.
8 R.G. Burnett, *Through the Mill*.
9 *The Master Millers*, p. 55.
10 *The Master Millers*, reprinted from *Milling*, 2 September 1922.
11 *Through the Mill*, p. 212.
12 ibid.
13 ibid.
14 ibid.

Chapter 2

1 *Through the Mill*, p. 103.
2 Wood, *Mr Rank*.
3 ibid.
4 ibid.
5 ibid.
6 ibid.

Chapter 3

1 The full story of Rank's Religious Films Ltd has never been told before. I am indebted to an extraordinary six-hour taped interview with Walter Knights, who died in 1989. He was with Rank from the very beginning. He was interviewed by Patrick O'B. Baker who made the recording purely out of his own interest. Towards the end of the tape Patrick says to Walter that he hopes one day someone will be able to use the information for a book.

2 Burnett and Martell, *The Devil's Camera: Menace of a Film-Ridden World*, p. 10.
3 ibid.
4 Originally it was called *The Mastership of Christ,* but the censor objected.
5 R.G. Burnett, *The Cinema for Christ*, p. 74.
6 C.T.V.C. was established by Rank in the late fifties to continue the work of Religious Films.
7 Despite Soper's reserve about Rank's involvement with films, it is suggested that he himself had encouraged some Wesleyan Methodists to follow Tiplady's example and start film services.
8 Wood, *Mr Rank*, p. 191.
9 Over the passage of half a century, the film *The Great Mr Handel* has achieved the status of a classic. It is occasionally seen at art cinemas throughout the country and on television, and is even available as a video.

Chapter 4

1 Wood, *Mr Rank.*
2 ibid. p. 67.
3 Geoffrey Macnab, *J. Arthur Rank and the British Film Industry* p. 17.
4 Other films BNF produced, such as *One of Our Aircraft is Missing* and *Pimpernel Smith*, have become cinema classics and most of the pictures they made were honest, straightforward and of good quality.
5 Wood, *Mr Rank*, p. 81.
6 Wyndham Portal was from the family firm, Portals Ltd and Wiggins Teape, who were paper manufacturers, supplying material for banknotes throughout the world. Macnab points out in his book (p. 21) that J. Arthur Rank and Lord Portal were both considered quite odd and 'different' to be part of the film world.
7 Macnab, *J. Arthur Rank and the British Film Industry.*
8 Wood, *Mr Rank*, p. 84.
9 Rank actually acquired 5,100 of the 10,000 voting shares. His competitors, 20th-Century Fox, owned the others. This shared ownership with Americans was the same for other properties including the Odeon chain, 27 per cent of which was owned by United Artists.
10 Macnab, *J. Arthur Rank and the British Film Industry*, p. 39.
11 ibid.
12 Macnab, *Kinematograph Weekly*, 11 Jan 1940, special supplement.
13 Macnab, *J. Arthur Rank and the British Film Industry*, p. 33.
14 The image of the strong man striking the gong was created in 1935 on a Sunday afternoon at Walton Hall Studios in Isleworth. The idea behind it was to symbolize the combination of power with sound. There have actually been three versions, with three different bare-chested men, to fit in with each new technological development in film production. The most famous was Bombardier Billy Wells, a former heavyweight boxing champion of Great Britain. Phil Nieman, a film extra and wrestler was second and finally, in 1955, Ken Richmond, an Olympic discus-thrower and British amateur champion wrestler took the role and still

bangs the gong today. Interestingly, none of them actually hit the gong since it was made of plaster and would have shattered if they had. The sound was dubbed on using the combined skills of percussionist James Blades and the Tam Tam, an ancient Japanese instrument.

15 Wood, *Mr Rank*, p. 89.
16 Published by Home & Van Thal, 1947.
17 Bob Monkhouse, *Crying With Laughter*, Century, 1993, p. 166.
18 Macnab, *J. Arthur Rank and the British Film Industry.*
19 Board of Trade 1944, paragraph 3.
20 Ken Russell, *Fire Over England—The British Cinema Comes under Friendly Fire*, Random House, 1993, p. 51.
21 From Rank's speech at his eightieth birthday party.
22 *Fortune* magazine, October 1945.
23 Wood, *Mr Rank*, p. 162.
24 ibid. p. 166.
25 ibid. p. 168.

Chapter 5

1 Wood, *Mr Rank*.
2 ibid. p. 223.
3 ibid. p. 225.
4 ibid. p. 226.
5 Pimlott, *Harold Wilson* , HarperCollins, 1992, p. 119.
6 Rank Organisation AGM, 1948.
7 Wood, *Mr Rank*, p. 235.
8 'Silhouette', *Daily Mail*, 1948.
9 *Daily Herald*, 15 July 1948.
10 Russell, *Fire Over England—The British Cinema Comes under Friendly Fire*, Random House, 1993, p. 34.
11 Wood, *Mr Rank*, p. 202.
12 ibid. p. 205.
13 ibid. p. 142.
14 ibid.p. 127.
15 ibid. p. 137.
16 R.J. Minney, *Talking of Films*, Home and Von Thal, 1947.
17 Wood, *Mr Rank*, p. 281.

Chapter 6

1 Wood, *Mr Rank*, p. 113.
2 From Rank's speech at his eightieth birthday party.
3 'Profile—J. Arthur Rank', *The Observer*, 13 November 1949.
4 Wood, *Mr Rank*, p. 110.
5 From Rank's speech at his eightieth birthday party.
6 Macnab, *J. Arthur Rank and the British Film Industry*, p. 205.
7 *Kinematograph Weekly*, 24 September 1948, quoted in Macnab, *J. Arthur Rank and the British Film Industry*, p. 208.

8 Macnab, *J. Arthur Rank and the British Film Industry*, p. 212.
9 *Manchester Guardian*, 11 October 1958.
10 Wood, *Mr Rank*, p. 237.
11 New talent has continued to keep the Rank Organisation among the top fifty companies and it is today one of the world's leading leisure and entertainment providers. Its work still includes film and television (distribution, duplication, Odeon Cinemas and Pinewood Studios), as well as leisure and entertainment concerns across Europe and North America (Butlins, Warner, Haven, Bingo and casinos). It still has an investment in Rank Xerox and is a partner in Universal Studios, Florida, a theme park in Orlando.
12 *Evening News*, 1 October 1957.

Chapter 7

1 Wood, *Mr Rank*, p. 122.
2 ibid. p. 123.

Chapter 8

1 Wood, *Mr Rank*.
2 ibid. p. 194.
3 During the period 1949-70 his labradors won sixty-eight first prizes at trials, forty-six second prizes and forty-six thirds. The Routledge-Rank Gold Cup for the dog with the highest marks was won in 1959, 1960 and 1961 by Field Trial Champion Scotney Jingle and by Field Trial Champion Scotney Crickleybarrow Pebble (Lord Rank's top runner-getter) in 1962, 1963 and 1964. The Scotney pointers chalked up 153 first prizes, 136 second prizes and 98 thirds, and have won eight championship stakes.
4 He was asked to be godfather to Robin Cowen's niece's child but he agreed only on condition that her middle name be Partridge. They didn't like that, but agreed to Pheasant. She is now Virginia Pheasant Powell.

Chapter 9

1 Extract from a letter written by J. Arthur Rank in December 1955. Quoted in *The Master Millers*.
2 Douglas Hutchinson's mother, Rank's sister, had also remained faithful to the church and was also a Sunday school teacher. She had married into another milling family with a business in Fife.
3 *The Master Millers*, p. 68.
4 ibid.
5 ibid. p. 94.
6 Just prior to his death Lord Rank left £1 million to fund two science prizes in areas which the Nobel Prizes did not cover: the sciences of nutrition, animal nutrition and crop husbandry; and the science of opto-electronics, the interface between electronics and optics as exemplified by television and lasers. A trust from the J. Arthur Rank Group Charity was set up. to administer the awards.
7 *The Master Millers*.

Chapter 10

1 Wood, *Mr Rank*, p. 190.
2 ibid. p. 50.
3 ibid. p. 50.
4 The Dawn Trust, run by Brian Hession, had nothing to do with the RFS. They had tried to get money from Rank but their ideas came to nothing. They had a 'studio' in Aylesbury which was really a shed, and no films were produced there. Hession went to the US to produce a film on the life of Christ, but he was taken ill with cancer. The Dawn Trust eventually faded out, ending up in Bournemouth where Hession had a large house, given by the Tate and Lyle Organization. His excellent engineer, a Mr Gosling, who invented the apparatus to show continuous 16mm film, came to work for the RFS.
5 *The Shield of Faith* showed the effect on a Welsh mining community of the death of eighty of its young men who were killed in a plane crash returning from a rugby international match. The story was suggested by the Llandow air disaster of 1950. Evans was a great rugby fan.
6 By 1971 Proctor and Buckler and their colleagues had developed their plans for an ecumenical centre for the rural church, to be based in Stoneleigh. So Buckler was sent to see 'the old man' again. They planned the centre to have a fourfold purpose: to act as a reception point for the National Agricultural Centre (NAC) as a whole; to provide social facilities for the NAC staff; to act as a permanent church pavilion for the Royal Show and to act as a base for chaplaincy work and conferences for the rest of the year. Buckler saw Rank again on 25 January 1972 at the Eaton Square office with Christopher Dadd, but despite their preparation, hopes were not high because they didn't know whether Rank had changed his mind about supporting building projects and it had been reported to them that Rank didn't want to spend any money until the new tax year in April.

Buckler recalled: 'He received us and heard us put the case for the building and a reception centre. He said, "We want this, don't we?" and he thought it was a good idea to "get it up for the Royal Show" ', (that was in six months' time and we hadn't even got planning permission!) Rank said there was only one problem; he was signing a cheque for £1 million the next day and that was going to make him a bit short, but he thought by April his situation should improve and he could afford the £22,000.'

Maybe his financial position had improved, but his health hadn't and he wasn't alive to honour his promise. Peter Buckler heard the news of Lord Rank's death while on a train at the start of a journey to the West Indies. He felt momentarily panic-stricken, since they had not got anything in writing from Rank about the promised money. However, the Rank family honoured the dead man's promise, and his daughters and son-in law were there at the opening, performed by the Queen, who was president of the RAS that year. The building was dedicated by the Bishop of Coventry.

It has now become the centre they wanted and has achieved their vision. The Arthur Rank Centre serves as the church pavilion for the

Royal Agricultural Show and for the Town and Country Festival over August Bank Holiday. It is also the Ecumenical Centre for the Rural Church and runs various conferences dealing not only with strictly church affairs but also with environmental issues. Farmhouse holidays are also run from the centre and it serves as a seed ground for new ideas. In its own leaflet it describes itself as 'concerned with the social context in which farming and the rural community and the rural churches operate... the centre seeks to analyse and comment on changes in the social and economic profile of the contemporary countryside, to contribute to the quality of rural life... and to improve the communications and understanding between the farming community and the non-farming community.'

After Rank died the family decided to keep at least one of his interests in rural affairs alive, so Robin Cowen invited the Stoneleigh team to Sutton Scotney to discuss Rank's various interests. They decided to pursue the establishment of the NAC Trust and, parallel with it, the NAC Rural Housing Association whose object was to provide houses for retired rural workers. Robin Cowen had suddenly remembered an incident after the war. All the time he worked with Rank he only received a written instruction once and that was on the back of an envelope! This particular instruction had been: 'All good Christian families depend on having a good home—please see that everyone has one!' The Rural Housing Association has the Princess Royal as its President and owns 1,437 houses in 183 villages.

Before he died, Rank had also made available £110,000 to provide a hall of residence at the NAC, but the project was postponed. But in 1978 work began on residential accommodation for herdsmen and women during the Royal Show which would also be available for visitors and delegates to conferences. This was made possible by a £320,000 donation from Rank Charities and has been named 'The Rank Village' in his honour.

Chapter 11

1 Wood, *Mr Rank*, p. 66.
2 The fact that Coggan 'touched the side of [Rank's] head' may have a deeper significance. Rank's father Joseph was very keen on phrenology—the feeling of the skull to ascertain character. He wouldn't appoint anyone to a position of responsibility who had not been to see a phrenologist, so it is very likely that he would have put his son through the test. Colin Rank speculates that Arthur may have seen this moment of touch from Donald Coggan as healing him of the influence of this occultic aberration.
3 Wood, *Mr Rank*, p. 193.

Chapter 12

1 Wood, *Mr Rank*, p. 69.

Chapter 13

1 Wood, *Mr Rank*, p. 280.

INDEX